AF616510

The Nature of a Humane Society

Contributors

ROBERT A. ALDRICH, Professor of Preventive Medicine and Pediatrics at the University of Colorado.

JAMES BALDWIN, Author and Essayist.

WERNHER VON BRAUN, President of the National Space Institute; Vice President, Engineering, of Fairchild Industries.

NORMAN COUSINS, Editor of *Saturday Review*.

ARCHIBALD COX, Williston Professor of Law at Harvard Law School.

MATINA S. HORNER, President of Radcliffe College.

CORETTA SCOTT KING, President of Martin Luther King Jr. Center for Social Change.

MARTIN E. MARTY, Associate Dean and Professor at the University of Chicago Divinity School.

TONI MORRISON, Author of numerous books and Editor of Random House, Inc.

MONRAD G. PAULSEN, Vice President for Legal Education at Yeshiva University.

JAROSLAV PELIKAN, Dean of the Graduate School of Arts and Sciences at Yale University.

JONAS E. SALK, Founding Director and Resident Fellow of the Salk Institute for Biological Studies.

ARTHUR M. SCHLESINGER, JR., Albert M. Schweitzer Professor of the Humanities at the City University of New York.

KRISTER STENDAHL, Dean of Harvard Divinity School.

The Nature of a Humane Society

A Symposium on the Bicentennial of the United States of America

Arthur M. Schlesinger, Jr.
Archibald Cox
Wernher von Braun
Jonas E. Salk
Matina S. Horner
James Baldwin
Norman Cousins
Jaroslav Pelikan
Monrad G. Paulsen
Krister Stendahl
Robert A. Aldrich
Coretta Scott King
Toni Morrison
Martin E. Marty

H. Ober Hess, editor

FORTRESS PRESS Philadelphia

Library of Congress Catalog Card Number 76–62616
ISBN 0–8006–0502–0

6181C77 Printed in U.S.A. 1–502

Contents

Contents

Preface

> A humane society is surely a society founded on the conviction, declared two hundred years ago in this city, that all human beings are created equal and possess certain unalienable rights, especially life, liberty and pursuit of happiness. This implies a blessed commonwealth in which men and women think and speak freely, criticize and review their government, live under just and equal laws, cultivate the arts and sciences, deal honorably and generously with one another, cherish human dignity as sacred, and leave a heritage of knowledge and beauty for those who come after.
>
> —Arthur M. Schlesinger, Jr.

In October, 1976, more than 900 persons attended a symposium on The Nature of a Humane Society. The symposium, sponsored by the Southeastern Pennsylvania Synod of the Lutheran Church in America and held on the campus of the University of Pennsylvania, was a forum for intellectual stock-taking on the occasion of the Bicentennial of the United States of America.

The symposium cannot be said to represent a new and original way of seeking the truth. It is not too much, however, to say that at many points it brought forward new perceptions of truth and new and attractive formulations of old truth, as, for example, Professor Schlesinger's definition of a humane society above. It is more than coincidence that one aspect or another of this definition was central to each of the fourteen presentations.

Six of the scholars whose work is included prepared their papers for distribution in advance of the symposium—James Baldwin, author and essayist; Wernher von Braun, President of the National Space Institute and Vice President, Engineering, of Fairchild Industries; Norman Cousins, Editor of *Saturday Review*; Archibald Cox, Williston Professor of Law at Harvard Law School; Matina S. Horner, President of Radcliffe College;

and Arthur M. Schlesinger, Jr., Albert M. Schweitzer Professor of the Humanities at the City University of New York. Five of them personally presented oral summaries of their papers at the symposium; Dr. von Braun was prevented by serious illness from being present.

The six papers prepared in advance were the subject of oral comment at the symposium by six other scholars. Their comments appear in this book following the work to which each related. The commentators were Coretta Scott King, President of Martin Luther King Jr. Center for Social Change; Martin E. Marty, Associate Dean and Professor at the University of Chicago Divinity School; Toni Morrison, author of numerous books and Editor of Random House Inc., Monrad G. Paulsen, Vice President for Legal Education at Yeshiva University; Jaroslav Pelikan, Dean of the Graduate School of Arts and Sciences at Yale University; and Krister Standahl, Dean of Harvard Divinity School.

Jonas E. Salk, Founding Director and Resident Fellow of the Salk Institute for Biological Studies, was originally scheduled to serve as a commentator upon a paper to be written by another, but because of a late change in the program he graciously consented to handle the basic Limits to Growth subtopic which he presented orally, with slide illustrations, based largely upon his book *Survival of the Wisest*. The text of his presentation is included in this volume with the kind permission of Harper & Row. Robert A. Aldrich, Professor of Preventive Medicine and Pediatrics at the University of Colorado, commented in turn upon Dr. Salk's material.

When the American Revolution Bicentennial Administration, the official governmental agency created by Act of Congress P.L. 93–179, gave official approval to the symposium project, it added these words of appraisal:

> We particularly welcome the emphasis which The Bicentennial Symposium on the Nature of a Humane Society places on the underlying values and assumptions of our society. The emphasis on the enduring nature of these values and their implications in the present and future is of great importance as we begin the third century of our national life.

Other distinguished persons confirmed these words of approbation by their presence and participation in other roles: Millard E. Gladfelter, Chancellor of Temple University, who served as chairman of the symposium sessions; Martin Meyerson, President of the University of Pennsylvania, on whose campus by his kindness the symposium was held and who contributed important introductory remarks at the opening session; and those who introduced the speakers at the several sessions: A. Leon Higginbotham Jr., Judge of the U.S. District Court for the Eastern District of Pennsylvania; William A. Janson, President of the Southeastern Pennsylvania Synod; Marciarose, journalist and T.V. newsperson; Robert J. Marshall, President of the Lutheran Church in America; John H. Morey, President of Muhlenberg College; and Marvin Wachman, President of Temple University.

It is the hope of the sponsors that the project will indeed have value to the minds of those who lead our land into its third century, and that it may, too, demonstrate a method by which the church can serve the commonweal in a significant way.

H. Ober Hess, Editor

The Lessons of History

Arthur M. Schlesinger, Jr.

Our collective concern in this symposium is to explore the idea of a humane society—its meaning, preconditions, potentialities. My particular charge is to consider what lessons history may have for us in this inquiry. But before we confront this question we must, I think, look at a couple of antecedent problems: whether indeed history offers any lessons at all; and whether, if history does have lessons to offer, mankind has much desire to learn them or will to abide by them. These problems are large, old, and perennial. I do not pretend to solve them now. I seek only to suggest some of the considerations involved in thinking about them.

History, as we all know, means two separate things. It means what happened in the past, and it means what people have written about what happened in the past. History existed once as event and exists now as text. The text only dimly reflects the event, and the relationship between event and text can be verified only up to a point. "History is poorly retain'd by what the technists call history," Walt Whitman observed a century ago, "and is not given out from their pages, except the learner has in himself the sense of the well-wrapt, never yet written, perhaps impossible to be written, history."[1]

The chasm between event and text is finally unbridgeable. Pending the construction of Mr. Wells's time machine, the past is beyond recapture. The air of confidence assumed by historians is a convention—or an illusion. "Everything historical has a strange and uncertain character," wrote Goethe, "and it really

1. Walt Whitman, *Democratic Vistas.*

becomes comical, when one considers how people convince themselves with complete certainty about the distant past."[2] No one understands the insubstantiality of history-as-text better than those who themselves have made history-as-event. "Suppose I have given an order," said Napoleon. "Who can read the bottom of my thought, my true intention? And yet everybody will take hold of that order, measure it by his own yardstick, make it bend to conform to his plans, his individual way of thinking. . . . And everybody will be so confident of his own version."[3]

Every historian measures the past by his own yardstick. No matter how hard he seeks to escape, he remains the prisoner of the problems, predilections, and values of his age. "No man," wrote Emerson, "can quite emanicpate himself from his age and country, or produce a model in which the education, the religion, the politics, usages, and arts of his times, shall have no share. Though he were never so original, never so wilful and fantastic, he cannot wipe out of his work every trace of the thoughts amidst which it grew."[4] Emerson, the greatest of transcendentalists, never supposed he could transcend his own culture. The historian sees the past only as the flickering light of his own day picks out objects in the caverns of time: new light, new objects. "The experience of each new age," said Emerson, "requires a new confession."[5] In this sense the present may be said to create, or at least to reinvent, the past. Oscar Wilde was everlastingly right: "The one duty we owe to history is to rewrite it."[6] Any reviewer who applies the adjective *definitive* to a work of history instantly proves his incomprehension of the historical enterprise.

So with the best will in the world history-as-text can only present a partial picture of hstory-as-event. But history does not always register the best will in the world. Most of the time through the ages society has invoked the past in order to justify the present. J. H. Plumb hardly exaggerated when he wrote,

2. Friedrich Meinecke, *Historism* (London, 1972), p. 427.
3. J. C. Herold, *ed., The Mind of Napoleon* (New York, 1955), pp. 50–51.
4. Ralph Waldo Emerson, "Art."
5. Emerson, "The Poet."
6. Oscar Wilde, *Intentions.*

"The past is always a created ideology with a purpose, designed to control individuals, or motivate societies, or inspire classes. Nothing has been so corruptly used as concepts of the past."[7] "To the essential incompleteness of history," as Schopenhauer cruelly put it, ". . . must be added the fact that Clio, the Muse of History, is as thoroughly infected with lies as a streetwalker is with syphilis."[8]

Confronted by the unbridgeable chasm, historians had two choices. The first was to keep on pursuing the inaccessible, employing all the artistry of the historical imagination and all the technology of the historical craft in the campaign to penetrate the mystery of the past. Wise scholars knew the goal was unattainable, but saw moral necessity, as well as intellectual discipline and challenge, in the striving. The historian's duty, as they saw it, was above all to honor the past for itself, to trace out its autonomous patterns, to liberate it, as far as humanly possible, from the preoccupations of the present. "I maintain," said that greatest of Lutheran historians, Leopold von Ranke, "that every epoch is directly before God; and its value is not dependent on what it produces, but on its intrinsic existence and its own distinctive identity."[9]

The other choice was to accept the inaccessibility of history-as-event and frankly use the past to serve the present and the future. Nietzsche, a most profound critic of the historical enterprise, believed that too much learning could be a dangerous thing. The nineteenth century, he said, was suffering from "a malignant historical fever." Life in any true sense was impossible without "the power of forgetting" as well as the passion to remember; in order to live fully, man must be "cured henceforth of taking history too seriously." Humanity needed history for action, not as a convenient way to avoid action. "We would serve history only so far it serves life."[10] This deep and percep-

7. J. H. Plumb, *The Death of the Past* (Boston, 1969), p. 17.

8. Arthur Schopenhauer, *Aphorisms.*

9. Meinecke, *Historism,* p. 505.

10. Friedrich Nietzsche, *Thoughts out of Season: The Use and Abuse of* History.

tive view—for Nietzsche at the same time appreciated the autonomy of historical inquiry—was subsequently reduced and to a degree trivialized by writers with a utilitarian, present-minded conception of history. "The use of history for cultivating a socialized intelligence," said John Dewey, "constitutes its moral significance."[11] Charles A. Beard, an able professional historian, nevertheless spoke of "written history as an act of faith" and announced his own faith in movement toward a "collectivist democracy."[12]

This view has a certain plausibility. It does not imply any rejection of "scientific," that is, critical, methods. It renounces what in any event cannot be achieved: a true and complete portrait of the past. It seeks to make explicit the values that are implicit in the historian's consciousness. It transforms history from an elitist hobby into a means of social cohesion and/or change. It responds to the recurrent, and not always contemptible, demand for "relevance." It places lessons at the forefront of the historical enterprise.

But the impression is inescapable that the lessons drawn from the past are precisely those that legitimate and underwrite what the writer thinks about the present. The subordination of the past *to* the present turns all too easily into the manipulation of the past *for* the present. The benign arguments of philosophers become the broadaxes of statesmen. "History became for me an inexhaustible source of understanding for the historical events of the present. . . . I do not want to 'learn' it, I want it to instruct me."[13] An unimpeachable Deweyite sentiment! The words are Adolf Hitler's. Other leaders were less self-deceived about the way they pressed history into their service. "History I conquered rather than studied," said Napoleon. ". . . I spurned what was of no use, and seized upon certain conclusions that pleased

11. John Dewey, *Democracy and Education*, p. 217.

12. Charles A. Beard, "Written History as an Act of Faith," *American Historical Review*, January 1934.

13. Adolf Hitler, *Mein Kampf*, ch. 1.

me."[14] Or, as de Gaulle remarked to Malraux, "History may vindicate life; it does not resemble it."[15]

Nietzsche recognized the consequences for the past when history was mobilized for the present: "The past itself suffers wrong. Whole tracts of it are forgotten and despised; they flow away like a dark unbroken river, with only a few gaily colored islands of fact rising above it." He added, anticipating the twentieth century, "Imagine this history in the hands—and the head—of a gifted egotist or an inspired scoundrel."[16] The true historian flinches from the maltreatment of history. He may have political loyalties and passions as a citizen. As a historian, he has a single passion and a single loyalty: the honest reconstruction of the past for its own sake. The historian, said Michael Oakeshott, loves the past "as a mistress of whom he never tires and whom he never expects to talk sense."[17]

The effort to reconstruct the past gives the historian one form or another of aesthetic satisfaction. Hume, a very competent working historian as well as a great philosopher, asked, "What more agreeable entertainment to the mind, than to be transported into the remotest ages of the world, and . . . to see all the human race, from the beginning of time, pass, as it were, in review before us, appearing in their true colours? . . . What amusement, either of the senses or imagination, can be compared with it?"[18]

That was the skeptical eighteenth century. In the romantic nineteenth, the historian changed from amused spectator to vicarious participant. One recalled Michelet, intoxicated by the vision of Vico, describing the historian as one who "taking history as something more than a game, makes the effort in good faith to enter into the life of the past. . . . Who can say here which are the living and which are the dead?" And later, work-

14. Herold, *Mind of Napoleon*, p. 50.
15. André Malraux, *Felled Oaks* (New York, 1971), p. 43.
16. Nietzsche, *The Use and Abuse of History*.
17. Michael Oakeshott, *Rationalism in Politics* (New York, 1962), p. 166.
18. David Hume, "On the Study of History."

ing on his history of the French Revolution: "I am accomplishing here the extremely tough task of reliving, reconstituting and suffering the Revolution. I have just gone through *September* and all the terrors of death; massacred at the Abbaye, I am on my way to the revolutionary tribunal, that is to say, to the guillotine."[19] "The historian," said R. G. Collingwood, "must re-enact the past in his own mind."[20]

All historical epochs are indeed immediate unto God. Who can say which are the living and which the dead? The past remains ultimately irretrievable. Still the historian must do the best he can. His is what Jacques Monod has called "the ethic of knowledge," where the supreme goal is objective knowledge itself.[21] Most professional historians privately regard history as its own regard. They study it for the intellectual, aesthetic and moral fulfillment they find in the disciplined attempt to reconstruct the past and perhaps for the ironic aftertaste in the contemptation of man's heroism and folly, but for no more utilitarian reason. To ransack the past for "lessons" that the historian himself, wittingly or not, plants there before he begins his search both discredits the lessons and distorts the past.

The purpose of history, then, is to examine the past for its own sake. But even if we abandon the notion that the function of the past is to serve up lessons for the present, this still does not mean that history may not yield lessons, even though not written for that purpose. There must be some other point to history beside the pleasure it gives historians. It obviously fills a primordial psychological need. What memory is for the individual, history is for the nation. It is the social form in which experience presents itself, the modern equivalent of ancient myth and legend, and experience is the source of practical judgment. A nation can no more make a decision without consulting social experience, that is, history, than an individual can make a decision without consulting personal experience.

19. Edmund Wilson, *To the Finland Station*, chs. 2, 4.

20. R. G. Collingwood, *The Idea of History* (London, 1946), p. 282.

21. Jacques Monod, *From Biology to Ethics* (San Diego, 1969), pp. 21–22.

Now if the past, its autonomy still honored, can nevertheless be made to deliver general laws of human development, history would overflow with lessons. A long tradition, philosophical and literary, has indeed supposed history to be governed by irrevocable laws: "If there is a single action due to free will," Tolstoi observed in *War and Peace,* "no historical law exists, and no conception of historical events can be formed." Great men, he wrote, were "but the labels that serve to give a name to an event and, like labels, they have the least possible connection with the event itself." If historical laws do not manifest themselves through one individual, they will do so through another. If Napoleon had not led the French Army across Europe, then someone else would have done so. The greater the man, "the more conspicuous is the inevitability and predestination of every act he commits." The hero, Tolstoi said, "is the slave of history."

The quest for the laws of history has been almost as old as written history itself. Hegel, Marx, Spencer, Spengler, Toynbee, and other prophets have outlined comprehensive schemes of historical determinism. But is history thus comprehensively determined? For determinism means, as William James said, that "those parts of the universe already laid down absolutely appoint and decree what the other parts shall be. The future has no ambiguous possibilities hidden in its womb. . . . Any other future . . . than the one fixed from eternity is impossible."[22]

This is stiff medicine. Nor does the rejection of historical inevitability by any means imply, as some have contended, the rejection of causal connections in history. Because antecedent circumstances "caused" something to happen does not prove that only this could have happened, that nothing else could possibly have occurred in its place. Causation is one thing; predestination another. "There is an infinite number of ways in which a thing that is in process of happening may materialize," wrote Sainte-Beuve a few weeks after the overthrow of Louis Philippe in 1848. "When it has happened people see only one way. What we saw last February is a fine case in point. The thing might have

22. William James, "The Dilemma of Determinism," in *The Will to Believe.*

turned out in many different ways. In fifty years people will maintain that the way in which it did turn out was a necessity."[23]

James admired *War and Peace* as "assuredly the greatest of human novels" but considered Tolstoi's philosophy "a false abstraction" savoring too much of "Oriental pessimism and nihilism."[24] James himself challenged the determinists directly by asking whether they really believed "the convergence of sociological pressures to have so impinged on Stratford-upon-Avon about the 26th of April, 1564, that a W. Shakespeare, with all his mental peculiarities, had to be born there." And did they further believe "that if the aforesaid W. Shakespeare had died of cholera infantum, another mother at Stratford-upon-Avon would needs have engendered a duplicate copy of him, to restore the sociologic equilibrium"?[25]

The idea of reducing historical change to a set of integrated general laws on the model of physics or chemistry has fascinated formidable intellects for centuries. The feebleness of the result, especially in view of the brililance of the minds engaged in the exercise, encourages the conclusion that the project of converting history into a science is inherently futile. In 1904 Bertrand Russell was laboring with Whitehead in the intensely abstract effort to deduce mathematics from the general principles of logic. Considering the problems of history, he threw up his hands: "In history, so many circumstances of a small and accidental nature are relevant, that no broad and simple uniformities are possible."[26] *Principia mathematica* were plainly easier to work out than *principia historica.*

In addition, even though observation may alter experiment, scientists have limited emotional commitment to the objects under their microscopes. But historians are too mixed up with

23. Sainte-Beuve, *Cahiers*, quoted by Gaetano Salvemini, *Historian and Scientist* (Cambridge, 1939), p. 123.

24. William James, "What Makes a Life Significant" in *Talks to Teachers.*

25. William James, "Great Men and their Environment," in *The Will to Believe.*

26. Bertrand Russell, "On History," *Independent Review*, July 1904.

the phenomena to eliminate subjective bias. Nor can historical reactions be tested in the laboratory. Gide once said that he distrusted history because of its "ifs" and much preferred science "in which we have a constant check on facts and can always refer back to them; in which the 'if' becomes an instrument of experiment, allowing new observations."[27]

Nor does science itself for that matter appear quite so solid in the twilight of the twentieth century as it did in the high noon of the mid-nineteenth century. James thought it folly "to speak of the 'laws of history' as of something inevitable, which science has only to discover, and whose consequences any one can then foretell but do nothing to alter or avert. Why, the very laws of physics are conditional, and deal with *ifs*."[28] More recently quantum mechanics has vindicated the idea of absolute chance. Heisenberg has instructed us in the principle of indeterminacy. The events that set off human evolution, according to Jacques Monod, were "fortuitous, and utterly without relation to whatever may be their effects upon teleonomic functioning." Monod sees humanity as "the product of an enormous lottery presided over by natural selection, blindly picking the rare winners from among numbers drawn at utter random." While it is not altogether clear whether Monod regards human history as lying finally in the realm of chance or of necessity, he brusquely dismisses existing systems of historical explanation as new versions of animistic myths.[29]

In addition to its scientific dubiety, determinism remains a psychological impossibility. Even determinists reject determinism in their own practice. Their very language involuntarily betrays their voluntarism. Lenin, after the July rising in 1917, proposed to the social revolutionaries and Mensheviks the formation of a government responsible to the soviets: "Now and only now, perhaps *only during a few days* or for only one or two weeks would it be possible to form and consolidate such a government

27. André Gide, *Journals*, 1889–1949, p. 723.

28. James, "Great Men and their Environment."

29. Jacques Monod, *Chance and Necessity* (New York, 1971), chs. 7, 9.

in perfect peace."[30] But either all things are determined, or all things are *not* determined. "The materialistic conception of history," remarked Max Weber, "is not to be compared to a cab that one can enter or alight from at will."[31] "The truth *must* lie with one side or the other," wrote James—either the universe is absolutely ruled by necessity or it is not—"and its lying with one side makes the other false."[32]

No human being could function in a world he profoundly perceived as determined. Anyone who rigorously accepted a determinstic view of life must, for example, surrender all notions of human responsibility, since it is manifestly unfair to reward or punish people for acts they were fated to commit. "No one should judge an action as right or wrong," Morton White has written, "unless he thinks it is voluntary."[33] Sir Isaiah Berlin has remarked of determinism, "If we begin to take it seriously, then, indeed, the changes in our language, our moral notions, our attitudes toward one another, our views of history, of society and of everything else will be too profound to be even adumbrated."[34]

Of course human freedom may remain an illusion, even if an invincible illusion. Still the matter is not quite beyond testing. Determinism sees the world as closed, as "one unbending unit of fact" in James's phrase, with the whole decreed in every part and everything fixed from eternity. Indeterminism, on the contrary, says that alternative futures may be possible, one future becoming impossible only at the very moment when the other excludes it by becoming real itself. "Actualities seem to float in a wider sea of possibilities from out of which they are chosen."[35]

If the world is one unbroken fact, as the determinists insist, then there follows, in James's words, that "prediction of all things

30. Quoted by Georg Lukacs, *The Historical Novel* (London, 1969), p. 115. Lenin's emphasis.

31. Quoted by Karl Mannheim, *Ideology and Utopia* (London, 1946), p. 67.

32. James, "Dilemma of Determinism."

33. Morton White, *Foundations of Historical Knowledge* (New York, 1965), pp. 273, 289.

34. Isaiah Berlin, *Historical Inevitability*.

35. James, "Dilemma of Determinism."

without exception must be ideally, even if not actually, possible."[36] The only conclusive proof of determinism therefore lies in prevision—the prediction of things before they happen. The test must obviously take place in advance of the event. Until the demonstration is made, the case for determinism is at best unproven.

Given the hopeless record of prevision, the determinist case, as a practical matter, is worse than that. The laws men have drawn from history have done little to prepare mankind for the future. On the contrary: experience teaches us that the future is filled with surprise and that history outwits all our certitudes. One has only to recall salient historic events of the twentieth century and reflect how many of them were foreseen—the First World War? the rise of Hitler? the Nazi-Soviet pact? the Tito heresy? the desanctification of Stalin? the overthrow of Khrushchev? Anyone predicting in 1945, as the Second World War came to an end, that by 1950 Germany and Japan would be well on the way to becoming intimate friends of the United States, would have been deemed slightly mad. So would be anyone who predicted in 1950, as the Russians and Chinese signed their thirty-year pact of amity and alliance, that they would be at each other's throats by 1960. General de Gaulle, candidly confessing his own failures in foresight ("I believed that Russia would never succeed in making the bomb; that in 1946 war was inevitable; that in 1947 France could not go on"[37]), finally said, "One should not insult the future."[38] Burckhardt even felt that foreknowledge of the future was not only probably beyond human power but undesirable as well. "Desire and endeavor can only unfold freely when they live and act 'blindly,' i.e. for their own sakes and in obedience to inward impulses. . . . A future known in advance is an absurdity."[39] The central point about history is surely not its inexorability but its inscrutability.

36. William James, *Principles of Psychology*, ch. 26.

37. Malraux, *Felled Oaks*, p. 122.

38. To the Tunisian ambassador to France, 1958. Françoise Giroud, *I Give You My Word* (Boston, 1974), p. 87.

39. Jacob Burckhardt, *Reflections on History*, ch. 1.

The failure to prove the case for determinism does not imply, of course, that man is totally self-determined. "Indeterminism," said James, "is not absolute."[40] The most powerful leaders have been conscious of their impotence. "I was not master of my actions," said Napoleon, "because I was not so insane as to attempt to bend events to conform to my policies."[41] "I claim not to have controlled events," said Lincoln, "but confess plainly that events have controlled me."[42] External circumstance and internal frailty circumscribe human freedom. But they do not abolish it. The future remains inscrutable. Tocqueville defined the human condition in his conclusion to the second volume of *Democracy in America*: "Around every man a fatal circle is traced beyond which he cannot pass; but within the wide verge of that circle he is powerful and free."

The fact that there are no laws in demonstrable command of history does not render the past meaningless to the present. History has always been held to provide moral consolation of an edifying sort. Polybius thus began his *History* by observing that "the most instructive, indeed, the only method of learning to bear with dignity the vicissitude of fortune, is to recall the catastrophes of others." "Wee may gather out of History," Sir Walter Raleigh wrote in the preface to his *History of the World*, "a policy no lesse wise than eternall; by the comparison and application of other mens fore-passed miseries, with our owne like errours and ill deseruings." History also places contemporaneous perplexities into perspective, thereby, in Reinhold Niebuhr's words, emancipating the individual "from the tyranny of the present. . . . The less the past is known and the human contrivance which entered into present unrealities is undisclosed, the more do present facts appear in the guise of irrevocable facts of nature."[43]

Nor does the absence of universal laws exclude the possibility

40. James, "Great Men and their Environment."
41. Herold, *Mind of Napoleon*, p. 240.
42. Letter to A. G. Hodges, April 4, 1864.
43. Reinhold Niebuhr, *Faith and History* (New York, 1949), p. 19.

of limited generalizations drawn from the past. But drawing these generalizations is a risky business. The first risk is that of overinterpretation: of imputing to the past a purpose, rationality, and general tidiness that express the historian's hunger for order much more than they do the fortuity and contingency of the historical process. "There is less intention in history than we ascribe to it," said Emerson rightly;[44] and, again, "I have no expectation that any man will read history aright who thinks that what was done in a remote age, by men whose names have resounded far, has any deeper sense than what he is doing today";[45] and, again, in words that should hang over every historian's desk: "In analysing history, do not be too profound, for often the causes are quite superficial."[46] In short, to read large, lucid and dogmatic schemes into the confusion of past events is in many cases to project onto the screen of the past what is deemed useful for the present.

A related risk is analogy. "The chief practical use of history," Bryce well said (alas, in vain), "is to deliver us from historical analogies."[47] We all know in our own time the mesmerizing power of analogy. "For a generation after World War II," Henry Kissinger said the other day, "statesmen and nations were traumatized by the experience of Munich"[48]—a remark that may have, one trusts, a certain effect in self-exorcism. Munich was unquestionably a mistake, and its lesson was that the appeasement of a highly wound-up and heavily armed totalitarian state in the context of a relatively firm and articulated equilibrium of power was likely to upset the balance and make further aggression inevitable. But to conclude from Munich, as some statesmen did thereafter, that all attempts at negotiation infallibly invited new aggression was an abuse of history. No one understood this better than that notable historian who was the greatest contemporary critic of Munich itself.

44. Ralph Waldo Emerson, "Spiritual Laws."
45. Ralph Waldo Emerson, "History."
46. Ralph Waldo Emerson, *Journals*, vol. 4, p. 160.
47. James Bryce, *The American Commonwealth* (New York, 1888), vol. 1, p. 8.
48. Speech in Boston, March 11, 1976.

> "No case of this kind," Churchill wrote in *The Gathering Storm,* can be judged apart from its circumstances. . . . Those who are prone by temperament and character to seek sharp and clear-cut solutions of difficult and obscure problems, who are ready to fight whenever some challenge comes from a foreign power, have not always been right. On the other hand, those whose inclination is to bow their heads, to seek patiently and faithfully for peaceful compromise, are not always wrong. On the contrary, in the majority of instances, they may be right, not only morally, but from a practical standpoint. . . . How many misunderstandings which led to war could have been removed by temporising! How often have countries fought cruel wars and then after a few years of peace found themselves not only friends but allies!

Perhaps in the end historians will conclude that the multitude of errors committed in the name of Munich may exceed the original error of 1938.

No case can be judged apart from its circumstances. The misuse of analogy justifies Tocqueville's observation: "The study of history often does illuminate the present, but it can also serve to befog it."[49] Analogy appears more often as an instrument of rationalization than of rationality. "The conclusions that we seek to draw from the likeness of events," said Montaigne, "are unreliable, because events are always unlike."[50] Mark Twain, as usual, put it most vividly: "We should be careful to get out of an experience only the wisdom that is in it—and stop there; lest we be like the cat that sits down on a hot stove lid. She will never sit down on a hot stove lid again—and that is well; but also she will never sit down on a cold one."[51]

Still, if historians can resist the seductions of overinterpretation and spurious analogy, history may, as Bertrand Russell put it, yield "maxims, whose truth, once they are propounded, can be seen without the help of the events that suggested them."[52] Some maxims of this order are chipped out of comprehensive systems. Thus Marx's contention that history is determined by changes

49. In his speech of 1852 to the French Academy, republished as "The Art and Science of Politics" in *Encounter*, January 1971.

50. Michel de Montaigne, "On Experience," *Essays*, Book 3, ch. 13.

51. Mark Twain, "Pudd'nhead Wilson's New Calendar," in *Following the Equator.*

52. Russell, "On History."

in the means of production—or McLuhan's that it is determined by changes in the means of communication—stand by themselves —as profound and powerful thoughts even if they fall far short of total explanations. Others are simply isolated precepts. Perhaps the fundamental historical generalization was set forth by Heraclitus in the sixth century before Christ: "Nothing stands still." Rousseau formulated a most important and original truth: "The ability to foresee that some things cannot be foreseen is a very necessary quality."[53] We all know Acton on the corruptions of power. Hume concluded from his study of history that "human nature remains still the same, in its principles and operations"; indeed, the "chief use" of history was "to discover the constant and universal principles of human nature, by shewing men in all varieties of circumstances and situations."[54] Vico criticized this proposition, and anthropologists have latterly amassed evidence against it; Christian theologians, I take it, abide by it.

Arnold Toynbee had a fairly elaborate system of his own; but in addition he drew from the past a miscellany of injunctions for modern man. Thus, like Hume, Toynbee read history as showing that "human nature and human conduct remain just what they have always been since modern Man's ancestors became human, at some date between 30,000 and 500,000 years ago." He proposed further lessons: that power is always transitory; that "the use of force for attaining objectives is, in the long run, counter-productive"; that "an ex-victim of ill-treatment is tempted to behave like his former persecutors"; that "it is disastrous to give paramountcy to a narrower loyalty over a wider one"; and other aphorisms of real or dubious validity.[55]

The founding fathers of the American republic were men steeped in the history of Greece and Rome. They had read Plutarch, Polybius, Livy, Cicero, Sallust, Tacitus. The lessons they derived from the classical past shaped their attitudes toward the revolutionary present. "Experience is the oracle of truth," Hamil-

53. Jean-Jacques Rousseau, *Social Contract*, bk. 4, chap. 6.

54. David Hume, *Enquiry Concerning Human Understanding*, sec. 8, pt. 1.

55. Arnold J. Toynbee, "What Modern Man Must Learn from History," *PHP*, February 1975.

ton and Madison wrote in the 20th Federalist, declining to apologize for having devoted several previous papers to a history of confederations. Like Hume, the founding fathers believed in the fixity of human nature. From the fate of the Greek city-states and the decline and fall of the Roman Empire they drew grave conclusions about dangers surrounding their own experiment in self-government. History persuaded them of the inevitability, not of progress, but of growth and decay. They were concerned with the problem of preserving republican virtue against vice and vicissitude. As they pondered the remote past, they decided that excessive disproportions in power, in property, in militarism, and in luxury led to tyranny, corruption, class conflict, and social dissolution. The remedy, they believed, was to disperse power and property, to prohibit large standing armies and to preserve republican virtue.

Professional historians in our own time have devised short-run generalizations that strengthen the lessons of history. They have, for example, identified a life-cycle of revolution that, if properly understood, might have spared us misconceptions about the Russian Revolution—first about its good will and later, after we abandoned belief in its good will, about the permanence of its fanatical purpose—and might later have spared us from the notion that the Chinese Revolution would be forever cast in its early mold. Historical generalizations in a number of areas—the processes of economic development, for example, or the impact of industrialization and urbanization, or the effect of population growth, or the influence of climate or sea power or the frontier, or the circulation of elites, or the conditions of entrepreneurial innovation—offer valuable lessons.

Nearly forty years ago my father sketched out the cyclical rhythm of American politics, showing the rather regular alternation between conservative and liberal predominance in the course of American history.[56] It has been noted that corruption appears to visit the White House in fifty-year cycles—the Grant

56. Arthur M. Schlesinger, "Tides of American Politics," *Yale Review*, December, 1939; revised as "Tides of National Politics" in *Paths to the Present* (New York, 1949).

scandals in 1873, the Harding scandals in 1923, the Nixon scandals in 1973—which suggests that around 2023 the American people would be well advised to go on the alert and start nailing down everything in sight.[57] Economists have traced cycles of fluctuation in the market economy—the forty-month Kitchin cycle, the ten-year Juglar cycle, the fifteen–twenty-five year Kuznets cycle, the forty-five–sixty-year Kondratieff cycle. Professor F. L. Klingberg has described the alternation of "extrovert" and "introvert" moods in American foreign policy. Klingberg found four introvert phases since 1776, averaging about 21 years in length, and three extrovert phases, averaging about 27 years. The fourth phase of extroversion began, in his view, around 1940. Writing in 1951, as the national commitment to globalism was rising to unprecedented heights, Klingberg ventured the prediction that the United States would "retreat, to some extent at least, from so much world involvement, and . . . do so sometime in the [late] 1960s."[58]

None of these things is a historical law in the Tolstoian sense. But the accumulation of wisdom about the past, confined or imperfect as each particular generalization may be, does provide something that might be called historical insight. It is comparable not to the conclusion of the physicist after long communion with his computer but to the judgment of the doctor after long experience with a variety of patients. It is essentially a diagnostic skill, a sense of what is possible and probable in human affairs, derived from immersion in the the perplexities of history and from a consequent feel for the continuities and discontinuities of social existence. This is certainly not to imply that historians are by virtue of their profession wiser than other people. Bancroft, Macaulay, Tocqueville, Guizot, Thiers, Morley, Bryce—one cannot say that their training as historians assured them success as statesmen. It is only to suggest that historical generalizations, sufficiently multiplied and interlaced, can generate incom-

57. Arthur M. Schlesinger, Jr., *The Imperial Presidency* (Boston, 1973). pp. 268, 418.

58. F. L. Klingberg, "The Historical Alternations of Moods in American Foreign Policy," *World Politics*, January 1952.

plete but not unhelpful insights into the shape of things to come.

From this one may conclude that, if the study of history has failed thus far to produce universal laws, it has produced a mass of suggestive thoughts, at various levels of sophistication and generality, and therefore offers lessons to those who wish to benefit by them. But is anyone listening? "What experience and history teach," wrote Hegel, "is this—that peoples and governments never have learned anything from history, or acted on principles deduced from it. Each period is involved in such peculiar circumstances, exhibits a condition of things so strictly idiosyncratic, that its conduct must be regulated by considerations connected with itself, and itself alone."[59] Hegel exaggerated; remember Madison arriving in Philadelphia for the Constitutional Convention bearing his analysis "Of Ancient and Modern Confederacies." Still, in the main, people turn to history for argument and legitimation, not for insight. The trouble is that the past is an enormous grab bag with a prize for everybody. "No one can draw more out of things, books included, than he already knows," Nietzsche wrote in *Ecce Homo*. "A man has no ears for that to which experience has given him no access."

Resistance to history's disagreeable lessons is part of the human condition. It becomes, I imagine, especially strong when a nation's historical consciousness itself has worn thin. In the American case, the intense historical-mindedness of the founding fathers was not of great duration. Several factors encouraged ahistorical attitudes in the new nation. Once liberal religion abandoned belief in original sin, there was no impediment to belief in virtue and perfectibility; and this helped take the American republic out of secular history. The country itself was populated by people fleeing from, or torn from, their own histories. For all the show-business clatter of the bicentennial, we have become in these two centuries an essentially history-less nation. Our intellectuals turn their backs on history in the rush to the ahistorical behavioral sciences. Our businessmen—and our young—simply announce, in the style of the elder Henry

59. G. W. F. Hegel, *The Philosophy of History*, Introduction, pt. 2.

Ford, that history is bunk. Confucius lived 2500 years ago, but he is still an impassioned issue in Communist China. As the American historical consciousness has thinned out, it seems unlikely that lessons of the past will find much sustenance or resonance in the American present.

Insofar as the lessons of history bear upon the creation of a humane society, these lessons are often equivocal. Nor is their power to enforce themselves, especially perhaps in contemporary America, unlimited. And what in any case do we mean by a humane society?

It seems appropriate this year to begin with a bicentennial definition. A humane society is surely a society founded on the conviction, declared two hundred years ago in this city, that all human beings are created equal and possess certain unalienable rights, especially life, liberty and the pursuit of happiness. This implies a blessed commonwealth in which men and women think and speak freely, criticize and review their government, live under just and equal laws, cultivate the arts and sciences, deal honorably and generously with each other, cherish human dignity as sacred, and leave a heritage of knowledge and beauty for those who come after.

Has there ever been such a society? For many centuries wise people would have voted for Periclean Athens as the model commonwealth—learned men and graceful women devoted to proportion, understanding and truth; philosophers, dramatists, and sculptors hardly equalled in the twenty four hundred years thereafter; noble leadership based on principles of civic equality; no pollution, no mugging, no Mafia; sublime temples and incomparable vistas. Thus Emerson:

> The Grecian state is the era of the bodily nature, the perfection of the senses—of the spiritual nature unfolded in strict unity with the body. In it existed those human forms which supplied the sculptor with his models of Hercules, Phoebus and Jove; not like the forms abounding in the streets of modern cities, wherein the face is a confused blur of features, but composed of incorrupt, sharply defined, and symmetrical features. . . . The reverence exhibited is for personal qualities, courage, address, self-command justice, strength, swift-

> ness, a loud voice, a broad chest. Luxury and elegance are not known. . . . From their superior organization, they have surpassed all.[60] Attica, Emerson said, was one tenth the size of Massachusetts but "still rules the intellect of men."[61]

Athens was beyond question an extraordinary human achievement. But a truly humane society? Athenian democracy was confined to about forty thousand adult males. Women were held in subordination. Economic life depended on slavery. The fate of Socrates reminds us what happened to dissenters. Moreover, the glorious era of Athens was a time of what we now call imperialism. Athenians sought greatness at the expense of other peoples. Pericles's oration at the funeral of the first of his fellow citizens to fall in the Peloponnesian War is accounted one of the loftiest utterances in history. Read today, it seems so shameless an exercise in chauvinist self-congratulation, so fulsome a eulogy of the city of which he was the leader, and therefore of himself, that, apart from the majesty of its language, it might have come from any third-rate American president.

In any case the glory of Greece was transient. The decline of Athens did not surprise the philosophers and historians of the ancient world. While they did not deny the possibility of progress, they denied its inevitability. They saw history as made up of eternal and endless recurrence—not as unilinear but as cyclical. This corresponded to the experience of the ancient world. Christianity eventually mounted the assault on the cyclical idea. Instead of cycles, *The City of God* discerned a preordained unitary pattern of human existence, a single linear movement from creation to millennium. But the pattern was known only to God. Man was a weak and sinful creature and, unless redeemed by the grace of God, more likely to fall than to rise.

Alaric sacked Rome in A.D. 410; Augustine completed *The City of God* in 426. The Augustinian vision thus emerged naturally from the age of decline and fall. It possessed the Western mind so long as it reflected Western experience. After a thousand years, material improvement began to undermine the vision and

60. Emerson, "History."

61. Ralph Waldo Emerson, "The Fugitive Slave Law."

finally produced by the eighteenth century a new and triumphant idea—the idea of progress as historical necessity, progress leading ineluctably toward a humane society. Condorcet was the new gospel's ardent and imaginative prophet, writing his *Progress of the Human Mind* "to show by appeal to reason and fact that nature has set no term to the perfection of human faculties; that the perfectibility of man is truly indefinite; and that the progress of this perfectibility, from now onwards independent of any power that might wish to halt it, has no other limit than the duration of the globe upon which nature has cast us." Alas, while he was prophesying "an Elysium created by reason and graced by the purest pleasures known to the love of mankind," he was in fact grimly hiding from Jacobin exponents of liberty, equality and fraternity. Yet he foresaw many things a later day would deem essential for the humane society: universal education, universal suffrage, freedom of thought and expression, the abolition of slavery, women's rights, the reform of penal codes, greater equalization of status and wealth.[62]

The idea now began to emerge of history as the bearer and guarantor of the humane society. The Christian millennium was secularized and transposed from heaven to earth. Even Kant, conceding that on its surface history appeared to be "woven out of folly and childish vanity and the frenzy of destruction," discerned "a universal purpose of nature in this paradoxical movement of things." He concluded that "when the play of the freedom of the human will is examined on the great scale of universal history . . . what appears to be tangled and unregulated in the case of individuals, will be recognized in the history of the whole species as a continually advancing, though slow, development."[63]

Kant retained a flavor of eighteenth century skepticism about history's guarantee of progress. His last paper on the subject ended with an ambiguous joke about a patient repeatedly assured by his doctor that he was growing better every day. Asked

62. Condorcet, *Progress of the Human Mind,* Introduction and "The Tenth Stage."

63. Immanuel Kant, "The Idea of a Universal History from a Cosmopolitical Point of View."

one day how his sickness was, the patient replied, "How should it be? I'm dying from pure improvement!"[64] The nineteenth century stopped making jokes about progress. Marx, Comte, Spencer and others composed majestic variations on the common theme. Darwin gave progress a scientific basis. Andrew Carnegie spoke for right-minded people when he described his first reading of Darwin and Spencer. "I remember that light came in as in a flood and all was clear. . . . 'All is well since all grows better' became my motto. Man was not created with an instinct for his own degradation, but from the lower he had risen to the higher forms. Nor is there any conceivable end to his march to perfection. His face is turned to the light; he stands in the sun and looks upward."[65]

Standing in the sun and looking upward proved to be a dangerous exercise. The effort blinded right-minded people and left them unprepared for the horrors of the twentieth century. Two world wars, Hitler and Stalin, concentration camps and slave labor and bureaucraticized criminality, terrorism and nuclear bombs—all challenged faith in the inevitability of progress. In retrospect the great weakness of the idea of progress was its benevolent view of human nature and its commitment to the perfectibility of man. It was a theology without a theodicy. It lacked a tragic sense. It offered no serious explanation for evil. It did not account for the destructiveness and demonry organized, unleashed, and relished in the twentieth century—for the irrationalism and violence that obviously flowed from deep springs in the soul of man.

Perhaps Augustine had a point about human nature after all; perhaps the classical pagans had a point about eternal recurrence. In any case modern man evidently could not rely on history to deliver the goods. After the Second World War Reinhold Niebuhr persuasively summed up the situation. The facts of contemporary experience, he said, were in glaring contradiction to optimistic interpretations of history, almost "as if history had

64. Immanuel Kant, "An Old Question Raised Again: Is the Human Race Constantly Progressing?"

65. Andrew Carnegie, *Autobiography* (Boston, 1920), p. 339.

been designed to refute the vain delusions of man." History was not Christ, nor was historical development a redemptive process. The idea of "salvation through history," Niebuhr said, was extinct.[66]

The neorealist mood could assume divine sovereignty over history (as describing the limits of the world's rationality, not as a theory of secondary causation), or it could follow Nietzsche and assume that God was dead. In either case it concluded that history was what men, within their fatal circle, had made it; that humanity had to save itself through its own will, whether as illuminated by the grace of God or by the human creation of meaning in a meaningless universe.

So we cannot rely on the automatic processes of history to lead us into the humane society. Progress, if it exists at all, is not self-executing; and history displays so many facets of progression and regression as to render the whole theory of inevitable progress useless as an historical generalization. Scientific and technological progress is demonstrable; spiritual, moral, artistic, philosophical progress is not; and, while science and technology may facilitate the humane society, decency, kindliness, reason and mercy are its essence. Who can prove human progress here? Where the idea of progress retains value is not as an historical law but as an ethical imperative. It explains neither the past nor the future. But it enjoins us to try and make the future better than the past.

What then should we do to move toward a more humane society? Tocqueville, one of the most humane of men, had an early vision of a regime of "balanced, regulated liberty, held in check by religion, custom and law."[67] Let us pursue Tocqueville's theory of the three checks as one entry into the larger problem. First, religion, in his view "indispensable to the maintenance of republican institutions"—indeed, more vital to democratic than to authoritarian societies. "How is it possible that society should

66. Niebuhr, *Faith and History*, pp. viii, 7, 31.
67. Alexis de Tocqueville, *Recollections*, part 2, ch. 1.

escape destruction if the moral tie is not strengthened as the political tie is relaxed?"[68] As that genial skeptic Benjamin Franklin put it, "If men are so wicked *with religion,* what would they be like *if without it*?"[69] Or, to put the issue another way, supernatural faith gave man's hunger for absolutes an outlet. The trouble when people stopped believing in God, G. K. Chesterton once said, was not that thereafter they believed in nothing; it was that thereafter they believed in anything.[70] The conjunction of the decline of supernatural faith and the rise of the totalitarian social religions of the twentieth century cannot be simply a coincidence.

It may be argued in addition that religious faith is essential to a humane society because of its salutary emphasis on the limits of human wisdom and the frailty of human striving in face of the impenetrable mystery of the cosmos. A decent doubt as to one's own infallibility is certainly a precondition to civilized living. On the other hand, religion can have the effect of inflating as well as deflating human pride. The Tocqueville argument overlooks the way in which the religious impulse, when discharged in fanaticism or organized in arbitrary institutions, has been one of the great sources of inhumanity in history. Even when humane, the dogmatic side of religion demands that, in order fully to grasp the blazing Christian insights into human nature and history, one must also accept an implausible cosmic melodrama about God and Satan, heaven and hell, sin and salvation.

At least the twentieth century finds the melodrama implausible except as symbolism; men in other times, far more intelligent than the speakers at this symposium, deemed it the ultimate and climactic reality. On Judgment Day they may well turn out to be right. But, for better or worse, religious faith hardly seems a living option for most of us today. God is dead; at least the serious God—the God of Augustine, Thomas Aquinas, Luther and Calvin—is dead. In how many lives nowadays is God, hour

68. Alexis de Tocqueville, *Democracy in America,* vol. 1, ch. 17.

69. Benjamin Franklin, *Complete Works,* ed., John Bigelow, vol. 9, p. 355.

70. Or so Malcolm Muggeridge once told me Chesterton had said; I have not located this splendid thought in Chesterton's writings.

by hour, the decisive force? Who believes in hell and damnation as St. Augustine and St. Thomas, Luther and Calvin, believed? God is a base to be touched ceremonially once a week, not a live, constant, supreme presence. And those who insist most clamorously on their intimacy with him—the John Foster Dulleses and Norman Vincent Peales, the Billy Grahams and Billy James Hargises—only bring the idea of divine sovereignty into greater disrepute. They do not get the basic point that, as Lincoln once said, "the Almighty has His own purposes."[71] Those who pretend to know personally the purposes of the Almighty are the betrayers of the faith.

So religion, it would appear, cannot—pending some new Great Awakening—play the part Tocqueville assigned to it in his scheme of balanced and regulated liberty. What about his other two checks: custom and law? Here too we encounter problems. The accelerating rush of change has shattered the mold of custom. There has been in recent times a logarithmic increase in the velocity of history. Man has been on earth, it has been estimated, for approximately eight hundred lifetimes, most of which he spent in caves. "Some five or six score people," William James said in 1895, "if each . . . could speak for his own generation, would carry us away to the black unknown of the human species, to days without a document or monument to tell their tale."[72] Man achieved movable type but eight lifetimes ago, industrialization only in the last three lifetimes. "The world did not [just] double or treble its movement between 1800 and 1900," Henry Adams wrote in 1909, "but, measured by any standard known to science—by horse-power, calories, volts, mass in any shape—the tension and vibration and volume and so-called progression of society were fully a thousand times greater in 1900 than in 1800."[73]

The rate of change, quickened by the self-accelerating internal dynamics of scientific inquiry, increased exponentially in the twentieth century. The eight hundredth lifetime has seen more

71. In his second Inaugural Address.

72. William James, "Is Life Worth Living?" in *Will to Believe.*

73. Henry Adams, "The Rule of Phase Applied to History."

prodigious scientific and technical achievement than the first 798 put together.[74] There is no apparent end. "Is it credible that such a mushroom knowledge, such a growth overnight as this," said James, "*can* represent more than the minutest glimpse of what the universe will really prove to be when adequately understood? No! our science is a drop, our ignorance a sea."[75]

Custom governs in static societies. It loses its force in the world of change where, as Aristophanes said, "Whirl is King, having driven out Zeus." Only the present is legitimate, and that not for long. So the experience of parents is increasingly irrelevant to the needs of their children. The old find themselves strangers in a strange land. Tradition, like God, is dead. And, if custom, like religion, no longer plays its regulative role, what of law? Here too the velocity of history has altered things. In static societies law might have a sacred, impartial, traditional character; it might seem, in Holmes's phrase, "a brooding omnipresence in the sky." But a world of change exposes the function of law as a manipulable instrument of rule—as, Holmes added, "the articulate voice of some sovereign or quasi-sovereign that can be identified."[76]

Tocqueville himself knew that his youthful vision was growing obsolete in his own lifetime. He did not despair, because he did not suppose there were rigid limits on human imagination and invention. He wrote in his *Recollections*:

> The more I study the former condition of the world and see the world of our own day in greater detail, the more I consider the prodigious variety to be met with not only in laws, but in the principles of law, and the different forms even now taken and retained, whatever one may say, by the rights of property on this earth—*the more I am tempted to believe that what we call necessary institutions are often no more than institutions to which we have grown accustomed*, and that in matters of social constitution the field of possibilities is much more extensive than men living in their various societies are ready to imagine.[77]

74. Cf. W. W. Hambleton, "The 800th Lifetime and the Energy Crisis," address to the Kansas Academy of Science, April 27, 1973.

75. James, "Is Life Worth Living?"

76. In Southern Pacific Co. v. Jensen, 244 U.S. 205, pp. 221–22.

77. Toqueville, *Recollections*, part 2, ch. 2 (italics mine).

When Whirl is King, philosophers tend toward pessimism. The threat to "what we call necessary institutions" appears a threat to the very framework of civil existence. Thus a school of social philosophy in our own day, oddly claiming Tocqueville as an ancestor, bemoans the contemporary disbelief in institutions of authority and suggests that authority *per se* must receive automatic respect if civilization is to survive. We heard such talk, for example, during the Watergate crisis. A sounder lesson from history surely is that authority is entitled only to the respect it earns. When Acton wrote those famous lines about power corrupting, he added a line that should be equally famous: "There is no worse heresy than that the office sanctifies the holder of it."[78] Nor is there any vainer enterprise than the artificial resuscitation of institutions that have lost their power to command respect.

In the quest for a humane society, what can we devise for the protection of the human personality to take the place of the checks the youthful Tocqueville saw in religion, custom, and law? This problem obsessed him when he came to the United States during the age of Jackson. Apart from specific American factors—antecedent traditions, geographical isolation, an open frontier—Tocqueville found comfort in such general features of government as federalism, democratic participation, voluntary association, and so on. But he laid particular stress on one point. "In order to combat the evils which equality may produce," he wrote, "there is only one effectual remedy: namely, political freedom."[79]

What are the conditions of political freedom? Plainly the basic condition is the right of political opposition—a right that we Americans strongly believe requires competing politcal parties, though, remembering Tocqueville's warning that necessary institutions may be only those to which we have grown accustomed, we cannot be eternally sure that this is the only form in which political opposition may be preserved. In any case,

78. Letter to Mandell Creighton, April 5, 1887.

79. Tocqueville, *Democracy in America*, vol. 2, bk. 2, ch. 4.

political opposition, in whatever form, requires a base safe from the easy invasion by those in power. "If men were angels," said the authors of the 51st Federalist, "no government would be necessary. If angels were to govern men, neither external nor internal controls on government would be necessary. In framing a government which is to be administered by men over men, the great difficulty lies in this: you must first enable the government to control the governed; and in the next place oblige it to control itself."

The structural solution devised by the founding fathers to the problem of obliging government to control itself was to deny the national government (and indeed any other claimant) a monopoly of power. Through the separation of powers and through federalism the Constitution sought to spread power about in ways that made each repository a check on the others. And the founding fathers were alive to substance as well as to form. They thoroughly understood the economic basis of politics and the dangers in the excessive concentration of wealth in private hands. "The most common and durable source of factions," observed Madison in the 10th Federalist, "has been the various and unequal distribution of property." Some of them believed therefore that small freeholds provided the only reliable foundation for a free state. "Those who labor in the earth," wrote Jefferson, "are the chosen people of God, if ever He had a chosen people, whose breasts He has made His peculiar deposit for substantial and genuine virtue. It is the focus in which He keeps alive that sacred fire, which otherwise might escape from the face of the earth."[80]

But Jefferson's rural arcadia is dead too, along with God and tradition. The problem now is to keep the sacred fire alive in industrial society. Still, a larger perception lay underneath the agricultural mystique: that political freedom required diffusion of property and diversification in its ownership. To concentrate property in a few hands was to concentrate political power, endanger political freedom, and cloud the hope for a humane so-

80. Thomas Jefferson, *Notes on Virginia*, query 19.

ciety. This was the general principle. Marx seized on a vital part of this, condemned the concentration of private property, and developed a theory of history, an analysis of industrial society and a revolutionary creed. But the Marxist revolution in the end failed to attack concentrated power; it only transferred power from the loose and vulnerable coalition of corporate barons to the totalitarian party and state. The result vindicated the general principle and was far more fatal to political freedom.

The general principle may be harder to enforce in industrial than in agricultural society, though even this is not self-evident when one recalls that power of great landholders through the ages. And Marx's prediction that class war in industrial society would lead inexorably to communist revolution has been, for a number of reasons, thwarted by history. "The feud between the capitalist and laborer, the house of Have and the house of Want," George Bancroft, historian and Jacksonian politician, wrote fourteen years before *The Communist Manifesto,* "is as old as social union, and can never be entirely quieted; but he who will act with moderation, prefer fact to theory, and remember that every thing in this world is relative and not absolute, will see that the violence of the contest may be stilled."[81]

Bancroft, the relativist, turned out to be in this case the better prophet. But absolutism has made a remarkable comeback in our time. A century ago John Morley could write that political freedom was "a finally accepted principle in some sense or other with every school of thought that has the smallest chance of commanding the future."[82] Ever since, political freedom has been in retreat. Yet it remains a constitutive element in the human society—because, among other things, it is the guarantee for access to a wider and richer spectrum of human rights. The longer list includes those inalienable rights to life, liberty, and the pursuit of happiness. It includes equal justice before the law. It includes the right to work out one's personal vision of truth and understanding, whether in religion, philosophy, liter-

81. Letter to the workingmen of Northampton, October 1, 1834, *Boston Courier*, October 22, 1834.

82. John Morley, *On Compromise* (1874).

ature, art, or life. And it implies the duty to respect the vision of others. Tolerance and compromise are part of the texture of civilization.

Political freedom, secured by resources relatively inaccessible to those in power, is thus not only a restraint against irresponsible power but the precondition to the serious exercise of other forms of freedom. Yet political freedom also unquestionably creates problems for the humane society. In particular, it presupposes the persistence of political conflict. Conflict cannot be expected always to take the most reasoned and agreeable forms. Moralists through the ages have argued with some justice that conflict brings out the most vicious human qualities—competition, envy, greed, aggression, hostility, malevolence, destructiveness. Political philosophers have dreamed of the cooperative commonwealth in which lions lie down with lambs and everyone loves his neighbor.

History, however, records that attempts to realize societies without political conflict have in practice only produced societies where conflict, denied constitutional outlets, becomes twisted, ugly and deadly (for example, Nazi Germany, Communist Russia, Communist China) and where the means of suppressing dissent, and with it liberty, becomes rapid and efficient. Pending the millennium, a world without conflict is a world of fantasy—or one of exceedingly cruel reality. The problem is not to abolish conflict but to contain and civilize it: as Bancroft said, to act with moderation, prefer fact to theory, and remember that everything in this world is relative and not absolute.

Still, political freedom defines the process, not the substance, of the humane society. "Freedom is a good horse," said Matthew Arnold, "but a horse to ride somewhere." The rider bound for the humane society presumably seeks a society committed to individual moral and intellectual fulfillment within an environment of collective kindness and decency. But how to civilize conflict? How to achieve kindness and decency in human relations? Obviously there is no final answer to these questions except in the dark recesses of the human heart. But it is also plain that some social arrangements are more likely than others to encourage kindness and decency. Thus unduly authoritarian or unduly acquisitive or unduly unequal societies place a premium on the less attractive qualities of man.

Must a humane society be an equal society? In the last year or two, eminent philosophers have expended much rigorous argument on the question of equality; and I would not dare challenge Messrs. Rawls and Novack on their own terrain. As a historian, I would retain the distinction between equality of rights and opportunities and equality of condition or result; the second having much merit only as it is the result of the first. Nor do I accept the current use of "elitism" as an epithet. History indicates that all government in developed states is in the end government by minorities; that Pareto was largely right when he wrote, "The history of man is the history of the continuous replacement of elites"[83]; and that most serious art and science has been the creation of men and women who preferred their individual vision to that of the majority. "I agree with you," Jefferson wrote John Adams, "that there is a natural aristocracy among men. The grounds of this are virtue and talents. . . . There is also an artificial aristocracy founded on wealth and birth, without either virtue or talents; for with these it would belong to the first class. The natural aristocracy I consider as the most precious gift of nature for the instruction, the trusts, and government of society."[84] Any conception of equality that repressed Jefferson's natural aristocracy would seem to me incompatible with a humane society. The humane society, in my view, would be an equalitarian but not an equal society. It would have significantly more equal distribution of income, liberty, power, and choice than any contemporary industrial state. But it would not expect or demand the compulsory equalization of the conditions of life.

If a humane society will thus not be a rigidly equalized society, if competition and conflict retain a role, the human ideal re-

83. Vilfredo Pareto, *The Rise and Fall of the Elites* (Totowa, New Jersey, 1968), p. 36.

84. Jefferson to Adams, October 28, 1813.

quires close attention to the relations between winners and losers. Kindness and decency in human relations demand above all, as Kant observed two centuries ago, the recognition that rational nature exists as an end in itself. From this proposition Kant drew his "practical imperative": *"So act as to treat humanity, whether in thine own person or in that of any other, in every case as an end withal, never as means only."*[85]

Kant's rule forbids the condemnation by society of men and women to poverty, squalor, and untouchability on the excuse that higher interests of society—the liberty of contract or the freedom of the market or the natural selection of the race—are thus served. It forbids the use of living human beings as means to some allegedly nobler, more abstract, or more distant end. Hawthorne described the danger in his portrayal of the world-saver Hollingsworth in that brilliant political novel *The Blithedale Romance.* Hollingsworth, Hawthorne wrote, had "a stern and dreadful peculiarity." While proclaiming his boundless love for humanity, he was himself inhuman. "This is always true of those men who have surrendered themselves to an overruling purpose." Such people, Hawthorne warned,

> have no heart, no sympathy, no reason, no conscience. They will keep no friend, unless he make himself the mirror of their purpose; they will smite and slay you, and trample your dead corpse under foot, all the more readily, if you take the first step with them and cannot take the second, and the third, and every other step of their terribly straight path. They have an idol to which they consecrate themselves high-priest, and deem it holy to offer sacrifices of whatever is most precious; and never once seem to suspect—so cunning has the Devil been with them—that this false deity . . . is but a spectrum of the very priest himself, projected upon the surrounding darkness. And the higher and purer the original object, and the more unselfishly it may have been taken up, the slighter is the probability that they can be led to recognize the process by which godlike benevolence has been debased into all-devouring egotism.[86]

85. Immanuel Kant, *Fundamental Principles of the Metaphysics of Morals,* sec. 2.

86. Hawthorne, *The Blithedale Romance,* ch. 9.

Mr. Dooley defined a fanatic as the man who does what he thinks "th' Lord wud do if He only knew the facts in th' case." And fanaticism—the willingness to sacrifice human beings to abstraction—is a mortal enemy of the humane society. "The duty of governments," wrote the young Winston Churchill in 1896, "is to be first of all practical. I am for makeshifts and expediency. I would like to make the people who live in this world at the same time as I do better fed and happier generally. If incidentally I benefit posterity—so much the better—but I would not sacrifice my own generation to a principle—however high, or a truth however great."[87]

Still the conception of persons as ends in themselves is itself an abstraction. How to make concrete and profound the sense of individual human beings? Here art becomes not only an aesthetic adornment but a social necessity for the human society. For it is art that reveals the specificity of life—and at the same time finds in specificity an ultimate heightening and clarification of common experience.

A humane society must be humane in its procedures, its values, and its face-to-face relations. It must, in addition, be prepared to defend its values against inhumane challenge. One of the lessons Toynbee extracted from history was the idea of the futility of wars. That is often the case, but it is not to be adopted as a general rule. Some wars—the American Civil War, for example, or the Second World War—were surely necessary wars in defense of the principle of humanity.

People on occasion will, and should, fight to save humane values. The question remains whether they will commit themselves unreservedly to these values short of manifest and mortal threat. History supports theology in raising doubts about the prospect. Human nature, as displayed in the one and revealed in the other, is, for all its glorious moments of heroism and sacrifice, too often weak in will, limited in wisdom, selfish in motives—its generosity

87. Churchill to Bourke Cockran, April 12, 1896. In Randolph S. Churchill, *Winston S. Churchill* (Boston, 1967), companion vol. 1, p. 668.

tainted with hostility, its capacity for love corrupted by its instinct for destruction. It is hard to suppose that such flawed creatures will ever attain a fully humane society short of the millennium.

But this does not render the value or the quest meaningless. After all, the West, even as it has contrived means to destroy civilization in a single fusillade, has also ended human sacrifices and mass infanticide, abolished slavery, reduced the ravages of disease, dismantled empires, established goals of employment and welfare, and started women on the ascent to equality. These are not inconsiderable gains for humanity. Our task is to widen and deepen them. The objectives are good in themselves, and so, in Whitman's phrase, is "the exercise of Democracy"—"To work for Democracy is good, the exercise is good—strength it makes and lessons it teaches."[88] What is essential is to comprehend the frailty of human striving but to strive nevertheless. Neibuhr has called Lincoln's "combination of moral resoluteness about the immediate issues with a religious awareness of another dimension of meaning and judgment" the almost perfect model of meeting the task at hand while preserving a vantage point over the struggle.[89]

This may perhaps be the final lesson of history in the quest for the humane society. Let us pursue the quest but do so without illusion. Satisfaction resides in small improvements—but small improvements can make vast differences in individual lives. I doubt whether the perfect society lies over the horizon. Having invoked Tocqueville so often in the course of these remarks, I can only conclude with his ruminations toward the end of his life: "Shall we arrive—as other prophets, perhaps as deluded as their predecessors, assure us—at a more complete and profound social transformation than our fathers foresaw or wished, and than we ourselves are able to foresee? . . . For

88. C. J. Furness, ed., *Walt Whitman's Workshop* (Cambridge, 1928), pp. 57–58.

89. Reinhold Niebuhr, *The Irony of American History* (New York, 1952), p. 172.

myself, I cannot say. I do not know when this long voyage will end. I am tired of seeing the shore in each successive mirage, and I often ask myself if the *terra firma* we have sought so long really exists or if we are not doomed to rove forever upon the seas."[90]

Response

Jaroslav Pelikan

When I accepted this invitation more than two years ago, it was with the observation that "Mr. Schlesinger and I read quite different kinds of historical sources," and with the hope that his presentation—based as I knew it would be on his wide and reflective study of American history—would provide a point of contact for a scholar who (within Professor Schlesinger's authorship) has been interested more in Orestes Brownson than in either Jackson or Roosevelt or Kennedy or, for that matter, any other "imperial president." With characteristic generosity and erudition, Arthur Schlesinger has provided the historian of Christian thought with several such points of contact. Not only has he spoken of the dangers of "a theology without a theodicy," but he has identified Augustine in *The City of God* as the spokesman for the most influential Western Christian view of "the lessons of history." And he has singled out "the fate of the Greek city-states and the decline and fall of the Roman Empire" as the historical instances from which the founding fathers of this Republic "drew grave conclusions" about such lessons.

For the founding fathers of the Republic, but also for Tocqueville, the history of Rome from Republic to Empire was a textbook to which to turn for instruction about the course of human affairs, the development of freedom and the fate of despotism.[1] And it was from this history that Augustine and the church fathers,

90. Tocqueville, *Recollections*, part 2, ch. 2.

1. Alexis de Tocqueville, *Democracy in America*, vol. 2, part 4, chap. 6; cf. also George Wilson Pierson, *Tocqueville in America* (New York, 1959), p. 73.

and with them most of European thought for a millennium or more in both East and West, derived the materials on which they based their views of "the lessons of history." As has been pointed out by several historical scholars elsewhere, the bicentennial of the Declaration of Independence coincides with the bicentennial of the publication of volume one of Edward Gibbon's *The History of the Decline and Fall of the Roman Empire.* That coincidence, combined with the role of the history of Rome as the fundamental paradigm both for Augustine and the church fathers and for Hamilton and Madison and the American fathers, would seem to justify an inquiry into the interpretation of the decline and fall of Rome by Christian theologians contemporary with the events of that history. I believe that we can distinguish three such interpretations, which I would identify as: the apocalyptic, the progressivist, and the dialectical.

Apocalyptic Interpretation

The Christian movement had in fact been preparing for the fall of Rome since its very beginnings. "Fallen, fallen is Babylon the great, she who made all nations drink the wine of her impure passion" the seer of the Apocalypse heard the angel say (Rev. 14:8). For him it was a lesson of history that the Roman Empire of Nero had violated the will of God and profaned the earth with its iniquities, and that its hegemony was now approaching its end. Based as it apparently was on Daniel's vision of the four beasts (Dan. 7)—representing the four empires of world history—the apocalyptic announcement of the imminent fall of Rome, the last empire, looked for the establishment of the reign of the Ancient of Days when all the thrones had been cast down (Dan. 7:9). While in the teachings of Jesus as reported in the Gospels, the coming of the end had been intertwined with the fall of Jerusalem, the Christians of the first two or three centuries more commonly connected the end with the fall of Rome—using the fall of Jerusalem instead as part of their argument that the old covenant with Israel had been superseded by the new covenant with the church.[2] Tertullian, the first important Christian

2. Tertullian *Apology* 26.

author to use Latin, incorporated these themes into his eschatology. "All nations," he said, "have possessed empire, each in its proper time . . . until at the last almost universal dominion has accrued to the Romans."[3] But this was soon to end; and at the conclusion of his treatise against theatrical performances and gladiatorial games, he described the performance soon to come on the great and terrible day of the Lord, when Caesars and governors, philosophers and poets would be led in triumphal procession at the unexpected return of Christ.[4] Yet elsewhere he also claimed that Christians "pray for the delay of the end" to give the empire and its citizens more time for repentance,[5] for he found it difficult to accept the implication of his own teaching that the Roman Empire, this "garden of the world,"[6] would soon collapse.

Writing a generation or so later, Tertullian's disciple Cyprian—though less flamboyant in his apocalypticism than his master—applied it more rigorously to the present status and the immediate prospects of the empire. Having experienced the persecution of the church—under the emperor Decius—which was followed by a devastating plague, Cyprian was persuaded "that the world is collapsing and is oppressed with the tempests of mischievous ills."[7] The "desolation of pestilence" and the prevalence of war were, he said elsewhere, evidence that "as the day of judgment is now approaching, the censure of a wrathful God is more and more aroused."[8] The forces of nature and the traditions of society were falling apart before his very eyes, confirming the law of all things that what has a beginning must also come to an end; so it was now with the Roman world.[9] "The whole world," he lamented, "is wet with mutual blood. And murder, which in the case of an individual is admitted to be a crime, is called a virtue when it is committed by the government."[10] The

3. Tertullian *To the Nations* 2.17.19.
4. Tertullian *The Spectacles* 30.
5. Tertullian *Apology* 39.2.
6. Tertullian *The Pallium* 9.
7. Cyprian *The Mortality* 25.
8. Cyprian *To Demetrianus* 5.
9. Ibid., 3.
10. Cyprian *To Donatus* 6.

Roman courts, which were intended to protect the innocent and to punish the guilty, "echo with the madness of strife"; and "wrong is being done in the midst of the laws themselves."[11] The vengeance of a just God was working its way in "the destruction of all things [*ruinis rerum*]" (or, if one accepts a variant reading, "the destruction of kings [*ruinis regum*]").[12]

Embedded as it thus was in the New Testament and in the writings of the earliest Latin fathers, the apocalyptic view of the lessons of history never disappeared from Christian thought, even after "apocalypticism [had been transformed into] the mother of all Christian theology."[13] But by the time the events of history had begun to catch up with the lessons of apocalyptic, the eschatological expectations of the church were no longer as vivid as they had been. More in sorrow than in either anger or glee, Jerome described the incursions of the barbarian tribes into the Roman Empire, which compelled "Rome to fight within her own borders, not for glory but for sheer life."[14] "The Roman world is falling," he said in another letter, "yet we hold up our heads instead of bowing them."[15] When Rome was sacked by Alaric and his Goths in A.D. 410, Jerome was in tears. "The city that had captured the whole world has itself been captured," he lamented.[16] "The world is sinking into ruin, [and] . . . the famous city, the capital of the Roman Empire, is being swallowed up in one tremendous conflagration."[17] For "the whole world has perished in one city," and "the mother of nations has also become their grave."[18] Now the Roman capitol was in shambles, and the temples of Jupiter had perished.[19] Through Jerome as well as through other sources, the apocalyptic definition of the lessons of history was transmitted to later genera-

11. Ibid., 10.
12. Cyprian *To Demetrianus* 17.
13. Ernst Käsemann, "Die Anfänge christlicher Theologie," *Exegetische Versuche und Besinnungen* (Göttingen, 1964), 2, 100.
14. Jerome *Epistles* 123.16-17.
15. Ibid., 60.16.
16. Ibid., 127.12.
17. Ibid., 128.4.
18. Jerome *Preface to Ezekiel.*
19. Jerome *To Jovinian* 2.38; Epistles 107.1.

tions, with the result that whenever it was to reassert itself in subsequent centuries, it was able to claim a legitimate place in the spectrum of Christian theories.

Progressivist View

As Jerome's observations about the transformation of Rome from paganism to Christianity suggest,[20] however, this apocalyptic definition had to yield to a belief in continuity and in a progression from imperial to Christian Rome. The principal locus of that belief was in the Greek-speaking Christian East, and its most articulate spokesman was the "father of church history," Eusebius, who wrote not only the first full-length history of the church, but a biography of the emperor Constantine as well. His predominant concern, as the opening words of his *Ecclesiastical History* make clear, was with "succession" and continuity.[21] Thus he gave an account of a "catechetical school" in Alexandria—where in succession Pantaenus, Clement, and Origen had taught—largely as a way of attributing to his hero Origen a continuity with the Christian past that he did not have, at least in so explicit a way; he likewise set down lists of bishops in various sees as documentation of the same "succession."[22] This was apparently part of an apologetic concern to prove that the church and the gospel had not sprung up all of a sudden in an obscure corner of the empire, but had in fact stood in a line with the best in both Jewish and Gentile belief. Therefore Abraham was, "in fact if not in name," a Christian.[23] It was characteristic of error, on the other hand, to be the product of "novelty-mongering" and to have no recognizable continuity or succession.

The persecution of the church by the empire was, in the light of this, to be seen as a betrayal of the best in the imperial tradition itself. Although the Christians had brought this calamity upon themselves by their sins,[24] the cause of the persecution was

20. Jerome *Epistles* 107.2.
21. Eusebius *Ecclesiastical History* 1.1.1.
22. Ibid., 5.10–11; 5.1.
23. Ibid., 1.4.6.
24. Ibid., 8.1.7.

the recrudescence of superstition and irrationality among the emperors.[25] Even imperial officials who had the reputation of being law-abiding and clement took arms against the church and persecuted it.[26] Yet in their martyrdom the believers continued to pray for the empire and to show themselves to be its most faithful supporters.[27] It was actually the persecutors rather than the persecuted who suffered most, not only in the world to come but also in the present life.[28] The persecution became the cause of calamity and confusion in the empire.[29] When this led to civil war, it was a respite for the church, for now the Romans directed against one another the fury that had been vented upon the Christians.[30] In Eusebius's own words, "that which had never been recorded in the annals of the Roman government from the beginning, now for the first time took place in our day contrary to all expectation. For the empire was rent in twain."[31] When the divine purpose of chastening and converting the church had been accomplished,[32] Providence intervened in the history of the empire to punish the persecutors and preserve the church.[33] But it was not only on behalf of the church that Providence intervened; it was also on behalf of the Roman Empire.

For the peace of the church and the conversion of the emperor Constantine to the faith meant, according to Eusebius, the restoration of the empire. "Constantine the most mighty victor . . . reconquered the East . . . and formed the Roman Empire, *as in the days of old,* into a single united whole."[34] Alone among all who had wielded the scepter over the Roman Empire until that time, Constantine was "the friend of God, who is the Sovereign of all,"[35] and through him God blessed and sustained the Roman

25. Ibid., 6.41.1–2.
26. Ibid., 8.12.7 ff.
27. Ibid., 7.11.8.
28. Eusebius *Life of Constantine* 2.27.
29. Eusebius *Ecclesiastical History* 8.14.18.
30. Ibid., 6.41.9.
31. Eusebius *Martyrs of Palestine* 13.13.
32. Eusebius *Ecclesiastical History* 7.30.21.
33. Ibid., 8.16.2; *Martyrs of Palestine* 11.31.
34. Eusebius *Ecclesiastical History* 10.9.6 (italics mine).
35. Eusebius *Life of Constantine* 35.

Empire. Like a new Moses, Constantine vanquished the enemies of God and of the empire and led his people into the Promised Land.[36] And although the experience of persecution may have aroused some Christians to think that as Christ had prophesied, the end of all things was at hand,[37] the end being worked out by Providence was not the end described in the language of Christian apocalypticism, but the progress of the Roman Empire from pagan to Christian. The Eusebian interest in the continuity of history found its ultimate expression in the belief that the Roman Empire had not fallen at all, but had continued and had progressed and would endure to the end of time.

Like Eusebius, Augustine insisted that "God can never be believed to have left the kingdoms of men, their dominations and servitudes, outside of the laws of his providence,"[38] and with Eusebius he affirmed that "the church has gone forward on its pilgrimage amid the persecutions of the world and the consolations of God."[39]

Dialectical Conception

In Augustine's philosophy of history, however, these beliefs did not lead either to an apocalyptic interpretation of the fall of Rome or to a progressivist view of the continuation and renewal of the empire in a new and Christian Rome, but to a conception of the lessons of history that may perhaps best be described as dialectical. That dialectical conception is the leitmotiv of his *City of God,* which treats of the city of God and the city of man, whose histories had been intertwined ever since their founding by, respectively, Abel and Cain.[40] The dialectic of the two cities was in part the dialectic between time and eternity,[41] for the city of God belonged to eternity but participated in time and history. But the dialectic also marked history itself; for only God in his secret counsels knew who belonged to which city, and therefore both cities had a "mortal course" and were

36. Eusebius *Ecclesiastical History* 9.9.5.
37. Ibid., 6.41.10.
38. Augustine *The City of God* 5.11.
39. Ibid., 18.51.
40. Ibid., 15.1.
41. Ibid., 11.6.

"mingled together from the beginning to the very end," and both shared in the good and in the ill of human history.[42] Only the Last Judgment would separate these two histories from each other, even though the judgment of God was going on constantly throughout human history.[43] "The present intermingling and the future separation"[44] of the two cities was described in the parable of the tares and the wheat, including its admonition: "Let both grow together until the harvest" (Matt. 13:30). In opposition to the classical theory of cycles in history, this dialectical theory stressed the linear character of time and history;[45] while against a view that transformed the historical dialectic into a metaphysical dualism, it stressed that the difference between the two cities was one of will—not one of nature, since both had been created by God.[46]

It was in this context that Augustine interpreted the history of Rome and the fall of Rome. Kingdoms and empires that neglected justice were nothing more than a form of "fancy larceny."[47] On the basis of Vergil's words about "the madness of war and the lust for possessions"[48] Augustine identified greed and conquest as the fundamental malaise of Roman history;[49] their yearning for peace and prosperity had as its ultimate goal licentious self-indulgence, which would use prosperity to produce "a moral pestilence a thousand times more disastrous than the fiercest enemies."[50] The secret of Rome's successes, especially in early days, lay in the positive virtues of which these vices were a distortion—the desire for glory, and with it the love of freedom.[51] Spurred on by these, Rome had conquered the world.[52] Quite

42. Ibid., 18.54.
43. Ibid., 20.1.
44. Ibid., 20.5.
45. Ibid., 14.20.
46. Ibid., 11.33.
47. Ibid., 4.4.
48. Vergil *Aeneid* 8.327.
49. Augustine *The City of God* 3.10.
50. Ibid., 1.30.
51. Ibid., 5.12.
52. Ibid., 18.22.

apart from the dialectic between the city of God and the city of man, then, even the history of the earthly city itself—epitomized in the history of Rome as narrated by pagan historians—was marked by conflict between virtue and vice, justice and tyranny, law and license.[53] And the God who in his providence "grants earthly kingdoms both to the good and to the evil"[54] had, through the conquest of the world by Rome, brought the nations into a "community of government and law."[55] Yet the Roman Empire was "like glass in its fragile splendor, about which one is always afraid that it will suddenly shatter into bits."[56] When it did finally shatter, that was not the fault of the city of God—which wanted and, historically speaking, needed the city of man to be at peace—[57] but the outcome of the dialectic in the history of the earthly city itself.

The Augustinian theology of history shaped the thought of the Middle Ages, but in the process the city of God came to be identified with the empirical church—with the result that the dialectic was seen as the theme of the conflicts between empire and papacy. In the Greek Church, on the other hand, the progressivist Eusebian theory of the continuity of Christian with pagan Rome gave to Byzantine historiography—and to Byzantine political philosophy—a characteristic belief in the uniqueness and sacredness of the Eastern Empire and in its historic mission. The apocalyptic definition of the laws of history did not—as, by definition, it could not—find similar embodiment in a continuing political and ecclesiastical institution; but it has repeatedly erupted within both Western and Eastern Christendom, as in Joachim of Fiore in the Middle Ages or in the radical sects of the Reformation. Beyond their theological formulations, moreover, these three views have also had a secularized afterlife, and even today it would be possible to identify their counterparts in historical philosophy and political thought.

53. Ibid., 2.18.
54. Ibid., 4.33.
55. Ibid., 18.22.
56. Ibid., 4.3.
57. Ibid., 19.17.

Law in the Governance of the Good Society

Archibald Cox

It would be comfortable while celebrating the bicentennial anniversary of the Declaration of Independence to feel assured of continued progress toward the good society under government of, by, and for the people. The founders' vision flowed from their belief in human perfectibility. They believed, and ask us to believe, that man is by nature a rational and social being; that each may grow in nobility and strength through the freedom and responsibility of each to choose the best he can discern; and further, that there is an ideal fitness of things suited to this belief which we have a duty to seek and to do what we can to realize, not just for ourselves but for our children and our children's children. The founders knew that pursuit of this commitment must be a joint adventure, even though the very ideas of personal liberty and responsibility presuppose diversity of goals and opinion. They looked to self-government as the form of political organization most likely to assure liberty, and also to reflect the worth of every man.

But while assurance of continued success in the adventure in self-government would be comfortable, the fact is that we have lost the buoyant optimism of our predecessors. The war and collapse of United States policy in Indo-china, the disclosures labelled "Watergate," the deterioration of the environment, the spread of crime in the cities, the empty future seeming to face millions of young men and women, idle, bored, deprived by unemployment of hope of usefulness, the injustices of an inflation which taught millions that the harder they worked the farther they fell behind, the disintegration of traditional moral themes, the divisiveness and drift throughout the nation—all these have shaken self-confidence and even produced cynicism, distrust, and despair. We are forced to ask questions seldom raised in American history. Was the dream of those who signed the Declaration a bubble destined sooner or later to burst? Is the form of self-government that served so well for two hundred years fatally unsuited to the crowded and complex society of the third century since independence?

The external conditions of the adventure have indeed changed in ways that test the vitality of essential elements in the founders vision. To the claim to individual liberty was linked a strong sense of personal responsibility. A man should be free, they thought, not because freedom would allow him to pursue his fancy but because freedom permitted him to choose between right and wrong, and thus to exercise man's noblest capacity. A man was responsible for himself and also for the progress of the enterprise. Responsibility went hand in hand with the opportunity and right of participation.

The very increase in our numbers weakens the sense of personal responsibility and lessens the appreciation of the commonalty of the enterprise. In 1776 there were less than three million people in the new United States. Today the population is two hundred million—a sixtyfold increase. Today New York City alone has more than twice the population of the colonies when they declared their independence. Seattle and Kansas City, each alone, has a population as large as the largest colony, Virginia. For three million people to govern themselves is one thing. For two hundred million people to govern themselves is quite another. The chance that an individual has of being heard, or of influencing public decisions, has shrunk by fifty-nine sixtieths. His view of his role in the enterprise is bound to be affected.

The industrial, scientific, and technological revolutions have also produced conditions which test the vitality of notions of personal responsibility. Harnessing the power unlocked by science and technology requires vast aggregations of wealth and human organization. The young ghetto-dwellers facing unemployment and bleak and empty lives in urban centers can no longer move to empty public lands and take up a homestead at trifling expense, as could the poor or dissatisfied two hundred years ago. The number of hours a farmer or artisan worked in 1776 depended chiefly upon his individual strength and will; the work week of the factory wage earner today depends upon how many automobiles General Motors schedules for production or how fast J. P. Stevens Co. can sell its cloth. The rancher or wheat-grower may find his best individual effort frustrated by a change in government policy or a sudden drop in market price. Whether there has really been a net loss of opportunities for self-determination seems debatable. Science and technology have greatly reduced man's vulnerability before three of the four horsemen of the apocalypse: ignorance, poverty, and disease. Men and women are less dependent upon the vagaries of weather and other natural forces. Most men and women, at least in the United States, have been freed from ceaseless toil for bare subsistence. Yet the price of the gains has been to create a complex system beyond the comprehension of most people, and to put most of them into the control of others wielding greater economic or political power or greater organizational authority. Somehow the substitution of a faulty, unmanageable human system for fate or an inscrutable God offering ultimate mercy makes it harder than it was to feel responsibility even for oneself, and still harder to feel responsibility for the progress of the human adventure.

These changes also affect two other moral forces vital to successful pursuit of the founders' dream. Alfred North Whitehead, when asked to explain the extraordinary achievements of the American people, replied that no other people in the history of mankind has ever shown such innate qualities of toleration and cooperation. The hardships of the wilderness taught our forbears that, despite the value they placed upon individual liberty, they were all fellow voyagers in the same boat, that no man can move very far towards his personal goals unless the vessel moves, and that the vessel cannot move while some voyagers pull ahead, some backwater, others demand a new boat, and more and more drop out to go fishing. Toleration and cooperation require more than the sense of personal responsibility which I have tried to suggest; they depend upon belief in the value of a common enterprise and from trust not only in the conduct of the enterprise but in those who participate. When these decline the spirit of toleration and cooperation vanishes along with any sense of personal responsibility. Men and women drop out, and factions press to achieve their separate aims not through general progress but by taking each other.

A third great change in the external circumstance is the emergence of big government with a central role even in a free society. Two hundred years ago Tom Paine could rightly say that the government which governs least, governs best. Although it was never the human lot that every man or woman could have at once all that he or she desired, even if what each desired might, viewed by itself, be wholly commendable, still, if the peace were kept, the inescapable conflicts and adjustments could once be left largely to individual ability, to the vagaries of nature, and to supposedly impersonal economic forces. The closing of the frontier and the industrial, scientific, and technological revolutions made this impossible. In the 1930s, because of the inequality of bargaining power between organized wealth, on the one hand, and individuals and smaller organizations, on the other hand—between farmers and food processors, between wage-earners and industrial employers, etc.—we took the revolutionary decision to temper the conflicts and work out at least portions of the inescapable adjustments through government. Government not only became big and central; it became the forum in which men and women, business corporations and other organized groups contend for individual or group advantage with all the selfishness and ambition, and sometimes the ruthlessness and deceit, which once characterized the marketplace. Too often politicians seem to win or lose according to their ability to satisfy those with preponderant power to influence elections. The weak are faithless to the trust reposed in them.

As government grows and moves to center stage in human affairs, it exerts ever greater influence not only upon the material conditions but upon moral and philosophical attitudes towards the whole human adventure, including the four driving forces I regard as essential to the continued pursuit of the American dream. Some are affected more than others. The value that law and government put upon human beings including the errant and unfortunate, not only reflects but helps to shape the prevailing philosophy, but government obviously has much less to do with the vision of human perfectibility than the home, the school, religion, literature, and the arts. The growth of big government, like the increase in population, adversely affects the individual's sense of participation and responsibility. The prime impact, however, lies in the people's perception of the value of the common enterprise in terms of both its goals and the way it is conducted, for government is now not only the chief instrument of societal endeavour but the principal exemplar of many of its values. The mood of cynicism, distrust, and despair to which I adverted earlier seems to flow from—or at least be blamed upon—chiefly the proven abuse of governmental power. More than one young man has written me: "Watergate makes it impossible to trust anyone in public life; it turned us from the system."

The current fashion is to put aside the task of improving the political system; it is to turn away from government. The fashion cannot be accepted for very long without disastrous consequences. The external changes brought by the past two hundred years are irreversible. We cannot cut a population of two hundred million back to three million. We yearn for simplicity and many can return to a simpler way of life, but nostalgia should not blind us to the enormous gains which complex technologies and industrial organization have won in the fight against ignorance, poverty, and disease. Nor is it likely that we shall significantly cut back the role of government and allow the exercise of unlimited power in the market place. Would men be nobler, more honest, or less avaricious in uncontrolled markets than in political forums? Would we achieve a fairer measure of distributive justice? For my part, I have no expectation of seeing the millenium either way, but having no greater faith in unregulated economic power than in the kind of armed bands which dominated society before the State achieved its monopoly of force, I see some gain in putting the contest in a forum which can be relatively open to public scrutiny, where men who are somewhat more disinterested, charged with a public trust, and ultimately amenable to the electorate can exercise some influence; and where every now and then someone or something can lift the public spirit to meet a great occasion.

Because the role of big government is central, a key question concerning the role of law in pursuing the good society becomes, What can be done by law to shape the goals, structure, and conduct of government so as to nourish the vitality of the moral forces essential to pursuit of the good society through freedom and self-government?

In addressing this question, I shall deal first with the contribution which law can make in shaping the nation's view of the good society, in nudging the country towards its aspirations, and thus, in helping sustain that belief in the value of the common enterprize which alone can bind the members of a free society together. In many societies law and legal institutions are primarily instruments used to effectuate ulterior purposes. With us, this is only partly true. Our faith in natural law as embodied in the Bill of Rights, the Fourteenth Amendment, and a constitutionalism expounded by an independent judiciary, charges judges and judge-made law with concern for formulating and protecting many of the enduring values of the nation.

The unique role of constitutional adjudication in the United States also dramatically illustrates some determinants of the usefulness of law in a free society. For although law carries nominally enforceable sanctions, in free society all law but especially constitutional law in truth depends upon its capacity to command uncoerced consent—a capacity which, in turn, depends upon the people's recognition that law and other restraints upon the means by which we pursue conflicting interests are the only means of accommodating freedom and social order.

After developing these themes, I turn to the uses of law as a tool for eliminating the sources of distrust of the manner in which government is conducted. Sidney Hillman was partly right when he defined politics as the science of who gets what, when, and why. Partly right, but fatally wrong because his definition excluded any element of moral aspiration. The political system that we substituted for the economic law of the jungle will be an improvement only to the context that politics is raised above Hillman's definition and public office is made a public trust. Because government is the most important teacher of respect or disrespect for law, putting better controls upon the heretofore lawless conduct of such agencies as the Federal Bureau of Investigation and the Central Intelligence Agency might do much to restore trust not only in the manner in which the common enterprise is conducted but in each other and in ourselves. Similarly, although legislation cannot eliminate all the sources of public distrust for government as presently conducted, the law could do more to set ethical standards and eliminate sources of temptation; and the conscious study and debate which precedes legislation can precipitate less formal judgments which will govern both official conduct and public expectations.

In the fourth part of this paper I shall suggest, all too sketchily, the need and possibilities for checking trends in the distribution and use of governmental power which have unnecessarily weakened the individual's sense of participation and responsibility.

It will be plain, as I proceed, that in all these areas the law at best is only one of the forces shaping the individual's view of government and society, and of himself. In some areas, the law can do very little. Yet the inability to do everything—or even to do very much—will hardly excuse not using the law for these purposes as best we can.

Law and the Goals of the Enterprise

Alexander Meiklejohn once observed that the Supreme Court of the United States "holds a unique place in the cultivating of our national intelligence. Other institutions may be more direct in their teaching influence. But no other institution is more deeply decisive in its effect upon our understanding of ourselves and our government."[1]

Dr. Meiklejohn's observation requires some qualification. There is little which the Supreme Court can do in fixing our notions of economic justice now that the political system has been freed from earlier constitutional impediments.[2] In this area, law is an instrument rather than a shaper of aspirations.

The Court's role is larger when it deals with the constitutional safeguards available to individuals and minorities against governmental oppression. Here, the Court's teaching does indeed shape our goals—in relation to liberty, human dignity, the avoidance of invidious discrimination, and the openness of the political system. Some of the founders foresaw its role at the beginning. During the debates in the First Congress upon the proposed Bill of Rights, James Madison argued that if they were incorporated into the Constitution, "independent tribunals of justice will consider themselves in a peculiar manner the guardians of those rights; they will be an impenetrable bulwark against every assumption of power in the Legislative or Executive."[3]

The flowering of the function was reserved for the current era. After World War II the multiplication and magnification of government activities increased sensitivity to threats to civil liberty. A wave of egalitarianism flowed from the rise of the peoples of Asia and Africa, both in their native lands and in the places to which they had been transported. Humanitarianism, aided by the prevailing teaching of the psychological and social science, cast doubt upon the sterner aspects of the criminal law. Later, a wave of subjectivism bred wide dissatisfaction with all constraints. These impulses beat stronger in the Supreme Court

1. Meiklejohn, *Political Freedom*, p. 32.

2. E.g., West Coast Hotel Co. v. Parrish, 300 U.S. 379 (1937); Olsen v. Nebraska, 313 U.S. 236 (1941), overturning earlier recognition of a liberty of contracts in such cases as Lochner v. New York, 198 U.S. 45 (1905).

3. *Annals of Congress* 439 (1789).

than in the political branches of government, perhaps because the justices are closer to the intellectual world, perhaps only by the chance which puts one man upon the Court rather than another.

The result was a period of extraordinary creativity in those areas of constitutional law which shape our view of the relation between the individual and society. As late as 1962 Alexander M. Bickel could write, "continuity is a chief concern of the Court, as it is a main reason for the Court's place in the hearts of its countrymen."[4] No one could say that today. In the Warren era the Court was converted from an instrument of continuity into an instrument of reform. *New York Times Co.* v. *Sullivan*[5] enlarged the freedom of the press to investigate and publish charges against public figures by sweeping away 175 years of settled libel law. The school desegregation cases[6] overturned not only the constitutional precedents built up over three-quarters of a century but the social structure of an entire region. When the Court held that the apportionment of seats in legislative bodies must achieve approximate per capita representation,[7] it was invalidating long-settled political arrangements and declaring that the composition of the legislatures of all but one or two of the fifty states was unconstitutional. It would be easy to multiply examples.

With the conversion came a new constitutional philosophy. The ultimate protection for minorities, for spiritual and political liberty, and for freedom of expression, and other personal liberties—it was said—comes rightfully from the judiciary. In these realms, the argument continued, the political process, subject to arbitrary compromises and responsive to short-term pressures as it must be in some degree, is inadequate to enforce the long-range values that bespeak our better judgment. A majority of the Court under Chief Justice Warren thus came to speak for minorities, for the oppressed, for the open and egalitarian opera-

4. *The Least Dangerous Branch* (1962), p. 32.
5. 376 U.S. 254 (1964).
6. Brown v. Board of Education, 347 U.S. 483 (1954).
7. Reynolds v. Sims, 377 U.S. 533 (1964).

tion of the political system, and for a variety of "rights" not adequately represented in the political process. At the same time the losers in the political process were becoming more conscious of the potentials of constitutional adjudication for achieving goals not attainable without the use of judicial weapons. More and more litigation came to be conducted by civil rights and civil liberties organizations, by radical political associations, and later by law offices funded to stimulate community action and provide legal services to the poor. Each successful appeal to the courts in lieu of the political process added to the momentum from previous steps.

President Nixon's four appointments, including Chief Justice Burger, have slowed the pace of change but the new justices do not seem to shrink from using constitutional law as an instrument of reform when an existing rule offends their preferences. The decisions in the abortion cases[8] invalidated statutes prohibiting or regulating abortion in at least forty states; they swept away established law, supported by recent votes as well as moral themes dominant in American life for more than a century. Similar reforming decisions have been rendered by the supposed "strict constructionists" in the area of "women's rights."[9]

The power of the Court in articulating and effectuating a vision of the good society is best illustrated by the consequences of the initial decisions condemning racial segregation in the public schools. The upshot also suggests that there are important limits upon the effective power of judge-made law although it is too soon to say where the balance should be struck.

Brown v. *Board of Education*[10] was the first clear expression for more than half a century of a national commitment to accomplishing an egalitarian revolution in race relations by and within the rule of law. The opinion restated the spirit of America and lighted a beacon of hope at a time when other voices were silent. Thereafter the American people could not evade the choice

8. Roe v. Wade, 410 U.S. 113 (1973).

9. E.g., Frontiero v. Richardson, 411 U.S. 677 (1973); Stanley v. Illinois, 405 U.S. 645 (1971); Reed v. Reed, 404 U.S. 71 (1973).

10. 347 U.S. 483 (1954).

between their pretensions and their practices, between their declared ideal that "all men are created equal" and the caste system engrained in soicety, North as well as South, since long before the Declaration of Independence. And the choice, so far as the Supreme Court could commit the people, would be the path marked by morality and natural justice.

We must come back to the qualification: "so far as the Supreme Court could commit the people." But consider first what *Brown* accomplished.

The moral and social pressures behind the *Brown* decision, the movement envigorated by that beacon of hope, and the force of the decision itself as both precedent and example joined to produce a veritable revolution in race relations. State laws enforcing a caste system were invalidated, and enforcement gradually stopped. New doctrines developed to extend the reach of the Equal Protection Clause.[11] New federal statutes were enacted in order to deal with acts and practices depriving black citizens of such rights as to vote, to enjoy equal treatment in places of public accommodation, to have equal employment opportunities, and to have equal access to housing.[12] Constitutional law changed and grew in order to sustain the new federal laws.[13]

Neither lawyers nor the legislative, executive, or judicial branch of government can claim sole credit for the reforms. The driving force came largely from the movement: from the Montgomery bus boycott, the freedom rides, the march in Washington, the march from Selma to Montgomery, and hundreds of smaller but equally courageous demonstrations. But those interested in law and government can justifiably take pride that the law did set greater racial equality as a goal of the national enterprise and did change to meet the needs of men. Where the law at its worst had been a tool of racial oppression and even at its best had been

11. E.g., Burton v. Wilmington Parking Authority, 365 U.S. 715 (1961); Reitman v. Mulkey, 387 U.S. 369 (1967).

12. Civil Rights Act of 1964, 78 Stat. 241, Voting Rights Act of 1965, 79 Stat. 437; Civil Rights Act of 1968, 82 Stat. 73.

13. E.g., Katzenbach v. McClung, 379 U.S. 294 (1964); South Carolina v. Katzenbach, 383 U.S. 301 (1966); Jones v. A.H. Mayer Co., 392 U.S. 409 (1968).

indifferent to racial wrongs, it became both spokesman and handmaiden of equality and human dignity—sometimes errant, sometimes ineffectual, often slow, but cleansed and committed so far as commitment can be written into law.

The revitalization of constitutional prohibitions against racial discrimination gave impetus to a review of other inequalities in American life. The opinions invalidating racial discrimination provided the doctrinal support for close judicial scrutiny of other invidious, governmental distinctions and of statutory classifications affecting the exercise of fundamental rights. The reapportionment decisions[14] are intellectually traceable to *Brown*, as are the rulings abolishing the poll tax,[15] property qualifications,[16] excessive resident requirements,[17] and other restrictions upon participation in elections.[18] Propelled by the decision, the courts later struck down a multitude of discriminations based upon sex,[19] alienage,[20] length of residence,[21] illegitimacy of birth,[22] and sometimes (but less often than one would wish) ability to pay.[23]

The influence of *Brown* also ran strong in the decisions reforming the administration of criminal law by requiring the states to supply paupers, in both courts and police stations, with the legal assistance that others can buy.[24] The consequences are not to be measured solely in terms of legal doctrine. The establishment of a constitutional requirement for the appointment of

14. Reynolds v. Sims, 377 U.S 533 (1964); Baker v. Carr, 369 U.S. 186 (1962).

15. Harper v. Virginia Board of Elections, 383 U.S. 663 (1966).

16. Cipriano v. City of Houma, 395 U.S. 701 (1969); City of Phoenix v. Kolodzieski, 399 U.S. 204 (1970).

17. E.g., Dunn v. Blumstein, 405 U.S. 330 (1972).

18. Union Free School District, 395 U.S. 621 (1969).

19. E.g., Frontiero v. Richardson, 411 U.S. 677 (1973); Reed v. Reed, 404 U.S. 133 (1973).

20. Graham v. Richardson, 403 US. 365 (1971).

21. E.g., Memorial Hospital v. Maricopa County, 415 U.S. 250 (1974); Shapiro v. Thompson, 394 U.S. 618 (1969).

22. Weber v. Aetna Casualty & Surety Co., 406 U.S. 164 (1972); Levy v. Louisiana, 391 U.S. 68 (1968). But cf. Labine v. Vincent, 401 U.S. 532 (1971).

23. Compare Boddie v. Connecticut, 401 U.S. 371 (1971) with United States v. Kras, 409 U.S. 434 (1973).

24. Gideon v. Wainwright, 372 U.S. 335 (1963); Miranda v. Arizona, 384 U.S. 436 (1966).

counsel in all criminal cases set in motion countless local reforms because the activity of assigned counsel brought to the attention of judges practices which had escaped their notice or which they had let slide, such as confining offenders for long periods without arraignment or advice upon their legal rights. The spirit engendered by the decisions supplied much of the stimulus for broader undertakings. The way a civilization values human life and dignity is shaped and reflected in the enforcement of its criminal law.

The difficulties in accomplishing actual school desegregation emphasize important limitations upon judicial power to set goals for society and then move society towards the goals under the influence of law. The vast enterprise flowing from *Brown* v. *Board of Education* is utterly unlike any previous judicial venture. Previously, the form of nearly all the Supreme Court's contributions to public policy had been negative. I do not mean to minimize the grandeur of John Marshall's conception of a politically and economically unified nation, the influence of the Court's great opinions upon the national consciousness, the momentum generated by important judgments legitimating assertions of state or congressional power, or the obvious fact that eliminating a governmental restraint upon private action may release forces that do more to shape the character of life than any governmental measure. The judgments, however—the effective disposition by the Court—did little more than validate or veto action by another arm of government: by the president, by the president and Congress, by the states and the state legislatures, governors and courts, and by other minor officials. Decrees telling state officials what programs they should institute or requiring legislatures to appropriate vast sums of money would have been unthinkable. When the Court entered its validation or veto, the Court was done with the matter.

One novel aspect of the school desegregation cases, therefore, is the affirmative character of the remedies judicially prescribed. The court determines what students will be assigned to each school, how teachers shall be selected, what security measures shall be adopted, and even where new schools shall be built.

When transportation is required, the court directs the expenditures of hundreds of thousands of dollars.

Second, the necessary components of any program of integrated education in a large city appear to commit the courts to constant executive or administrative supervision of the organization, employment practices, curriculum and extracurricular activities of entire school systems. In Boston, for example, the city was induced by fear of fiscal disaster to plan the elimination of 191 teachers. The federal court went down the list, school by school, even hearing the personal pleas of individual teachers, and decided to allow sixty layoffs and to disallow 131.[25]

Third, desegregation decrees have all the qualities of social legislation. They pertain to the future. They are mandatory. They govern millions of people. They reorder people's lives in a way that benefits some and disappoints others in order to achieve social objectives.

Fourth, they regulate the lives of millions of people without voice in the decision.

These characteristics of the school desegregation decrees are typical of legislative rather than judicial action. In emphasizing this observation, I do not mean to imply that the courts should have omitted the undertaking. Quite likely it was the only way to instill conviction that the constitutional promise of equality was genuine and capable of realization. But approval of the aim and even of the means chosen should not blind us either to the novel aspects of the judicial venture or to the resulting degree of judicial dependence upon political support. The courts cannot possibly go it alone. At the very minimum the community's professional educators must cooperate. The support of the executive and legislative branches may be essential. For half a decade after the Brown decision there was no significant executive or legislative support for school desegregation, and progress was halting under judicial decree. From 1961 to 1969 integration progressed faster because the political branches gave varying measures of effective support in the area of education in addition to enacting

25. *Boston Globe*, March 21, 1976, p. 1, col. 5.

legislation striking at discriminatory racial practices in such related fields as housing, employment, voting, and public accommodations. After 1969, resistance became stiffer and compliance slowed while President Nixon pressed for legislation to deprive the courts of power to remedy past denials of equal protection through programs of affirmative action. Judicial decrees of a quasi-legislative character may prove slender reeds when the political community withholds its support and the people are recalcitrant, for judicial decrees lacked the legitimacy which flows from popular participation.

One sees the consequences at their worst in the violence, hatreds, and frustration consequent upon the effort to integrate previously segregated schools in Boston. Part of the city is an extraordinarily homogeneous, proud and self-conscious Irish Roman Catholic community, politically powerful in eastern Massachusetts yet in many ways isolated and inward-looking, perhaps because of earlier decades of discrimination against the Irish because of their race and religion. As a whole, this South Boston community has not shared the affluence of the suburbs. Perhaps some of its members fear the upward movement of the black people of the neighbouring Roxbury district from the bottom of the economic ladder, especially into the building trades and the fire and police departments, as a further threat to their economic well-being. Although Boston escaped the riots which occurred in a number of cities in the 1960s, there was occasional violence along the fringes. Worst of all, too many local politicians had run too long for the School Committee and other local offices upon the promise that Boston's schools would never be integrated; and such are the delays of reform through litigation that integration was indeed held off until the autumn of 1974. The result was an outbreak of violence followed by fear, frustration, and ever-growing hatred. The judicial decrees directing integration of the black with white students by bussing are being executed only in the most formal sense. Hatred grows, education suffers, and time alone can tell whether Boston will become Belfast.

School desegregation is not the only area in which the use of constitutional law as an instrument of social reform has led the courts into new ventures requiring affirmative action threatening judicial prestige and testing the power of judge-made law. Several federal courts have ruled that the Due Process Clause of the Fourteenth Amendment implies that patients involuntarily committed to a state mental health facility "unquestionably have a constitutional right to receive such individual treatment as will give each of them a realistic opportunity to be cured or to improve his or her mental condition."[26] The courts have then gone on to enter long and detailed orders for the renovation of the physical facilities and the conduct of the medical program.[27]

Other federal courts have undertaken to require not only the rewriting of prison rules and regulations but the rebuilding of prison facilities. In Texas, a federal court undertook to specify the work load of each staff social worker, the level of training to be possessed by prison psychologists, the size of the classes in teaching mathematics and languages to be provided inmates, and the social environment, including "a coeducational living environment, allowing frequent and regular contacts with members of the opposite sex." In Boston, in May 1976, the federal judge handling school desegregation is also threatening the City Council with citation for contempt of court for failure to comply with his order to issue city bonds with which to finance the construction of a new prison.[28]

Although the Supreme Court of the United States dismissed a similar suit,[29] the California[30] and New Jersey courts[31] have held that financing public education out of local property taxes where school districts vary widely in the value of the taxable property per pupil is unconstitutional because it results in smallest expenditures per pupil in the areas with lowest tax base.

26. Wyatt v. Stickney, 344 F.Supp. 373, 374 (M.D. Ala. 1972).

27. Wyatt v. Stickney, supra n.26; Davis v. Watkins, 384 F.Supp. 1196 (N.D. Ohio, 1974).

28. *Boston Globe*, May 1976.

29. San Antonio Independent School District v. Rodriquez, 411 U.S. 1 (1973).

30. Serrano v. Priest, 5 Cal.3d 584, 487 P.2d 1241 (1971).

31. Robinson v. Cahill, 62 N.J. 473, 303 A.2d 373 (1973).

Such judicial attempts at social reform multiply the occasions for collision between the courts and the political branches. When a constitutional mandate requires affirmative action, that is, the revision, or adoption and implementation, of an ongoing governmental program, the Court must either rely upon the goodwill of the legislature or else itself take over essentially legislative functions. To induce the political branches to adopt and implement an ongoing, affirmative program conforming to a constitutional decision puts judicial power to a much severer test than the traditional order to stop governmental interference with private action. The difficulties are intensified when judicial decrees take on the characteristics of social legislation without the consent of the people expressed through elected representatives. It is not yet clear whether the courts can fulfill these new functions successfully where there is determined opposition. School desegregation has not succeeded in Boston. In New Jersey the State Supreme Court undertook to particularize the broad ideal of equality of opportunity into a ruling that the dollars spent on a child's education in the state's public schools may not vary with the value of the taxable property in the district in which he lives. The New Jersey legislature refused to enact the revenue laws necessary for equalization. The court forbade the expenditure under the old system.[32] The legislature again refused. In May 1976 the impasse had not been broken.

Later, I shall speak of the dependence of law upon its power to command uncoerced compliance and support even from those it frustrates—a point all too vividly illustrated by South Boston's resistance to school desegregation. For the moment, it is important and also enough to emphasize that judicial decrees, such as orders requiring busing as an instrument of school desegregation, have none of the legitimacy which legislation derives from the participation of the people through elected representatives and the principle of majority rule. The conventional explanation of the legal profession is that ability to rationalize a constitutional judgment honestly in terms of principles referrable to legal

32. Robinson v. Cahill, Supreme Court of New Jersey, May 13, 1976.

precedent and other accepted sources of law is the essential major ingredient of the judicial power to command uncoerced consent. The power of legitimacy is thought to flow largely from the realization that the major influences in judicial decisions are not personal fiat, but principles which bind the judges as well as the litigants, and which apply uniformly to all men not only today but yesterday and tomorrow. *If* this is true, the constitutional decisions of recent years strain the chief source of their legitimacy. Swift judicial reform of areas left untouched by legislation over a period of years is by definition a departure from the traditional judicial function.

Yet the prestige of the Supreme Court is surely greater today than that of other branches of government, and I am inclined to think that it has never been higher. Possibly, we have been living on the momentum of a legitimacy won by earlier adherence to a system of law, which is bound to decline if unelected judges continue to take over functions once thought to be suitable only to the political branches. Perhaps, the decisions appeal to other, stronger sources of the power to command consent because both the process of decision and the goals set exemplify essential aspects of the good society better than other governmental institutions.

A few years ago I put to my constitutional law class a hypothetical bill forbidding strikes for higher wages in the construction industry, and then developed to the best of my ability all the considerations pro and con that would be taken into account by a detached, conscientious, and wise legislator, uninfluenced by personal ambition, party loyalty, or other commitment. I then asked what, if this was the function of the legislator, was the function of the Court when it came to determine the statute's constitutionality? A student replied that my question was based upon a false hypothesis because no legislator acted or was even expected to act in the manner I had described. What I had described, he insisted, was the process of decision to be followed by the Court. While I reject the student's description of the judicial function in constitutional adjudication, he struck near a different truth. The political branches are the forums where group interests are served, coalitions are built, loyalties are formed, and obligations respected. The function of the Court—the role implicitly assigned to it by history as well as the fact of its having been created as a court—is illuminated by contrast with the political branches. The core of the Court's strength is impartiality, independence, and freedom from every form of loyalty or self-interest. Its decisions draw authority from the commitment to judge by higher, disinterested, and more objective standards.

At this point the deep-seated and enduring American belief in natural law becomes important. The Bill of Rights was, for its framers, a codification of natural law. We should use different words today: "impersonal and durable principles," "enduring values," "fundamental aspirations," "vital lessons of liberty and equal opportunity," "human rights," and so on; but the very persistence of such evocative, rather than sharply definitive, phrases attests the strength of our natural law inheritance. "What drives us back from time to time to search further, to question outright what are our purposes," Lord Radcliffe observed, "is the insistence of the layman, the man who is not versed in law, that it shall stand for something more, for some vindication of a sense of right and wrong that is not merely provisional nor just the product of a historical process."[33] The Court's judgments gain respect when the people perceive that they deserve it.

Constitutional adjudication depends upon a delicate, symbiotic relation. The Court should sometimes be the voice of the spirit, telling us what we are by reminding us of what we may be. But while the opinions of the Court can help to shape our national understanding of ourselves, the roots of its decisions must be already in the nation. The Court cannot do much to coerce either the political branches or the masses of people. The aspirations voiced by the Court must be those the community is willing not only to avow but in the end to live by. The contribution of great constitutional decisions to the evolution of a more humane society depends, I think, upon the accuracy of the Court's per-

33. Radcliffe, *The Law and its Compass* (1960), p. 78.

ception of the goals of the enterprise and upon the Court's ability, by expressing its perception ultimately to command not only a passive but a supportive consensus.

The Morality of Procedure

Although constitutional decisions present unusual difficulty because they are reached without any form of popular participation and often override or seek to constrain the political process, the contribution that any form of law can make to a good and free society, whether as teacher or tool, seems to depend upon its capacity to command compliance even where obedience cannot be forced. I think this almost as true of criminal codes, revenue laws, and directives distributing welfare or managing the economy as it is of Supreme Court decisions. Indeed, I am inclined to think that although law has special qualities, it is one part of a broader group of social bonds depending upon the society's sense of the importance of a basic morality of procedure.

The adventure in liberty and self-government launched two hundred years ago includes an inherent contradiction. The very notion of a free society posits liberty to select and pursue our own objectives. That individual choices should conflict is unavoidable, even desirable because conflicts are creative. Yet the preservation of any society at all requires some restraints upon self-interest. Our predecessors' success in resolving the contradiction seems to me to rest upon their voluntary acceptance of limits upon the means by which the struggle for self-interest—or to serve an altruistic interest in others—would be pushed. Justice Brandeis wrote, "One can never be sure of ends, political, social economic. *There* there must always be doubt and difference of opinion. There is not the same margin of doubt as to *means.* Here fundamentals do not change; centuries of thought have established standards. Lying and sneaking are always *bad,* no matter what the ends."[34]

The history of the past ten years reveals what mutually destruc-

34. Quoted in A. Mason, *Brandeis: A Free Man's Life*, p. 569.

tive forces are unleashed by disregard of this perception. The tactics of physical confrontation pursued by student activists during the wave of unrest in 1968–71—the physical seizure of buildings, the bombing of the laboratory at the University of Wisconsin or of Harvard's Center for International Affairs Library, the burning of R.O.T.C. buildings, and the disruption of public meetings so that views distasteful to the activists were denied expression—led directly and I think inevitably to the seige mentality of the Nixon White House, to political snooping and deceitful harassment by the FBI, to the suppression of civil liberties, and to the stepped-up resort to other lawless measures in the name of internal security. Daniel Ellsberg, who took away and released copies of the Pentagon Papers, and Egil Krogh, the head of the White House "plumbers," had much in common. Dr. Ellsberg, if I understand the fact, intentionally violated a trust he had knowingly accepted when—in common but not legal parlance—he "stole" the Pentagon Papers. Egil Krogh planned and directed the burglary of Dr. Fielding's office in an effort to "steal" Daniel Ellsberg's psychiatric files in the hope of obtaining information with which to destroy Ellsberg's public image. Both thought of themselves as highly moral men. Each was sincerely convinced, although their goals were diametrically opposed, that he was performing a service to his country and all humanity.

Both men, I submit, were tragically wrong. In both instances the conduct was wrong because it violated standards that must be accepted if free men are to live together. In both cases, the actor believed his wrong to be justified by the righteousness of his cause and the need for drastic means to achieve his objective. Similarly, the willingness of student activists and their counterparts in the peace movement to override constraints upon the means of pursuing social, political, moral, or other human objectives generated willingness to override them on the part of others in the Nixon White House, who had different goals but believed with equal conviction in their righteousness of purpose. In my view, each incident marked and contributed its share to some crumbling of the moral order which enables free men to live together. Each lessened the bonds of trust.

Likening the role of Egil Krogh in the Ellsberg-Fielding break-in to Daniel Ellsberg's breach of trust and to the radical tactics of physical confrontation has been criticized upon the ground that Krogh was a government man while the others were outsiders, and that Krogh possessed, while the others lacked, a high degree of power. These differences are important, but I wish to insist a little that the argument gets the perspective wrong if pushed to the length of attempting to justify breach of trust or deceitful means by those who are out of power. It is the forgetting of the constraints upon methods of working our wills that counts, because despite short-run frustrations such constraints furnish the best hope of combining liberty, change, and progress. Constraints upon means cannot survive exceptions for those who think their influence too small in proportion to the justice of their cause. Those who assert freedom to override the constraints in attacking the government cannot seriously suppose that government will observe the constraints if frightened, nor that they themselves will suddenly observe the constraints if, as they hope, they come to power.

The point seems vital. If man is by nature a social being—if we are destined to live and work together yet allow freedom for each to choose the best he can discern—if we are to tolerate the diversity which liberty implies—then surely some virtually absolute constraints upon the ways in which we individually pursue even the worthiest objectives (insofar as their worth can then be judged) furnish the best, perhaps the only, liberty and progress. What the constraints even upon means should be may be debatable around the periphery but surely the core includes refraining from physical aggression, lying and cheating, and breach of a trust voluntarily undertaken, and respecting the rights of speech, privacy, dignity and other fundamental liberties, by both government and private persons. Call the constraints "standards," as Brandeis did, the "rule of law," "civility," or the "liberal tradition," as you will, any serious erosion carries the greatest threat to the dream of the good society. Disregard of the constraints by some breeds further disregard upon the part of others. Trust dissipates. Brute power and skill in subterfuge become the determinants of what is falsely labeled "justice." To those who say, "It is the only way to action. We know that we are right," I would reply that many of the greatest wrongs known to history were committed by men who were acting, according to the contemporary judgment of society as well as by their own lights, in the cause of human welfare.

Perhaps it is only a lawyer's prejudice, but I am inclined to think that commitment to the rule of law is but one, although perhaps the most important, of the procedural restraints which men must accept as the foundation of the mutual trust underlying a free and good society. Law can be said to differ because the state imposes sanctions for violation. The policeman's billy will be an indispensable part of every legal system until we reach the millennium. That swift enforcement can and must follow disobedience, even by a state against constitutional judgments, is evidenced by our early constitutional history as well as by the enforcement of civil rights in Mississippi and Alabama during the 1960s. In cases affecting individuals, whether civil or criminal, the sheriff stands behind the court's decree. Nonetheless, even in the case of individuals, force can be invoked only in exceptional cases. The frightening rise in crime, the lagging criminal dockets and the cruelly overcrowded prisons are all testimony to the declining power of legitimacy. Often, and especially in the case of constitutional restraints upon the executive, there is no satisfactory answer to the question, how should the law be enforced. On some occasions there is no practical power, on others no practical power we are willing to use. The former would have been true in 1952, when the Supreme Court invalidated President Truman's seizure of the steel mills, if the President had said, "I do not intend to comply with the Court's decision. I think that it is morally wrong." It would probably have been true in the summer of 1963 if the railroad workers had persisted by the thousands in going on strike, regardless of what statute Congress might enact or what decree a court might enter. As the litigation over the Watergate tapes moved toward a crisis in the summer and autumn of 1974, the great question became, how would the country respond if President Nixon refused to comply with the order enforcing the subpoena for the tapes. Courts possess neither the purse nor the sword. Constitutionalism, especially as a constraint upon government depends, in the first instance, upon the habit of voluntary compliance and, in the last resort, upon a people's realization that their freedom depends upon observance of the rule of law. The realization must be strong enough for the community to rise up and overwhelm, morally and politically, any notable offender. Conversely, each time a political body or a community withholds compliance or attempts to frustrate a court decree, it weakens the chief safeguard of liberty.

You may object that this is indeed a lawyer's view and that if a law is truly unjust, there is no reason to preserve it. I think that there is good reason, and wish to insist upon it at a little length because the intense subjectivism of the day, including assertions of the higher morality of civil disobedience, seems to me to threaten the present development of a more nearly humane society. My answer to those who would disobey an evil law is that we are concerned with the basic ideal of law—with a force binding all men—and that you cannot pick and choose among good laws and bad laws according to each individual's conscience without undermining the entire structure. Nor do I attach value to the rule of law just because it is law. Law is a human instrument, constructed by men to meet men's needs; it must justify itself by what it does for men in meeting their needs, including their ethical judgments and moral aspirations. Here our constitutionalism—our rules of law—offers three ultimately moral justifications:

First, it secures for men the maximum of individual liberty, freedom of speech and association, religion and privacy, and equality before the law.

Second, it secures the greatest opportunities for peaceful change not only today but in the future.

Third, the ultimate commitment of those devoted to the rule of law is to the belief that the growth of each individual toward responsibility and the freedom to choose the best he can discern is a purpose which must never be made subservient to other objectives.

Men can be lifted from savagery to a form of civilization solely through the pacification achieved by concentrating power in the hands of the State, but neither pacification nor the concentration of physical power will secure individual liberty and opportunities for each generation to remake society, if it is able. To achieve those goals, even the power of the government must be restrained, and ways must be found by which men can live together not by power, be it physical, economic, or in some cases even political, but by what reason tells them is just. To achieve both civility and freedom, and opportunities for change, there must be a substitute for power. Our substitute is the force of legitimacy—the capacity of law to command consent and conversely the habit of voluntary compliance.

The rule of law is not a static code but a process. Law is a civilizing and liberating influence only so long as it arises out of the conditions of contemporary society and serves the current needs of men. The capacity for change and growth is as essential an element of the rule of law as reason and voluntary compliance. Indeed, voluntary compliance cannot be severed from the other side of the coin—to win acceptance the law must deserve it. When the pace of social change or the growth of social conscience is revolutionary, so must be the changes in the law.

Social protest and even civil disobedience serve the law's need for growth. Ideally, reform would come according to reason and justice without self-help and disturbing, almost violent, forms of protest. Resort to such pressures is hardly consistent with the ideals of reason and civility. Those who use direct action eschew reason in favor of a form of force, whether it be economic power or simply the power to upset the community by interfering with its normal life. No little cause will justify their action. Still, candor compels one to acknowledge the gap between the ideal and the reality. Short of the millennium, sharp changes in the law depend partly upon the stimulus of protest.

History affords abundant examples. The extension of the

rule of law to millions of workers in industrial establishments is one of the great creative accomplishments of law in the present century, but the stimulus came from strikes, boycotts, and picketing that, under the older precedents, were quite plainly illegal. Similarly, while we may take some measure of reassurance from the demonstrated capacity of our statutory, judge-made, and constitutional law to grow in response to demands for racial justice, that satisfaction must be tempered by the admission that for decades the law was blind to racial wrongs and its eyes were opened by picketing, boycotts, sit-ins, marches, and other demonstrations creating the specter of violence.

Thus, the law itself faces a dilemma. To approve or condemn all civil disobedience is neither quite right nor altogether wrong even from the viewpoint of the law. The most we can say with any confidence is that the test is not always whether the action is consistent with the rights of others under *existing* rules and finds sanction in *existing* precedents. Perhaps this is a workable distinction: 1) Those who resort to self-help and other nonviolent action in disobedience to civil authority do no moral wrong if their cause is just provided they can honestly say to themselves that their conduct does not violate the becoming-law as they reasonably hope the courts will now declare it. 2) Those who cross that line—those who violate a court decree resolving the issue for today or who violate a law that no lawyer could conscientiously predict might be held unconstitutional, can claim no social or moral justification.

The civil rights movement observed the distinction. Except for excesses outside the mainstream, none of the great events in the history of the movement involved more than the exercise of what could be claimed—honestly and nearly always correctly—to be the exercise of a constitutionally protected right. Not more than the exercise of such rights was involved at Tuscaloosa in 1956, at Little Rock in 1957, in the freedom rides of 1961, at Oxford in 1962, or even in the events at Selma in 1965. The failure of many liberals to note this essential distinction explains many of the excesses of the radical peace movement, the student dissidents, and the governmental repression of later years.

I speak of principles applicable to all men and women but again the action of government is a central influence. Violations of law by high officials in their own self-interest or of the restraints of decency towards other human beings erode the morality of procedure. Violations as part of planned and systematic government policy are even more destructive. "Our Government," Justice Brandeis wrote, "is the potent, the omnipresent teacher. For good or for ill, it teaches the whole people by its example. Crime is contagious. If the Government becomes a law-breaker, it breeds contempt for law; it invites every man to become a law unto himself; it invites anarchy. To declare that in the administration of the criminal law"—and I would add "and in the search for security"—"the end justifies the means . . . would bring terrible retribution."[35]

There is no need to recount the findings of several congressional committees.

What is to be done? A special committee of the American Bar Association and the Watergate Special Prosecution Force have called for closer congressional oversight and clearer executive statement of policy with respect to the missions and practices of the FBI, the Internal Revenue Service, and like law enforcement agencies. These are the remedies projected in Congress. The ABA Committee also wisely adds that legislation should be enacted sharply restricting the circulation of materials gathered by such agencies.

Helpful as these measures will be, two more are necessary:

First, the burglaries, buggings, mail openings, and other "dirty business" which flowed from practices begun in war and continued in cold war surely should be enough to convince us all of the costs of skipping the safeguard of a judicial warrant issued only upon a showing of probable cause. Attorney General Levi's guidelines are a major step, but insufficient. Legislation should be enacted to repudiate and proscribe such tactics absolutely.

A more fundamental vice has been targeting individuals and groups for investigation because of political beliefs or activities.

35. Olmstead v. United States, 277 U.S. 438, 471, 481 (1928) (dissenting opinion).

The FBI has a duty to prevent crime as well as to catch the perpetrators of crimes already committed, but surely a society that values political liberty cannot continue to allow its law enforcement agencies to draw from his ideology, speech or political activities, or membership in a lawful political organization, the inference that a man has engaged, or is likely to engage, in criminal misconduct. It is not beyond the power of a skilled draftsman to put the principle in statutory form where it may be approved by Congress and a President as a declaration of national conscience. Enacting a law does not guarantee the cessation of dirty business but it helps, and more important, it tells us unequivocally where we stand and gives us a standard by which to measure the conduct of our officials. Executive orders can never fully serve this purpose.

As the armed forces have no charter to prevent or detect crimes in civilian society, their domestic intelligence activities should be halted by legislation.

The evil in the course the government has followed is not merely the threat to civil liberty. The greater danger is the threat to the fundamentals of decency. A special committee created to advise President Eisenhower on the duties of the CIA observed:

> We are facing an implacable enemy whose avowed objective is world domination by whatever means at whatever cost. There are no rules in such a game. Hitherto acceptable norms of human conduct do not apply. If the United States is to survive, long-standing American concepts of American fair play must be reconsidered.

If the government will not play fair, who else will be willing? If the government does not trust the citizens, how can they trust the government? Trust is given in return for trust. If there is no trust between government and the people, the people are not likely to trust one another. Unless there is change, history may well characterize our times as the Age of Distrust. Law cannot be the fabric of mutual confidence, but if there is the will, law can be used as a tool to limit the activities of government which breed distrust.

Justice Brandeis gave the proper answer in words to the advice given by President Eisenhower's committee:

> Those who won our independence believed that the final end of the state was to make men free to develop their faculties; and that in its government the deliberative forces should prevail over the arbitrary. They valued liberty both as an end and as a means. . . . They recognized the risks to which all human institutions are subject. But they knew that order cannot be secured merely through fear of punishment for its infraction; that it is hazardous to discourage thought, hope and imagination; that fear breeds repression; that repression breeds hate. . . . Those who won our independence by revolution were not cowards.

They were willing, the justice rightly implied, to take risks in order to found a society based upon mutual respect and decency among men whose views and interests would often clash. The lesson of the past two decades is surely that we cannot follow the advice of both the committee and those who won our independence. Nor can we fudge the choice.

Law and Trust in the Conduct of Government

The progress of a society in which government has a central role requires not only belief in the value of the common goals but also confidence in the manner in which government is conducted. Representative government could hardly survive corrosion of the honor and integrity of official decisions, and the resulting alienation of the citizenry from the political system. In the United States, these dangers have been shown to be neither hypothetical nor remote. The temptations of office and the dangers of abuse multiplied as government became the chief buyer of goods, the largest employer, the dispenser of subsidies through direct benefit or tax advantage, the manager of the economy, and the adjuster of conflicts among many economic interests.

The lawmaker has no magic wand with which to instill honor and integrity into the character of public officials, nor would it be useful to enact a law declaring it to be the duty of voters to place more value upon these qualities in casting their ballots and to choose more perceptively. Law and the legal process can make other contributions. The laws which structure the political system can reduce temptation and provide procedural safeguards. Some practices can be outlawed. Both the debate which precedes legislation and any resulting enactment provide moral education. They focus attention upon the problem, force men and women to decide where they stand, and often precipitate, articulate, and broaden the consensus. Consider two examples.

First, the customary methods of financing campaigns for election to public office were, and in the absence of further reforms will remain, a source of much distrust of the political system. Prior to the enactment of the Federal Election Campaign Act of 1972 and the amendments of 1974, expenditures in federal election campaigns had been growing by leaps and bounds. The staggering cost increased the pressure to accept, and even to extort, very large gifts from men whose personal ambitions or business affairs would be directly and substantially affected by government decisions which the successful candidate or political party could influence. As the role of money rose, so increased the obligation which the successful candidate or party owes to the large contributors who supply the means of victory. No one seriously denied either the sense of obligaton or the pressure to make repayment in some form. The larger the contribution, the greater the pressure to repay.

Most large campaign contributors have business interests likely to be affected by decisions of the Congress and federal agencies. A contributor of $100,000 during the 1972 presidential election campaign testified that he was seeking not so much to help in the election as to secure the lifting of an order suspending him from taking construction contracts. The Milk Producers Association pledged $2,000,000 to the 1972 campaign just as the beneficiaries were deciding whether to raise the support price for milk. Other large contributors testified they were moved by fear that unless they match their rivals' contributions, their competitors would fare better than they in dealing with government agencies. Still others hoped only to obtain entree to the offices of high government officials charged with decisions affecting their business interests, preferably under the auspices of an influential figure in Congress, the White House, or a political party, whose pleasure or displeasure could affect the responsible official. Whatever the true motives of those who give or receive the money, public confidence in government is gravely weakened by acceptance of a $2 million pledge from the Milk Producers Association by an administration which concurrently grants an increase in the support price of milk; by the approval of American Airlines' route applications shortly after a large corporate contribution to the party in power; and by the settlement of antitrust litigation against International Telephone & Telegraph Corporation, shortly after an ITT subsidiary agreed to underwrite a large proportion of the expenses of that party's national convention. Government becomes, or is seen as, a "rip-off." The chilling cycle which begins with ever-larger campaign spending ends in alienation of the people from all aspects of the political process.

The Federal Election Campaign Act of 1972 and 1974 amendments went a long way to meet these evils by providing a five-part remedy.

(a) One part struck at the source of the evil, the pressure to raise vast war chests, by placing ceilings upon the aggregate expenditures which may be made by or on behalf of candidates for federal office: $10 million in seeking nomination, and $20 million in seeking election, as president; $70,000, plus $14,000 for fund-raising, in seeking nomination or election as representative.

(b) Individuals were prohibited from contributing more than $1000 to any one candidate in any one primary or genereal election, or more than $25,000 to all candidates in any election year.

(c) Ceilings were placed upon the sum a candidate could lawfully expend from personal or family funds. The $1000 limit upon contributions was extended to expenditures made to elect a candidate without obtaining his consent.

(d) Detailed reporting and disclosure was required of all contributions and expenditures within the statutory limits.

(e) Provision was made for public financing of presidential

election campaigns by matching funds in the primaries and, in the general election, by substitution for private contributions.

The act was to be administered by a six-member Federal Election Commission, two appointed by the president, two by the president pro tem of the Senate, and two by the Speaker of the House of Representatives.

In January the Supreme Court of the United States held the ceilings upon expenditures unconstitutional, but upheld the restrictions upon the size of any contributions to a candidate, the requirements for reporting and disclosure, and the public financing of presidential election campaigns including accompanying expenditure ceilings. The method prescribed of selecting FEC members was held unconstitutional because inconsistent with the president's constitutional right to appoint officers of the United States. Congress belatedly and grudingly corrected the error.

The present law, in short, eliminates the worst sources of improper financial influence and public distrust. The absence of financial limits upon candidates expenditures, however, will leave candidates under pressure to raise and spend enormous sums and the public fearful that money is still a predominant influence in the outcome of elections. The very wealthy are free to spend unlimited sums upon their own campaigns for Senator and Congressman. The advantage is now even greater than before because the men who lack personal wealth may not seek or accept large sums from financial angels. The Supreme Court struck down the prohibition against individual expenditure of more than $1000 to elect a candidate even though made without his or her request or approval, in the belief that the ban would prevent individuals from spending money to publish their own writings or broadcast their own speeches. News reports concerning the 1976 presidential primary campaigns suggest that in fact such expenditures will be made and pooled simply to hire the services of an advertising agency. The first two inadequacies can readily be corrected by extending the plan of public financing applicable to presidential elections to races for senator and representative.

A second source of public misgivings about the conduct of government is the danger that public office will be used for forms of private or political advantage other than obtaining campaign contributions.

The activities of government now touch so large a part of business enterprise as to create a wide variety of actual or potential conflicts of interest. Some perhaps are too subtle to handle by rule of law or even by a code of ethics. Can one deal by rule with the situation of a general charged with military procurement who is reaching the age of compulsory retirement but might expect to find employment with a firm holding procurement contracts? Or with that of the experienced member of a regulatory agency who knows that, despite his knowledge of the industry, he will not be reappointed when his term expires? In March or April 1976 it came to light that President Ford's campaign manager at that time, while he was secretary of war, had held a conversation in his office in the Department of Defense with employees of the Forest Service in which he urged them to expand the area allocated by permit to a resort in which he had a financial interest. The Senate investigation seemingly was made to turn upon whether Mr. Callaway attempted to use improper pressure. In my judgment the standard is shockingly lax. There can be no firm public confidence in the integrity of a government whose senior officials holding presidential appointments use their offices as a place in which to press their private financial interests upon others lower in government rank. Whether my view is correct is less important, however, than that more conscious thought be given to developing and articulating clearer standards and then dealing unequivocally with violations.

The conflicts between party loyalty in laying out a course of official action need more thoughtful attention. No one should have difficulty in perceiving that the FBI or IRS should not be used for political purposes, or that it will not do to pressure the SEC or NLRB to give favorable treatment to a large contributor. But the lines are not always so clear. Suppose that a lawyer representing the Widget manufacturers, and also influential in the same political party, tells the assistant attorney-general in charge of the Antitrust Division that executives in the industry made generous contributions in the past election but that, although he will sincerely try to raise the money, he fears no contributions will be forthcoming if the assistant attorney-general decides to press an antitrust case against the industry upon the new and debatable legal and economic theory recommended by the staff. Plainly, one should disregard the information. Suppose that the projected action is one to break up General Motors; that the president points out that bringing the suit will send shock waves through industry, and that loss of business confidence may cause a downturn in the economy and possibly a recession? May either the president or the attorney-general properly take into account the effect upon a forthcoming campaign for reelection? In proposing remedies for unconstitutional racial segregation in a city's schools may the Department of Justice properly take into account the reaction of different groups not only in the particular community, but throughout the nation? Is the effect upon elections to be considered or ignored?

The lines between law and policy and between policy and politics are often hazy, but surely conscious study might do much to separate the clear cases from the judgmental, to prepare the novitiate for the decisions he must face, and to clarify the implications for the long-run strength of the legal system and the processes of government.

Conscious attention also might identify and eliminate practices that involve the legislative branch which tend to blur lines otherwise clear in principle. Few senior attorneys in the Department of Justice have not received calls from a senator or congressman expressing interest in learning the status of a case; or telling, with only a desire to be helpful, about his knowledge of the high repute of the opposing party; or arranging a conference for the opposing party and his attorneys. In 999 cases out of one thousand the Department of Justice attorney handles the case—and the senator or congressman expects him to handle the case—exactly as if the call had not been made or the conference had not been held; part of the attorney's job is to have a bit of backbone and sophistication. But still . . . but still . . . I wonder.

Is it wholly honest to look upon these only as the courtesies that enable men to work together? Can the attorney be *sure* that he was not affected by the telephone call, especially if it came from the chairman of the Judiciary Committee or an aide to the President? Does the constituent or contributor suppose that he has gotten nothing? Is confidence in the honor and integrity of the administration of justice really unaffected?

It is the habit of law professors to ask questions which they cannot or will not answer, yet possibly the course is justified in this instance because I wish to emphasize only that the questions have gone unattended for too long. There was a flurry of concern late in the Eisenhower administration because of the gifts accepted by President Eisenhower's chief assistant and the misconduct of a few members of regulatory commissions. Watergate produced another, somewhat different flurry. Except on these occasions, however, we have concentrated on expanding governmental programs without much conscious effort to ensure that public office will be filled as a public trust.

Government and Personal Responsibility

The duty of each individual to choose the best he can discern and to contribute what he can to to the good society belongs more to moral than political philosophy. Yet the frame of government and the manner in which decisions are reached influence the extent of the citizens opportunities for meaningful participation, and the extent of his opportunities is likely to determine his feeling of responsibility or alienation.

The original frame of government under the Constitution as ratified in 1789, coupled with the limited nature of total governmental activities, achieved a remarkable balance of unity and diversity. The division of power between the federal government and the states left wide scope for local autonomy upon most matters of daily concern to the people. The states, in turn, delegated a large proportion of governmental activity to town or county government, and in densely populated areas to the cities. Given the relatively small population of a township or county, and even of a state in comparison to current numbers, it seems likely that any male citizen with sufficient interest could not only make himself heard but exert significant influence. Opportunities for meaningful participation give authenticity to ideas of civil duty.

In the beginning, the opportunities for participation through the ballot box were not unlimited, but they have been gradually extended. The franchise was extended to black people in 1879,[36] to women in 1920,[37] and to those between 18 and 21 years of age in 1970–71.[38] The Voting Rights Act of 1965[39] gave reality to the Fifteenth Amendment. Property qualifications,[40] the poll tax,[41] and literacy tests[42] have been eliminated, some by statute and some by court decision. The "one man, one vote" decisions prevent use of malapportionment of representatives as a device for frustrating majority rule.[43]

Every significant change in the past two centuries, except the extension of the franchise, has so greatly increased the distance between the average citizen and the direction of governmental affairs that the meaning of self-government in 1976 is altogether different from its meaning at the time of independence. Some of the forces are beyond our control. Because the poulation has increased sixty fold, the average citizen has one sixtieth the opportunity for influence. Because questions of policy and programs are becoming infinitely complex, the average citizen has neither the time nor the training and experience to master them. Two important changes involve the distribution of power within

36. Amendment 15.

37. Amendment 19.

38. The decision in Oregon v. Mitchell, 400 U.S. 112 (1970), upholding federal legislation reducing to eighteen years of age the requirement for voting for president and vice-president, had the practical effect of impelling the states to reduce to eighteen years the age at which a person would qualify to vote in state elections.

39. 79 Stat. 437.

40. Cipriano v. City of Houma, 395 U.S. 701 (1969); City of Phoenix v. Kolodzieski, 399 U.S. 204 (1970). See also Harper v. Virginia Board of Elections, 383 U.S. 663 (1966).

41. Harper v. Virginia Board of Elections, 383 U.S. 663 (1966).

42. Voting Rights Act of 1965, 79 Stat. 437 Voting Rights Act Amendment of 1970, 84 Stat. 314.

43. Reynolds v. Sims, 377 U.S. 533 (1964); Baker v. Carr, 369 U.S. 186 (1962).

the frame of government: the drift of power to a central government in Washington, and the growth and isolation of a presidential establishment. Both developments separate power and responsibility from the people. The challenge to find ways of restoring opportunities for meaningful participation is so important to the success of the founders' vision that I say a few words under each head by way of emphasis though I have no full solution.

(1) The transfer of power from states to national government was required by the improvement of transportation and communications, the development of national markets, and the growth of giant industrial and commercial enterprises; and the increasing economic interdependence of individual localities raises problems requiring measures of national planning and regulation. Returning power to the individual states, even if they could do the job effectively, would not significantly increase the individual citizen's sense of participation or recognition. One can feel involved in the government of a town of 5000 or even 15,000 people as an ordinary citizen, but the degree of felt involvement in the affairs of state government where the state's population is even one billion will scarcely differ from the degree of felt involvement in the affairs of the nation.

Plainly, more imaginative solutions are required if the people are to be involved as authentic participants in governmental activities which even more directly affect an ever-larger share of daily living. The solution may lie in identifying activities for which direction and execution responsibility could be delegated to identifiable neighborhoods along with a portion of the necessary funds. Performance should be judged not solely by financial and economic measures but by the improvement of civil responsibility and the quality of neighborhood life.

(2) Since the 1930s the size and power of the executive branch have grown at an extraordinary rate, partly because the revolutionary decision to use government to meet the social and economic problems of industrial and urban society requires masses of information and skills from numerous disciplines which Congress lacks and only an executive bureaucracy can provide; partly

because the United States's assumption of a leading role in world affairs built up the presidency by focusing world attention upon the president; and partly because radio and television give a president unique ability to focus attention upon *his* acts and words, and thus to choose the subjects and frame the terms of political debate in a way that neither senator nor congressman, nor all senators and congressmen together, can emulate.

By the 1960s presidents were exercising lawmaking power with little or no congressional authority, on a scale unthinkable thirty years before. Often the pressures were great and the results commendable, even though in retrospect one has doubts about the method. President Kennedy, for example, issued an executive order prohibiting racial discrimination in housing affected by federal loans or guarantees at a time when Congress would have rejected such legislation.[44] In some cases, even the results seem questionable. Presidents Johnson and Nixon asserted the inherent executive power to conduct electronic "bugging" and other secret domestic intelligence operations without specific statutory authority or even general congressional authorization.[45] President Nixon asserted an executive right to seek judicial aid to suppress publication of the Pentagon Papers,[46] without even a vague legislative foundation. Presidents Johnson and Nixon asserted the constitutional right to carry on large-scale military operations in Indochina without a declaration of war or any other clear-cut authorization from Congress.[47] President Nixon claimed even the power to undo what Congress had done by impounding funds appropriated by Congress for various programs of expenditures.[48]

Watergate was a major engagement in the long war between the legislative and executive branches which began under the

44. Executive Order No. 11063, 27 Fed. Reg. 11527 (1962).

45. United States v. United States District Court, 407 U.S. 297 (1972).

46. New York Times Co. v. United States, 403 U.S. 713 (1971).

47. A useful introduction to the debate is Note, Congress, the President, and the Power to Commit Forces to Combat, 81 *Harv.L.Rev.* 1771 (1968).

48. Subsequent judicial opinions rejected the claim. E.g., Train v. City of New York, 420 U.S. 35 (1975); Pennsylvania v. Lynn, 501 F.2d 848 (D.C. 1974); State Highway Comm. v. Volpe, 479 F.2d 1099 (8th Cir. 1973).

first president. The battle went to the legislative branch because of pervasive wrongdoing within the Executive Offices. The legislative victory was the more complete and extended to foreign policy because of the country's repudiation of presidential involvement in Vietnam. Yet I think it a mistake to draw from recent events a general, vaguely worded conclusion that the power of the executive should be lessened and the power of Congress increased. The practice of committing the country to major policies by executive action without the effective participation of the people or their representatives should stop, but I do not expect our presidents to lose the power of strong leadership, nor would I wish them to cease to exercise it. The forces just mentioned will continue to operate. The times require novel policies, energetic programs, and a voice capable of restating our common aspirations and restoring our self-confidence. These are tasks which the president can perform much better than Congress. For a legislative body to initiate and formulate policies and programs successfully requires a degree of party discipline and cohesiveness which is unthinkable without presidential leadership in a country as large and comprising as many diverse local interests as the United States.

What did go wrong in the past decade was the growth of an alien philosophy concerning the nature of presidential leadership. For the adventure in self-government to go forward we need presidents and presidential aides who—as Thomas Jefferson said —"identify themselves with the people, have confidence in them, cherish them and consider them as the most honest and safe,"[49] and who—I add—put above all else the right of the people to share in, and make, all major decisions. American involvement in Vietnam—whatever the wisdom or folly of the substantive policy—is the best example of the fault because two presidents attempted to commit the nation upon questions even of life and death without ever putting the issue fairly before either the people or their representatives.

President Johnson never succeeded in convincing the public of his faith in self-government; his years in the Senate bred into

49. Letter to Harry Lee, August 10, 1824.

him a secretive and manipulative style. At the end of one of the briefs filed in support of the claim of executive privilege in the litigation over the Watergate tapes, President Nixon's attorneys wrote: "The right of Presidential confidentiality is not a mystical prerogative. It is, rather, the raw essence of the Presidential process, the institutionalized recognition of the crucial role played by human personality in the negotiation, *manipulation* and disposition of human affairs."[50]

It seems to me now, as it did during the litigation, that the plea for power to engage in presidential *manipulation* revealed a fatal flaw. Self-government does not end on election day. Government by consent of the governed is not made up of quadrennial referenda or even the formal action of elected representatives. Consent is infinitely subtler and more complex. Momentary numerical majorities are not always nor in all cases its most reliable expression. Conversely, the sense of participation which binds a nation together, the sense of sharing, at least remotely, in the decisions that determine our fate, springs not merely from casting a ballot but from continuous openness and widespread discussion. Election as president is not a four-year license to manipulate the people.

The defect is chiefly one of attitude, but political philosophy and institutions have a symbiotic relation.

One structural fault is the aggrandizement of the presidential establishment, at the expense of the cabinet members, departments, and agencies. Under recent presidents, the White House staff grew rapidly in size and power. Increasing control passed to men like the director of the Office of Budget and Management who lack political status, who are not subject to senatorial confirmation, and who claim immunity from testifying before the congressional committees which are the principal means of congressional oversight. Presidential aides began to expect and obtain unquestioning obedience even from cabinet members, who were sometimes actually denied access to the president. The growth began with need to extend the president's eyes and ears.

50. Nixon v. Sirica, U.S. Court of Appeals for the D.C. Circuit, No. 73-1962, Brief of Petitioner p. 93.

It spread in the effort to rationalize and energize an increasingly unwieldy bureaucracy, and still later, in the belief that a presidential establishment was needed to overcome the hostility of established departments with vested attitudes and interests. But other means of dealing with departments and agencies are available, and the cost of this means is excessive. The power of presidential aides is like that of royal courtiers. They are responsive, and responsible, to only one man. Unlike many cabinet officers and agency heads, White House aides usually have no independent sources of support, no constituency or other group whose response, being of concern to them, limits their behavior. Unlike cabinet officers and agency heads, White House aides are subject to almost none of the checks of regularized procedure, of speaking for an organization, and of having to respond to it. If the president exposes himself, directly and often, to all the ideas and pressures which can be brought to bear by other centers of power and responsibility, then his aides may be a useful way of extending the president's eyes and ears. But if the president's own style is monarchical or if the Palace Guard succeeds in isolating the president because of excessive protectiveness towards him or concern for their own influence, then the power of White House aides breeds an obsessive concern for secrecy and an arrogant sense not only that the king, but also the king's favorites, can do no wrong.

George Reedy, a longtime friend and press secretary, drew a chilling picture of these tendencies as he observed them in President Johnson's White House.[51]. The tendencies intensified under President Nixon. We have from Jeb Magruder the acknowledgement that those close to the center of the Nixon Administration came to believe that nothing done in pursuit of their objectives could ever be found wrong. Robert Haldeman's television interview early in 1975 displayed before all the world not only chilling moral insensibility but the almost paranoid sense of the White House courtiers that Congress and all other outsiders are enemies to be fought and destroyed if possible.

51. Reedy, *The Twilight of the Presidency,* (Mentor Books, 1971).

The monarchical view of the presidency is encouraged by the doctrine of executive privilege which asserted the constitutional right of the president to withhold information from Congress whenever he asserted that secrecy would be in the public interest. The privilege to withhold has been asserted from time to time throughout our history, beginning with President Washington, but the claims proliferated during recent Republican administrations, which were dealing with a hostile Congress. President Eisenhower was the first to claim explicitly an executive privilege based simply upon an undifferentiated interest in preserving the confidentiality of deliberations and advice throughout the executive branch. On at least forty-four other occasions between June 1955 and June 1960 executive officials sought to justify withholding matters from Congress on grounds of executive privilege, although the claims were often abandoned. There were only rare claims under Presidents Kennedy and Johnson, but President Nixon began making very extensive use of the claim before the Watergate investigations.

Devising appropriate remedies for the growth in the power and isolation of the White House establishment and consequent lessening of popular participation raises puzzling questions concerning what can be done by law and what must be left to the political process. In the theory, Congress can limit the size of the White House staff by curtailing appropriations; it can require senatorial confirmation for men named to positions of authority; and it can put an end to the practice of giving more and more power to formulate executive policy to men and women who claim immunity from testifying before congressional committees. Practically speaking, only the president—a succession of individual presidents—can determine the pattern for the organization and style of the administration. Presidents may find it easier to work with courtiers and to manipulate levers of power without appointing strong public figures, with their own sources of political support, to head the executive departments, making substantial use of them as a cabinet, to the members of which the President would owe and who would owe each other a duty of candid consultation; but perhaps they too will read recent history and conclude that the solid accomplishment is likely to be less, just as the danger to self-government is greater.

Similarly, there are difficulties in dealing by law with excessive claims of executive privilege to withhold information from Congress. In the past the debate was often cast in constitutional terms, but the appeal was to political theory, history, and common sense. The distance the contest was pushed depended upon political considerations. The sanctions available to the House or Senate (as the case might be) were wholly political. Their use depended upon public reaction and political power. The controversies have been rather infrequent, and one can discern little tendency to develop anything that could be called settled practice carrying a degree of legitimacy even though without legal sanction. Moreover, insofar as one can learn from history, the national interest was not injured by the absence of legal remedies.

The situation seems different today. For one thing, executive power has grown to the point where the privilege is no longer necessary to prevent subjecting the executive branch to legislative oppression.

Second, if the executive branch were left to itself, the practice would surely grow. Secrecy, when sanctified by a plausible claim of constitutional privilege, is the easiest way of hiding inefficiency, maladministration, breach of trust or corruption, and also a variety of potentially controversial executive practices adopted without authority from Congress. Ability to control what information to disclose and when to disclose it is a potent political weapon.

Third, the doctrine of executive privilege is closely related to the grave problems of government secrecy. In 1791, when the First Amendment was adopted, governmental repression posed the chief threat to an alert and informed electorate. Men could be pretty sure of obtaining the facts and of communicating with each other in the ways necessary to self-government, provided that men could speak, write and publish, and associate together without fear of reprisal by rulers or elected representatives. This condition no longer prevails. Because of their scale and complexity, coupled with the interdependence of all aspects of society, government itself is often the chief, if not the only, source of information to be the people's agents. The central problem today is how to deal with governmental secrecy and—at times—with governmental deception. Congressional power to inquire, freely exercised, could help. The people cannot govern when the president insists on secrecy. What the president withholds from Congress, he withholds from the people.

The matter may be within congressional control. Last year a bill was introduced in the Senate to establish a law office to challenge, on behalf of Congress, claims of executive privilege and other alleged executive usurpations in the courts. I am appalled by the congressional confession of impotence implicit in turning to the courts for definition of the rights of Congress, and by the damage likely to be done to the judiciary by interjecting it repeatedly into disputes involving no interests of normal legal cognizance but only the relative powers of the two political branches. Nor do I see how a court is to weigh the legislative need for information of any particular kind or in any practical situation.

A better solution, assuming the constitutional difficulties can be overcome, would be to enact legislation vesting the responsibility in the Congress by making it the legal duty of the president and any other official in the executive branch to respond to a subpoena approved by the full Senate or House of Representatives. Under present practice, investigations in aid of legislation or pursuant to congressional oversight over the conduct of the executive branch are conducted by sundry standing committees of the Senate and House of Representatives. A single committee, or subcommittee, because it offers little guarantee of restraint upon individual passion or political ambition, is the greatest threat to the values of confidentiality and carries the greatest danger of legislative irresponsibility or oppression. Requiring the vote of an entire chamber would not only provide a forum in which the executive's arguments could be deliberately considered, but the uncertainty of the outcome would press all concerned to negotiate an accommodation. A vote of the entire Senate or House of Representatives is required to cite a private person for contempt of Congress, and that requirement has proved useful. If either house did vote to require the information, supplying it should become a legal duty enforceable by judicial subpoena, as in the case of the Watergate tapes.

These two changes would help to restore our older and sounder political philosophy concerning the role of presidential leadership. They would leave unsolved the far greater challenge to find ways of delegating self-determination back to smaller groups of citizens, but they should help to revive the sense that self-government is a joint adventure in which all share both power and responsibility.

Law can contribute little to building the good society—indeed, law can have neither vitality nor value—without belief in social progress and the perfectibility of man. Today such confidence comes with difficulty. We have become extraordinarily honest in facing our ugliness, cruelty, indifference, and capacity for evil. It is right to see ourselves for what we are. The danger is that we become obsessed by human failings, lose perspective, and forget the true nature of the enterprise bequeathed to us. Contemporary literature and the arts tell of man the absurd, the pervert, and the dropout, but rarely of man the hero or even man the tragic, for the tragic requires a degree of nobility, and it is the fashion to forget Prometheus's reach and see only the chains.

We are not the first. The founders had no illusions about human weakness. Their experience show them government's power of evil. They did not use Pogo's words, "We have met the enemy and he is us," but their religion taught them the same truth in the language of original sin. The men and women who sought freedom across the seas, who crossed the prairies and the great plains to conquer the mountains and build gardens in the desert, knew the costs, the struggle, the defeats and disappointments. They knew their fallibility and capacity for evil. They also had the insight for a nobler vision and the courage to pursue it even when they knew that neither they nor their children nor their children's children could wholly achieve the dream.

Response

Monrad G. Paulsen

When we ask what law can *do,* we also ask what is the *nature* of law.

In one sense, law is what actually happens in the police station, in the courts, in the agencies of the executive and the independent administrative authorities. In another aspect, law is a large number of binding formulations, each applicable to certain situations but without any *necessary* connection to moral or societal values.

Professor Cox reflects yet a third point of view. Law is not simply an accurate description of what actually happens in the administration of justice nor is its nature fully grasped when one understands and accurately states legal propositions which, as we have said, may be morally neutral or even detrimental to the achievement of the highest human aspirations. No, these conceptions of law though partially valid, leave out something essential to the term. Law is normative. It is a great teacher, a moral force shaping "the goals, structure, and conduct of government so as to nourish the vitality of the moral forces essential to pursuit of the good society through freedom and self-government." A society governed by law is governed by propositions and principles of some universality and generality directed toward a great goal. Remember, Professor Cox's essay is entitled "Law in the Governance of the Good Society"—a society in which humans, "by nature" rational and social beings, seek full development and therefore "will require the form of political organization most likely to assure liberty, and also to reflect the worth of every man."

The planners of this Bicentennial Symposium suggested that each inquiry should be concerned with some aspect of "The Nature of a Humane Society." This is, I take it, something more than an inquiry into the just society or a social organization which nurtures freedom and responsibility.

Humane, my dictionary tells me, means "characterized by tenderness and compassion for the suffering or the distressed."

Humane takes into account the noble aspects of man such as "benevolence in treatment of fellows or helpless animals." In short, part of our task is to ask can law hope to make an important contribution to the "humane" aspect of human life. We must ask not only "what is essentially human" but also whether the instruments and institutions of law can bring "humaneness."

There are those, in contrast to Professor Cox, who see law and authority as an impediment to human development. Professor Robert Wolff, a philosophical anarchist, writes: "Neither majority rule nor any other method of making decisions in the absence of unanimity can be shown to preserve the autonomy of the individual citizens. . . . Each of us must make himself the author of his actions and take responsibility for them by refusing to act save on the basis of reasons he can see for himself to be good. . . . [In] and of themselves, the acts of police and the commands of the legislature and have no peculiar legitimacy or sanction."[1]

Wolff contrasts authority with anarchy. Authority says "Do this!" not "*Let* me suggest this for your consideration." There are, he admits "utilitarian arguments for submitting to the State and its agents" but the state's claim to *legitimacy* is "unfounded."[2]

I read Professor Cox to affirm that the benefit of a regime of law lies in its ultimate aims of providing the conditions for personal liberty and for the dignity of every person. Legislation, in such an order of things, derives its legitimacy "from the participation of the people through elected representatives and the principle of majority rule." Cox refers to "that belief in the value of the common enterprise which alone can bind the members of a free society together." Fundamental trust in the processes of government is essential.

Law depends in the main on "uncoerced consent" ("most properly," the anarchist would agree). Such consent "depends upon the people's recognition that law and other restraints . . . are the only means of accommodating freedom and social order."

The general position of the Cox paper has much in common with the ideas of "natural law" as formulated in the philosophy of Aristotle and St. Thomas Aquinas. The modern Thomist,

1. Robert Wolff, ed., *Violence and the Law* (1971), pp. 54, 61.
2. Ibid., p. 56.

Jacques Maritain, has formulated a definition:

> Since man is endowed with intelligence and determines his own ends, it is up to him to put himself in tune with the ends necessarily demanded by his nature. This means that there is, by virtue of human nature, *an order or a disposition which human reason can discover and according to which the human will must act in order to attune itself to the necessary ends of the human being. The unwritten law, or natural law, is nothing more than that.*[3]

Maritain distinguishes several classes of human rights which would be guaranteed in a regime paying heed to the law of nature. First there are the rights of the human person *as such* (my list is a partial one): the right to existence, personal liberty, to the free exercise of spiritual activity and the right to property.[4]

The rights of the civic person include the right to participate in public life, the right of association, political discussion and organization, and of a right to independent judiciary.[5]

The rights of the social person (especially the rights of working persons) include the right to choose work, to form unions, to a just wage, and to social benefits such as unemployment and health insurance and care in old age. Under this rubric, "the right to have a part, free of charge, depending on the possibilities of the community, in the elementary goods, both material and spiritual, of civilization."[6]

Professor Cox considers carefully the role of the Supreme Court of the United States. The function of that institution obviously sets a problem for him because of his assertion that the legitimacy of law is bound up with the citizens' participation in the law-making process.

The Supreme Court obviously exercises enormous authority without its members having been subjected to the electoral process. It's constitutional decisions can be changed only by the Court itself or by the cumbersome process of constitutional amendment.

Professor Cox recognizes that some of the Court's decisions look very much like legislative determinations. He calls particular

3. Jacques Maritain, *The Rights of Man and the Natural Law* (1958), p. 35.
4. Ibid., p. 60.
5. Ibid., p. 61.
6. Ibid., p. 62.

attention to those cases which prescribe remedies of an affirmative character, listing some of the recent busing decisions, and cases in the lower federal courts which have undertaken to prescribe detailed standards for the running of prisons. One might add the Supreme Court's decisions in the fields of abortion and the death penalty as among those that present difficulties to whoever would support the Court's role.

Professor Cox has an interesting resolution of the issue put by these observations:

> Constitutional adjudication depends upon a delicate, symbiotic relation. The Court should sometimes be the voice of the spirit, telling us what we are by reminding us of what we may be. But while the opinions of the Court can help to shape our national understanding of ourselves, the roots of its decisions must be already in the nation. The Court cannot do much to coerce either the political branches or the masses of people. The aspirations voiced by the Court must be those the community is willing not only to avow but in the end to live by. The contribution of great constitutional decisions to the evolution of a more humane society depends, I think, upon the accuracy of the Court's perception of the goals of the enterprise and upon the Court's ability, by expressing its perception ultimately to command not only a passive but a supportive consensus.

Even acknowledging its great power, the Supreme Court can do little to change the system of distribution of wealth. Aside from relatively recent judicial opinions (having to do with such things as a state's duty to supply counsel in a criminal case, to arrange for a fair hearing before welfare benefits are cut off, to spend for the improvement of prison facilities and, in some states, to provide public funds, in an equitable manner, for elementary and secondary education) the spending, taxing, and regulatory priorities—those decisions which determine who gets "what, when and how"—are made by the legislature although the pattern of distribution can, of course, be influenced by independent administrative agencies or the executive in its participation in lawmaking.

Professor Cox's position on civil disobedience is bound to be controversial. The reader will recall that he had few kind words to say about those who break the law to achieve results which seem to the lawbreaker to serve a "higher morality." He wrote, "Assertions of the higher morality of civil disobedience [seem to me to] threaten the present development of a more nearly humane society." Those who protested the war in Vietnam by means of unlawful conduct chose a dangerous path which could lead (and Cox argues did lead) to other unlawful conduct by the government.

It must be said that his condemnation of almost all civil disobedience is a judgment made in a free society where law is made legitimate by general participation in lawmaking. He does not write of the proper and justifiable acts of persons in Hitler's Germany or the present day Eastern Europe.

Professor Cox does have one qualification to his general argument. If protestors can "honestly say to themselves that their conduct does not violate the becoming-law as they reasonably hope the courts will now declare it," their position may be morally acceptable. This qualification is narrow. Literally, it speaks of the *protestor's* acts as becoming lawful as the existing law is now, developing not to the unlawful acts of protestors who seek by unlawful acts, to move government to change its policy in respect to a different matter, that is, the war in Vietnam. To make a contrast, the late Professor Harry Kalven of the University of Chicago Law School once said of civil disobedience, "one should punish it and listen to it."

In the legislature, the essence of the governmental process is compromise. Very little legislation reflects high principle with great clarity. Arbitrary distinctions are the order of the day. Does it make moral sense that a person offering public accommodations for a total of four persons may discriminate on racial grounds, yet those who serve more must take in everyone? Such a compromise was necessary to enact the Civil Rights Act of 1964. A majority of legislators were wise enough not to permit the best to be the enemy of the good. A valuable little book by the late T. V. Smith, a professor of philosophy at Chicago, a legislator in the State Senate of Illinois and, later, in the United States House of Representatives saw a democracy's legislative process as a civilizing achievement which provides a means for curbing the egoism and self-righteousness of persons as they attempt to solve difficult problems. A society with an effective legislative process, he wrote, had "a method of spreading the element of sociality across all broad crevices of disunion." Compromise he saw as the keeper of the peace. The process gives all a chance to be heard and to take the interests of all into account.

> If we are civilized, we draw, not the conclusion that we will have our way regardless, but a more modest conclusion—the conclusion that, since no one can adequately represent the opposing point of view, each must be allowed to state his own case, to represent his own cause.
>
> "It is, you see, upon the elemental and universal fact of conflict that the legislative way of life is built; it is inescapable conflict which makes legislation necessary and which alone renders tolerable its imperfections. Once we admit that if opposing points of view are to be acknowledged, we must allow partisans to represent them, then we must begin to provide an institution under which all points of view can meet on equal terms and have it out. That is precisely what a legislature is. It is an institution which every important point of view sends its own partisans to see after its interests, sends them as lobbyists if not as legislators. Such an institution must exist in order to make possible the peaceable adjustment of issues.[7]

New forms and the participation of citizens in policy-making are emerging, likely to be more widely accepted and present more challenges for the legal system. A recent book (1975) sponsored by the American Assembly entitled *Law and the American Future* contains essays with the following titles: "Representation in Rule-Making"; "Public Interest Law: Problems and Prospect"; "Legal Services for Citizens of Moderate Income and Civil Legal Services for the Poor." These writings are subsumed under the title "The Representation of the Unrepresented." Participation in the legal process by large numbers of people, some of whom will entertain new and striking points of view, is bound to fuel change in the United States.

Professor Cox is rightly concerned with the expanding power of the presidency. We can agree that election as president is not

7. T. V. Smith, *The Legislative Way of Life* (1940), pp. 14–15. This impressive hymn to the methods and results of the legislative process was first delivered as a set of three lectures at Westminster College, Fulton, Mo. It is kept in print by the University of Chicago Press.

a four-year license to manipulate the people and yet doubt whether in the long run the power of presidents will give way in a very significant fashion. I put it that the office of president in the modern day of wide-ranging federal government is inevitably the center of leadership and practical power. Problems can be solved by the state only if there is the power to solve them. A significant reestablishment of congressional power is unlikely. Only the president has a mandate from the nation. Senators and representatives have special constituencies with special interest but they are not (for that reason) perceived as leaders on the national level.

The president alone can easily command radio and television time. By his actions and statements he receives the attention of the press. The cabinet, the members of which are always subject to dismissal, cannot provide independent leadership unless the president permits it. They have no constituency either as elected officials, or necessarily as leaders in their party. Absent major changes in our Constitution, the president is likely to remain the central force—and a very great one—in the federal government.

Turning to another matter, a great concern today is trust in government. Professor Cox's essay is an eloquent example of that concern. What puzzles me is the notion that lack of trust in government is new in American history. I first heard this point of view from my grandfather and also my father: "All politicians are alike, they promise you everything and accomplish nothing; officials are in office for their own selfish purposes, they are all tax eaters." Maybe these views from Eastern Iowa in the 1920s were unusual but I am inclined to doubt it. I do believe, however, that such attitudes of mistrust are heard more widely today because life is so filled with problems of staggering proportions that seem to arise from apparently impersonal institutions.

It must be remembered that most of our personal concerns do not yield to government intervention at all. Ask what problem kept you restless last night and follow the answer with a question: What could government do to bring that problem to a satisfactory resolution?

Of course, some actions and attitudes of public officials can make the atmosphere of mistrust considerably worse. Yet Watergate and its coverup seem to grow less important in the minds of most persons. If that is true, perhaps it is because it seems to many persons as simply another example of government as it ordinarily functions. The question (in one aspect) is not whether such an attitude should be deplored but whether it exists.

In closing, I should like to return to consider the word *humane* as my dictionary has defined it and ask whether law can truly generate "humaneness." Law, and I think Professor Cox agrees, is an instrument which assists in the perfection of mankind, but its importance is as a teacher about conduct which can harm others, and a guide which points out what a political and social order for beings of reason might be. Yet, quite often law is seen to be a rough teacher. Luther, as I recall, spoke of Law as a hammer and anvil which would dissuade wicked acts "even in respect to regenerate man to whom much of the flesh still clings."

In Professor Cox's essay, he makes the point that the role of law is limited. It cannot do everything. Something else is necessary to call all persons to true "humaneness."

Jacques Maritain in *The Peasant of the Garonne* develops the position by quoting a text by his wife, Raissa:

> Law is, in a certain manner, opposed to love. God has made it insofar as he is the Creator of being. But insofar as he is our end and our beatitude, he calls us beyond it.
>
> The law is proposed Externally, it implies a subjection—in itself it seems to have nothing to do with mercy—nor with the equality of friendship—nor with familiarity.
>
> It is truly a necessity; only a necessity.
>
> Love gives over the head of the Law.
>
> It forgives.
>
> Love creates trust—freedom of spirit—equality—familiarity.[8]

8. Jacques Maritain, *The Peasant of the Garonne* (1965), p. 260.

Responsible Scientific Investigation and Application

Wernher von Braun

Motivations for Scientific Study and Research

Ralph Waldo Emerson once said, "Men love to wonder, and that is the seed of science." Wonder, curiosity, is indeed the mainspring of all scientific research. Since time immemorial there have always been some men and women who felt a burning desire to know what was under the rock, beyond the hills, or on the far side of the open seas. With all the rocks and hills and oceans explored, this restless breed now wants to know the nature of subatomic particles, the mechanism through which given forms of life can make duplicates of themselves, whether there is life on Mars, or whether the whole cosmos started with a big bang.

Why does man want to know all these things? Why are we so eager to learn more about the universe in which we live? I cannot provide you a better answer than a quote from that great explorer and humanitarian, Friedjof Nansen: "The history of the human race is a continual struggle from darkness toward light. It is, therefore, of no purpose to discuss the use of knowledge. Man wants to know and when he ceases to do so, he is no longer man."

Even from the purely materialistic angle, man's pursuit of his innate curiosity has stood him in good stead. All material advances enjoyed today, whether color television or miracle drugs, jetliners or aqualungs, sewing machines or artificial kidneys, can be traced back to the fact that at some time, somewhere, someone was curious about something.

As a man whose entire life has been devoted to rocketry and space exploration, I should like to make a few remarks about the relationship between space research, scientific education, and motivation of the young who we expect to continue where my generation leaves off.

The space program really did not begin with Sputnik, Explorer I, and the first manned flights into orbit. Our program of space exploration is simply the latest chapter in a continuing scientific revolution that dates back to Copernicus, Kepler, and Galileo. It was their observations, and their ability to draw inferences from what they saw, that moved the earth from its exalted position as the center of the universe. That was a profound blow to the human ego, and it called for some very painful reassessments of man's place in the universe. But it was a very necessary step in the continuing search for truth and the advancement of knowledge.

Today every school child is aware that our small planet, its neighbors in the solar system, and even our sun itself, are in what someone has described as the suburb of a minor galaxy in a dynamic universe populated by galaxies and supergalaxies in numbers that probably surpass our comprehension.

The average citizen today, of course, has far more scientific information at his disposal than did those greatest of intellects of earlier times. Yet paradoxically I think there has never been a greater need for increased understanding and appreciation of science and technology.

The noted educator Dr. Lindley J. Stiles of the University of Wisconsin addressed himself to this question of scientific literacy some years ago. Dr. Stiles said that, although the choice of direction for our civilization will be determined through the democratic process, it is there that the problem begins. To make rational choices, he pointed out, the average citizen must understand the nature and role of science at a time when its breadth and complexity are increasing almost exponentially.

Conversely, the scientist, at a time when he can barely keep up to date in his speciality, must not isolate himself in his parochial interests. Instead, he should see his profession as a part of the larger world, to evaluate himself and his work in relation to all forces, especially the humanities, which shape and advance society.

The need, then, is for an educational process resulting in more scientific literacy for the layperson, and more literacy in the humanities for the scientists. It is also important that the layperson not attach too much importance to the scientists' opinions on issues outside their special disciplines. Scientists are not experts in everything just because they are scientists.

Man in this scientific and technological age is free only to the extent that he has a grasp on himself and his surroundings. Freedom—the ability to speak, think, act, and vote intelligently—is based largely on our ability to make choices growing out of our understanding of the issues involved. With each advance of science, and with each invention of technology and its uses, there is an invitation to more understanding. This is the essence of the burden borne by all peoples since the dawn of humanity and toolmaking. This is the imperative for scientific literacy and, we should add, technological literacy. There must be widespread understanding of the role of science and technology in modern society, both as to their limits and our dependence on their basic function as tools for our survival.

How do we encourage scientific and technological literacy? I think the problem is how to instill in students a permanent desire to learn. All youth is endowed with curiosity from the very beginning. What can the educational process do, not only to keep this natural curiosity alive, but to make it a permanent part of the individual drive?

Professor Okey of Indiana University offers one approach: "In addition to learning facts," he wrote, "students should learn to examine facts, how to answer questions or solve problems using facts, and how to produce facts." This is essentially the scientific method. By learning the scientific method, students will understand its role in society and at the same time learn to think for themselves. Learning to think for oneself, in turn, imparts a deep sense of freedom. Once tasted, an appetite for it is formed which may well endure throughout life.

But if our young people are going to gain this appetite, our schools, our colleges, our universities, must bear an ever greater responsibility. All too many times in the past, education—particularly in the scientific disciplines—has placed extremely heavy emphasis on transmitting the established knowledge of the past. There has been a tendency for teachers to assign reading and to encourage rote learning instead of taking the admittedly more difficult path of encouraging students to think for themselves.

A serious trend that I see emerging is the intellectual effort to bridge the gap between the natural sciences and the social sciences. This effort must by its very nature involve the educational processes at all levels. We see it manifested today in the pronouncements of many of the professional associations of science as well as of prestigious natural scientists. We see less of a realization of its importance among the social scientists and humanists. But here, too, the realization is beginning to grow in the writings and pronouncements of such prophets as Buckminster Fuller and the poet Archibald MacLeish. In my opinion, democratic society cannot survive if the masses of the population are lacking in understanding of the fundamental principles of science: it is through science and its related technology that more and more of the operations of society and the decisions that will have to be made concerning these operations are based. From an educational point of view this effort to bridge the gap involves, as I see it, reorientation of curricula in both the natural sciences and the social sciences. This, of course, takes time and thought, because the curricula in each of these fields have tended to go more and more their independent ways.

Never has there been a greater opportunity or a greater incentive for the young people to learn to think for themselves. The body of knowledge is advancing at an absolutely incredible rate, and new tools are constantly being made available to the researcher that were previously not only unavailable, but often not even dreamed of.

Without wanting to seem overly partisan, I would like simply to point out that the space program has by all standards become America's greatest generator of new ideas in science and technology. It is essentially an organization for opening new frontiers, physically and intellectually. Today we live in a different world because in 1958 Americans accepted the challenge of space and made the required national investment to meet it.

Young people today are learning a new science, but even more importantly, they are viewing the earth and man's relationship to it quite differently—and I think perhaps more humanly—than we did fifteen years ago. The space program is the first large scientific and technological activity in history that offers to bring the people of all nations together instead of setting them further apart.

Science, Technology, Morality, and the Question of Taboos

One of the most disconcerting issues of our time lies in the fact that modern science, along with miracle drugs and communications satellites, has also produced nuclear bombs. What makes it even worse, science has utterly failed to provide an answer to how to cope with them. As a result, science and scientists have often been blamed for the desperate dilemma in which mankind finds itself today.

Science all by itself has no moral dimension. The same poison-containing drug which cures when taken in small doses may kill when taken in excess. The same nuclear chain reaction that produces badly needed electrical energy when harnessed in a reactor may kill thousands when abruptly released in an atomic bomb. Thus it does not make sense to ask a biochemist or a nuclear physicist whether his research in the field of toxic substances or nuclear processes is good or bad for mankind. In most cases the scientist will be fully aware of the possibility of an abuse of his discoveries, but aside from his innate scientific curiosity he will be motivated by a deep-seated hope and belief that something of value for his fellow man may emerge from his labors.

The same applies to technology, through which most advances in the natural sciences are put to practical use. No sooner had man learned to make iron than he beat it into axes to fell trees so he could till more land, and into swords to defend himself or help him grab land from his neighbors. The modern offspring of that axe, the knife, may save a life when wielded by a skillful surgeon, but will kill if thrust only a few inches deeper. Aircraft carry millions of people across oceans and continents, thus forging ever-closer ties of understanding, friendship, and trade between nations, but they are just as capable of carrying troops, war material, or even nuclear bombs. Technology all by itself thus does not have a moral dimension, either.

The deplorable fact that neither science nor technology have a moral dimension, of course, does not help solve the problem we are trying to address here today. Science and technology have made such rapid advances in so many fields that the public is almost ready to expect they can solve any of mankind's problems if we only set our mind to it and make the necessary resources available. "If we can send people to the moon," many people seem to feel, "why can't we . . ." and then we hear an endless enumeration of all the grim problems besetting humanity.

Many of mankind's problems are, of course, outside the domain of science and technology, but probably just as many are profoundly affected by them. And we have reached the point in many fields of scientific and technological endeavor where we can expect success of a new project with a very high degree of probability, provided we are willing to spend an adequate amount of effort and money. The decision whether a proposed new objective should be pursued must therefore often be made not on the basis of whether it is attainable or not, but on its general desirability, its intrinsic value, its future growth potential, its inherent dangers, its environmental impact, or its cost compared to other competing science projects.

The choice must also be based on a new value system. The old American standards of material wealth or technological efficiency obviously require some reappraisal, since in these terms we are already the greatest society in history. As Professor Herbert J. Muller, professor of English and government at Cal Tech, once formulated it, we should adopt "some civilized standard, involving moral, cultural, spiritual values, the kinds of achievements recognized in the broad agreements upon what were the great societies and the golden ages of the past."

Also we are squarely confronted with the ethical question, Is everything that is scientifically possible, also permissible? There can be no question that unless we find a more effective mechanism to steer scientific investigations and their practical applications into constructive and safe channels, the future of mankind will be exposed to ever-growing dangers. As we have learned to harness and unleash fantastic new sources of energy, both our potential to create a life of abundance for everybody and to bring about a sudden apocalyptic end has grown immensely. In the horse-and-buggy days, no one was exposed to great risk if the coachman had a drink too many. Today, the driver of a high-powered automobile can become a killer in one careless moment. Tighter rules of the road have become a necessity for survival. But how do we write a set of rules of the road for scientific investigations? Should we attempt to develop a set of taboos declaring certain scientific studies off-limits? If so, who should be entrusted with the task of setting those taboos?

Looking back to mankind's slow emergence from caveman to spaceman, from cannibal to cardinal, we may well doubt whether we would have ever succeeded, had such taboos been strictly enforced in the past. Take the case of Prometheus. Clearly, had he not defied the Olympic taboo we would still sit shivering in unheated caves. And yet, suppose Zeus in all his wisdom had convened an Olympic committee, complete with futurologists and environmental impact appraisers, to advise him on the foreseeable human sufferings that had to be expected from hearth fires running out of control or from the use of fire in war. Is it not likely that that committee would have produced powerful reasons supporting Zeus's final decision to pronounce the Prometheus taboo? And in retrospect, are we not fortunate indeed that Prometheus defied the ruling?

How much smarter are we today? Could we really convene a group of academic Olympians wise enough to set the green and red traffic lights for fundamental research in such equally promising and dangerous areas as genetic engineering, breeder reactors, high power lasers, or the harnessing of thermonuclear power?

Dire predictions have been made that even the next generation must gird itself to cope with near-hopeless problems resulting from the divergence between the growing demands of a rapidly expanding world population and the shrinking supply of nonrenewable resources of our planet.

Is this really the time to put shackles on scientific research in areas that are both highly promising and fraught with grave hazards? Is this the time to put Prometheus in chains before he can carry the new fire to man? Don't we need all the new insights that only unfettered scientific research can give us if we want mankind to survive not just the next generation but for a few more million years, and hopefully the remaining four billion years the earth is expected to remain inhabitable by man (unless he himself deprives himself of that chance)?

And yet has mankind really a chance to survive the remaining several million or even billion years—or even just the next generation—if we refrain from imposing any effective controls? I think the majority of scientists are convinced that very wise and cautious statesmanship and ironclad international treaties are absolutely mandatory to protect mankind from the abuse of its newly-won scientific capabilities.

The question, therefore, boils down to what is the best point in time between gestation, birth, childhood, adolescence, and maturity of a new potentially dangerous discovery or invention at which these controls should be imposed. It appears to me that the time to flash up the red no-go sign is *not* at the very early stage of any basic scientific pursuit. As Plato said, "We can easily forgive a child who is afraid of the dark; the real tragedy of life is when men are afraid of the light."

Controls should rather be established only after the area of potentially dangerous abuse of an otherwise promising and beneficial scientific discovery can be clearly identified and isolated. No judge would condemn a human embryo to death because it has the potential to become a criminal. Laws of *dos* and *don'ts* are rather applied to children and grownups with clearly identified legal and illegal options, and the law is enforced by policing and the imposition of penalties in case of violations.

I fervently believe that not everything that is scientifically possible is per se permissible—in the ethical or religious sense. But the stop light for scientific research and application should be appled only after we can discern the beneficial from the detrimental, the good from the evil.

Do we need a new organizational structure to administer whatever new controls in the field of scientific investigation and application may become desirable? I do not think so. In the medical and health fields the National Institute of Health, the National Cancer Institute, and the National Food and Drug Administration are examples of organizations already deeply involved. In the food production area the Department of Agriculture must continue to work out its differences over fertilizer and pesticide uses with the Environmental Protection Agency. And on the question of nuclear safety for our many new nuclear power plants we simply cannot find any more competent people than in the Energy Research and Development Agency and the Nuclear Regulatory Commission.

Wherever fundamental new research is required to provide a better base for future legislation—for instance, in the field of absorption of pollutant and toxic metals by the whole complex food chain of marine organisms living in our river estuaries and on our continental shelves—the National Science Academy, the National Science Foundation, and the National Oceanic and Atmospheric Agency are competent, eager, and busy formulating the necessary programs.

Mankind's Most Pressing Problems

The most pressing problems of our generation are easily identified. There is probably little fundamental disagreement over their identity among most Americans, and many are shared by mankind as a whole. None of them can be solved by science and technology alone. All have economical, social, philosophical, aesthetical, political, and other aspects which are often in conflict with one another.

My paper deals with responsible scientific investigation and application and attempts to identify such problem areas where science can really help. For this reason I have intentionally omitted problem areas on which science policy has no profound effect—such as Africa's new search for identity, the painful evolution of democracy in some Latin American countries, or the immensely complex Middle East problem with all its ramifications. I excluded these problem areas not because I underestimate their possible fateful significance, but solely to bring my science-related message into better focus.

A dome supported by five pillars offers a somewhat simplified model for the hierarchy of our key problems. The dome itself represents the all-embracing objective, "Survival of Mankind as a Species." The five pillars supporting the dome are:

(1) Resources survival. Here we are talking about the continuing availability of the material and energy resources required to feed, clothe, house, and provide jobs for the world's growing population.

(2) Environmental survival. We must drastically clean up and protect from further deterioration the precious life-support system of our thin biosphere, the thin layer of soil, water, and air that supports all life on earth. This will require continuous monitoring of the land and ocean surface and its atmosphere.

(3) Spiritual survival. We must accomplish all this and more without drifting into a regimented, coercive society. To restore and protect inalienable personal freedom we must provide more elbowroom for the individual. This requires a reversal of the trend toward urbanization.

(4) Nuclear survival, which is tantamount to avoidance of a self-inflicted nuclear holocaust.

(5) Scientific survival. Unless the United States retains leadership in the natural sciences and in technology, these four support pillars for the dome we called "Survival of Mankind as a Species" are bound to erode and collapse. Scientific survival,

therefore, is a vitally needed fifth pillar. We live in a dynamic, fast-moving world. The great races for superiority in aviation, nuclear, and space technology between the superpowers have dramatically illustrated that he who relaxes his efforts in science and technology even for a few years can be easily confronted with a momentous, fateful, and possibly hopeless task of catching up again. But in continuing our pursuits in applied science we must never neglect scientific effort for its own sake, for the continued search for the basic laws of creation. It is basic research which lays the groundwork for any scientific application.

A Hierarchy of Scientific Priorities

Using our dome-and-five-pillars model, we can now attempt to identify some of the most promising contributions of applied science and technology.

Let us look at each pillar and see how science and technology can protect and strengthen it. Needless to say, science and technology have so many facets that my list of scientific priority projects is incomplete and should be extended to include other relevant programs aimed at protecting our five pillars.

Resources Survival

It has been said that earth is a spaceship with three and one half billion astronauts and no captain, coasting through the universe to an unknown destination. And while they are rapidly depleting the ship's limited supplies, those astronauts are multiplying like rabbits.

Well, regardless of where you stand on that unqualified demand for "limits to growth" expressed in some quarters, and the dire predictions of the Club of Rome—which very nearly comes to the conclusion that we are doomed no matter what we do—it should be obvious that a systematic survey of the earth's resources should have one of the highest priorities for science and technology. It is in this field that space technology has provided us with a most timely breakthrough.

In space parlance, we call "resources" everything man needs for his survival: food crops, timber to build houses, fresh water, wildlife and marine life to hunt and fish, cattle and grazing land, minerals, fossil fuel and other energy sources (such as solar energy and uranium), and last but not least, remaining land for his future use.

Two NASA-built LANDSAT satellites, orbiting the slowly revolving earth fourteen times a day in near-polar orbits, are swamping the data centers on the ground with a wealth of new information, and it will probably be quite a while until we are able to completely interpret the maze of new orbital data on resources contained in their multispectral images. But we have already come down the road quite a bit. A customer anywhere on earth buying images from both satellites gets a picture of the same place every ninth day. As of October 1975 more than 155,000 different pictures of parts of the earth's surface were taken, each in four spectral bands, stored at and available to the public from a data center in South Dakota.

NASA trains foreign scientists to interpret the images; data goes to more than one hundred research teams around the world, giving many less developed nations their first report on natural resources. Data have taken polluters to court, led geologists to oil, given land planners a regional picture faster and at far less cost than traditional surveys, analyzed plant health for farmers and foresters; corrected maps, showed the Sahel (African drought-famine region) that some land had been preserved from encroaching desert by controlled grazing, and so on. Such information from satellites has been called as epoch-making as the first use of fire as a tool, or the first practical use of the wheel.

There are, of course, many other areas where science and technology can make great contributions to mankind's growing resources dilemma. But there can be no doubt that continued aggressive research and development programs aimed at improved resources surveys from orbit is one of our best bets.

Let me now touch upon the vital subject of our continuing supply of energy. We must distinguish here between the energy problem for mankind as a whole and our national energy problem which is overshadowed by the desire to minimize our dependence on imports which, as recent events have shown, make the United States vulnerable to undesirable pressures on our foreign and domestic policies. I quote from a recent publication from ERDA, our new Energy Research and Development Administration:

> The national energy system currently relies most on the least plentiful domestic energy resources and least on the most abundant resources.
>
> Over 75 percent of the Nation's energy consumption is based on petroleum and natural gas. Domestic supplies of these commodities are dwindling.
>
> Coal, the most abundant domestic fossil fuel, provides less than 20 percent of current energy needs.
>
> Uranium, the domestic energy source with the greatest energy potential, provides about 2 percent of the Nation's energy.
>
> Solar energy, available to all, but diffuse, provides a negligibly small percentage of current needs.

In response to this situation, and after a careful analysis of projected needs, the status of candidate technologies, and the extent of the resources they would use, a ranking list for ERDA's priorities has been developed and submitted to Congress. The list breaks the priorities down into three categories—and here I am quoting again directly from ERDA's official plan:

> For the near-term (now to 1985) and beyond the priorities are:
>
> To preserve and expand major domestic energy systems; coal, light water reactors (the highest nuclear priority), and gas and oil from both new sources and from enhanced recovery techniques
>
> To increase the efficiency of energy used in all sectors of the economy and to extract more energy from waste materials.
>
> For the mid-term (1985–2000) and beyond the priorities are:
>
> To accelerate the development of new processes for production of synthetic fuel from coal and extraction of oil from shale
>
> To increase the use of under-used fuel forms, such as geothermal energy, solar energy for room heating and cooling, and extraction of more usable energy from waste heat. None of these technologies has a major long-term impact, but each can be quite useful in relieving mid-term shortages.
>
> For the long-term (past 2000) the priorities are:

> To pursue vigorously those candidate technologies which will permit the use of essentially inexhaustible resources:
>
> —Nuclear breeders
>
> —Controlled thermonuclear fusion
>
> —Solar electric energy from a variety of technological options, including wind power, thermal and photovoltaic approaches, and use of ocean thermal gradients.
>
> None of these three technologies is assured of large-scale applications. All have unique unresolved questions in one or more areas: technical, economic, environmental, or social. The benefits to be gained in achieving success in one or more of these approaches require that vigorous development efforts proceed now on all three.

In the context of my paper, "Responsible Scientific Investigation and Application," I cannot take issue with any elements of this ERDA program. I think it is a mature and well thought out plan which, as all plans aimed at broad objectives, will require repeated reviews and adjustments to the ever-changing realities of costs, needs, encountered difficulties, accomplished scientific and technological breakthroughs, and even national moods.

There is one item buried in the multitude of ERDA goals that requires particular attention, however. As we have seen, ERDA recommends for the near term a great expansion in the building of light water reactors which power the conventional nuclear utilities already providing a small percentage of our electrical power needs. For the long term, ERDA plans to pursue the breeder reactor program, so called because it produces more nuclear fuel than it consumes.

I am personally convinced that the nuclear safety aspects of both conventional and breeder-type power plants can be met if the same standards of perfection and careful scrutiny are applied that made our lunar landing program so successful. However, both types of reactors produce an ever-increasing amount of plutonium. The question of how to avoid an uncontrolled proliferation of this material which can be used to make atomic bombs is serious indeed. I shall address this question later in context with the nuclear survival pillar of our pillar-and-dome model.

Man's most precious resource undoubtedly is his brain, but the vast majority of mankind uses it most sparingly. The reason, of course, is inadequate education.

I have already talked a bit about scientific education, which we need to provide the world with new generations of scientists. Important as it is, the education of new scientists, of course, directly involves only a tiny minority of mankind. The sorry fact is that the bulk of the three and one half billion astronauts of Spaceship Earth are illiterate. If we want to improve the quality of their lives, we must literally start with the ABCs.

In the summer of 1975 the United States, implementing a state treaty with the government of India, placed a unique geosynchronous communications satellite above the African east coast, from which it is sending educational television programs to twenty-five hundred villages in India. The programs themselves —the "three Rs" for the kids, and topics like farmer instruction, animal husbandry, and family planning for the adults, have been prepared by the Indians themselves and are beamed up to the satellite from a large transmitter station in Ahmedabad, near Bombay. The satellite, equipped with a huge thirty-foot parabolic antenna and a powerful transmitter, beams the amplified signal back onto the entire Indian subcontinent where it can be received in any village equipped with a normal TV receiver attached through a special black box to a six-foot chicken-wire antenna. The entire TV village setup, a twentieth-century version of the little one-room red schoolhouse of early America, costs less than one thousand dollars.

Both from the technical viewpoint and from the aspect of audience acceptance the Indian program has been a great success. However, we should not lose sight of the fact that it was only the first large-scale experiment of carrying education via a direct broadcast television satellite to a predominantly illiterate population. From this first experiment to an operational educational system for all of India is still a long and difficult road.

Just look at a few figures which illustrate the immensity of the problem. India is a very large, diverse country with an area of over one million square miles. It has fourteen languages and about eight hundred different dialects. Approximately thirty percent of its five hundred million people live in rural areas. There are about 560,000 villages, many without access roads, electricity, hospitals, or schools. Seven out of ten people are illiterate. Even though the literacy rate has doubled over the past twenty years, the number of illiterates has actually increased by over eighty million during that period due to the high population growth rate. There is a serious shortage of qualified teachers, which grows worse as the population increases. In 1975, there were already about five hundred primary school students for every qualified teacher.

It is clear that if India is to bring enough education to its rural population to mount an effective nationwide campaign to increase its food production and control the population growth rate in time to avert a national catastrophe, the traditional teacher-classroom concept of education must be bypassed, or at least supplemented, with modern techniques utilizing audio-visual aids. The most flexible and effective of those is modern television. But how can a developing country, without benefit of a nationwide network of ground TV stations, reach a large enough segment of a rural population with conventional educational TV methods in time to meet its pressing needs and at a price it can afford? The answer clearly is the Direct Broadcast Television Satellite.

There are, of course, very serious questions concerning this marvelous new product of science that can bring education and enlightenment to the illiterate and poor of a vast country: Can we—or can the Indians themselves, for that matter—really assess the impact of bringing within the time span of a single generation literacy to half a billion people? What changes will that cause to the social and political fabric of a predominantly rural country? Will there be enough challenging job opportunities for the next educated generation? If not, will there be widespread frustration? Will the Indian population as a whole, known for its calm acceptance of fate and the individual's station in life, become more restless, with resulting turmoil and bloodshed?

It seems we are right back to my earlier question. Should we put Prometheus in chains? Clearly, here again science and technology help to carry the fire of knowledge and enlightenment about the rest of the world to people who had not known it. I am personally deeply involved in this particular satellite and the Indian educational experiment. Many of my friends and associates, who for many years have worked in this program with unbounded enthusiasm because of its epoch-making humanitarian potential, have quietly confided to me their concern and moral scruples, as no one can fathom the long-term consequences of such an educational revolution.

Speaking for myself, I hold the strong belief (and so told my friends) that now that science and technology have given us the capability to bring education to the illiterates in the world we have no moral right to deny it to them. Maybe the fact that I spent twenty years of my life in Huntsville, Alabama has something to do with that conclusion. When I arrived there in 1950, the opinion was widespread among the predominantly white population of Huntsville that most black children were either not ready for first-class education, or that a general rise in their educational standards would only lead to trouble with job placements. Today, Huntsville has some of the finest integrated schools in the nation and few, if any, of the predicted problems have arisen.

Environmental Survival

The three and one half billion astronauts not only deplete the dwindling resources of Spaceship Earth like drunken sailors, but they also poison their life-support system as though they were implementing a global suicide pact.

Many of our environmental problems can be solved with existing scientific knowledge and technology, provided we are willing to pay the price for it and ready to sternly enforce present and future water and air pollution and waste disposal laws. These laws frequently collide with the economics of a factory or the realities of a community budget, and we must probably be a little patient before all our rivers are again safe to swim in and full of fish, and smog is an unpleasant memory of the past. But as far as the United States is concerned, I am confident that we shall see drastic and obvious improvements within the next decade.

It is almost ironical that some of civilization's most applauded accomplishments have become the most serious threats to our environment. The earliest cities in antiquity were built on riverbanks because of the convenience the river offerd as a combination sewer and source of fresh water. The river as a convenient sewer led to the invention of the flush toilet, which some environmental experts in modern sewage treatment now consider one of the most disastrous inventions ever made by man. It led to the habit of committing not just our body wastes, but most of our other wastes as well, to sewage water, which we now find we must remove from that water in expensive sewage treatment plants before committing it to the river. In retrospect, an earlier invention of the chemical toilet and of energy-producing incineration of dry garbage might have been a better overall approach.

During the early days of the industrial revolution, a belching factory chimney was a visible sign of progress and the pride of the community. In most developing countries it still is. Today, in the United States any plan for a new factory or public utility plant with smokestacks is subjected to rigorous reviews of the scrubbing equipment and often never materializes because of local aesthetic or environmental objections.

Collisions between the requirements of those responsible for meeting our ever-increasing electric energy demands and those who are to protect our environment can be expected to continue for years to come. While a few other industrialized nations established effective mechanisms to resolve these issues before we did, the United States now has set up machinery that makes me confident that we shall see a steady rate of improvement of our environment.

Let us just take a quick look at how this machinery works. In 1970, by a presidential act, the Environmental Protection Agency was established to formulate federal standards, spelling out in chapter and verse the type and amount of permissible pollutants that may be added to our air, rivers, and lakes. As thousands of factories and service operations, ranging from steel plants to car wash facilities and millions of automobiles, were outside the new legal limits, target dates were set by which everybody had to comply or be in violation of the law. This new Environmental Protection Agency was given the authority to police the progress and take the violators to court.

Under the act, cleaning up our air and water will actually be a step-by-step process. The rationale behind this approach was that applying new yardsticks to industries employing millions of people is a painful and time-consuming process. While great improvements can often be made at moderate cost, true perfection is always costly. Thus a set of target dates, spread several years apart, was established under which the screw was tightened gradually and the permissible amount of pollutants reduced in steps.

Law enforcement, however, is only one side of the problem of environmental survival. It clearly also has a scientific aspect which touches more directly on the topic of my paper. In fact, the protection of our environment has so many scientific facets that I must limit my discussion to two examples and what remedial steps could be taken through responsible scientific investigation and application.

My first example involves water pollution. Our rivers, lakes, and estuaries are populated by thousands of species from microorganisms to oysters and game fish, which feed upon each other in an extremely complex food chain. This chain produces a snowballing effect with the result that some organisms accumulate many hundred thousand times the pollution concentration of the water in which they live. Stories you read about oyster beds being closed by the Food and Drug Administration, or mercury-contaminated fish being taken off the market, are based on this multiplication phenomenon.

The sorry fact is that we understand the interaction between pollutants and marine life only in a very sketchy fashion. More scientific research in this field, supported by well-equipped marine laboratories and research ships, should be accorded highest priority. As Captain Jacques-Ives Cousteau has pointed out, river pollution is even endangering the survival of the earth's continental shelves, which support most of the life in the open oceans.

Now as to remedies, permit me to become a little parochial again and tell you how the space program can help. The two LANDSAT satellites I talked about earlier have detected numerous hitherto unknown sources of river and lake pollution. Their images have been successfully used as evidence in court action against offenders. They have also detected oil slicks in mid-ocean and identified the tankers whose skippers decided to clean their bilge under cover of night.

Satellites as monitors and protectors of our environment lead me to my second example, which involves air pollution. You have undoubtedly read about the controversy raging on the subject of the atmosphere's protective ozone layer, and whether or not supersonic airliners or the freon gas escaping from spray bottles may decompose that layer. Statistics, little contested, show that any reduction of the layer's ozone content increases the amount of solar ultraviolet radiation which reaches the earth's surface—and with it the statistical occurrance of skin cancer. One of our satellites now has been monitoring the earth's ozone layer on a global scale for several years. It has identified numerous occasions where a sudden burst of protons emanating from the sun did indeed produce a noticeable drop in the layer's ozone content, but the old balance, itself produced by solar radiation, was soon restored. Only a single man-made phenomenon was detected that produced a similar if somewhat lesser effect: a high-altitude explosion of a French nuclear bomb over the Pacific, a test program since terminated by the French government. Evidence of any effects in the ozone layer caused by supersonic aircraft, which are in widespread use by air forces all over the world, or by freon spray bottles, has not yet been found. But let me hurry to add here that I am not ready to conclude that there may not be some problem after all. Research in this area should continue as a high priority.

Another field which in my opinion deserves much more attention, priority, and resources is that of marine biology. You can study the food and behavioral pattern of a large mammal pretty accurately in captivity or in a wildlife preserve. But when it comes to the question of how the thousands of pollutants and toxic metals that come down with the river water are absorbed by the thousands of different marine organisms ranging from microorganisms to oysters, shrimp, and game fish, we have to establish more marine laboratories in more estuaries to study these processes in situ. Being affected by tides, temperatures, silt, soil, speed of water movement, and what have you, the conditions differ from place to place, and simulation in test tanks and aquariums has turned out to be hopeless.

Before I leave the subject of environmental survival, let me leave you with some food for thought and maybe a smile:

Our rightful concern about the environment has led to the legal requirement in the United States to file an environmental impact statement for practically every major new undertaking. This requirement may be easy to applaud, but it is not always so easy to implement. Suppose the elder Henry Ford, before committing himself to mass-produce his Model T, had had to file an environmental impact statement. In his contagious optimism, that statement would undoubtedly have included the highly desirable effect of personal mobility for every citizen and the ensuing subsequent public demand for better roads. A critical reviewer of Mr. Ford's first draft might have added the unpleasant odor of exhaust gas, but it is not likely that that particular aspect would have bothered the authorities. Had that reviewer also added that the automobile would become so popular that in 1975 in America alone over 46,000 people would be killed and over two million people injured in car accidents, no government appraiser of that environmental impact statement would have believed that figure anyway.

But I am sure that both Mr. Ford and his critical reviewer would have missed what was probably the most important item in their impact statement: the fact that the automobile would rid American cities of the housefly. As a carrier of contagious diseases the housefly is one of the worst killers known to man. Its home and breeding ground in the horse-and-buggy days was the horse stable in the city, and it fed on what it found in the horse manure on the streets. No one can deny that the automobile drove the horse and with it the horse stable out of the American city. It thus surely made the cities healthier. True, we traded this gain for the health-impairing effects of smog, but that will probably be a temporary nuisance which with cleaner cars will soon disappear.

The moral of my little story on the effect of the automobile on the housefly is that our crystal ball may often not be clear enough to predict the long-range environmental impact of an innovation.

Spiritual Survival

The often colliding demands of those expected to satisfy mankind's insatiable needs for material resources and energy, and those responsible for the protection of the earth's life-supporting biosphere, are bound to lead to an ever-increasing regimentation of many aspects of our lives. Not one of the many candidates for the 1976 presidential election failed to mention the undesirability of the continuous growth of the Washington bureaucracy in his campaign speeches, and every one was applauded when he pledged to stop or reverse that trend. After all, one of the basic premises of the founding fathers of our great republic had been that the best government for the newborn nation would be the smallest government, which would interfere as little as possible with individual freedom and initiative. Yet as we are celebrating the bicentennial we find the number of people on the federal payroll far exceeding the total population of the United States at the time of its birth.

Having served in the U.S. Civil Service myself for over twenty years, I have always resented the widespread belief that government employees are some sort of drones in near-permanent hibernation, who show some temporary signs of life only when presented with their bimonthly paychecks. I have also never shared the view that government has grown so big mainly because it is so difficult to lay off civil service employees, or because they cling more tenaciously to their jobs than other people. I have met the finest, most capable and hard-working people in the U.S. Civil

Service, and can assure you that Americans would not have landed on the moon without their leadership qualities and dedication to what most of them considered a great patriotic challenge.

Why then is it that "big government" is in the doghouse? Let us look at what has made government grow as big as it is. Two hundred years ago the United States consisted of thirteen states. Today it has fifty states, while the total population has grown from a little under four million to nearly 216 million. But equally important is that life in our highly industrialized civilization has become infinitely more complex. A whole string of unprecedented regulatory or public safety needs arose which simply could not be turned over to the private sector. George Washington had no need for government agencies such as the Federal Communications Commission that would allot radio frequencies or issue permits and operating rules to the telephone, television, and radio industries. Nor did he need a Federal Aviation Agency to operate airport towers and a nationwide air traffic control system with radar-equipped centers and thousands of navigational aids.

Unfortunately government agencies, like human beings, have a tendency to put on a little fat as they grow older, and to slow down their pace. By the same token young agencies, charged with exciting and difficult new tasks, display more vigor and vitality. The youngest members of our ever-growing fraternity of United States government agencies are the Energy Resources Council, the Energy Research and Development Agency, and the Environmental Protection Agency. Obviously they play a vital role in the protection of two of the five pillars of our priority dome—resources survival and environmental survival—and should therefore be welcomed with applause.

But the American public has just become weary of any further growth in our federal bureaucracy, no matter how noble their objective or how pressing their need may be. For one thing, John Q. Public grouches about the higher taxes he feels he will undoubtedly have to pay in one way or another to support any new agency. Even more important, he shudders at the relentlessly creeping growth of government interference with his business affairs and his private life. That, undoubtedly, is the underlying cause for the widespread interest in the congressional hearings on the CIA and the FBI—two types of institutions without which no large country can survive in this dangerous world. It is also the main reason why any pledge of a presidential candidate to lower the boom on "big government" always assures him a big hand from the audience. Americans just have a profound dislike for anything that smacks of "big brother" or "Daddy knows best." Instinctively, they have a deep-seated concern for our spiritual survival.

A mere hundred years ago, this was a nation of open frontiers and unlimited possibilities. Many people have told me, with a tone of nostalgia in their voice, that with the end of the Western pioneering days the wind has gone out of the sails of the United States. They say a person can no longer build up his own life as he pleases—that he is being trained, tutored, and manipulated from cradle to grave. Now as a native European I must admit that I do not see it all that glumly. There are still vast untapped opportunities even for rustic pioneers and settlers in many thinly populated parts of this huge country. But I concur that even in the vastness of the American West and Southwest the prospective pioneer and settler of 1976 is bound to collide with the plans of some energy or mineral-related agency that wants to develop and exploit a local natural resource, or some environmental protective group desirous of stopping local settlement and economic development altogether because it interferes with their plan for a wilderness area or a national park. Nevertheless, in this respect America is still a lot better off than much of the rest of the world. In countries with a high population density there are usually no undeveloped areas left at all, and opportunities for a rustic pioneer to start his own homestead from scratch have been nonexistent for centuries.

The threat of an imminent collision between an expanding world population and the limited space and resources of a finite planet has given rise to the battle cries of "limits to growth" or even "zero growth." As so many new ideological concepts that feed on a grain of truth, "zero growth" has been enthusiastically embraced by many. And yet in its simplistic form I am convinced it should be rejected as half-cocked and downright dangerous.

There is no question, of course, that some growth trends should indeed be of great concern, but continued growth in other areas is a vital necessity for the survival of humanity. Better land use, prudent family planning, protection of our environment, and conservation of energy and all of the earth's precious resources are vital necessities that we should wholeheartedly endorse.

On the other hand, growth in food production, development of our hardly-tapped ocean resources, reduction of human suffering by provision for better health care in remote areas, or improvement of the worldwide level of literacy are areas in which we should support a continuous and vigorous growth. To subject ourselves to drastic across-the-board curtailment in producduction of necessary goods and services I think is unacceptable both from the practical and spiritual viewpoint. The indiscriminate philosophy of "no growth" makes no difference between growth of population and growth of means for continuing survival. We must reject this simplistic concept. Indiscriminate "no growth" would remove the good with the bad, and in the process condemn that part of the world now living below subsistence levels to eternal poverty and misery, a brutal policy that would deprive mankind of hope.

In connection with my remarks on resources survival I mentioned the capability of our new LANDSAT satellites to monitor the worldwide status of food crops and to find new mineral and fossil-fuel sources. These satellites can also be used as survey tools to make better use of the many unused parts of the earth. Central Brazil, for instance, is almost uninhabited, while Brazil's coastal areas are densely populated. Java is bursting with people, while adjacent Sumatra and Borneo's population density is exceedingly low. It is neither poor climate nor governmental desire that prevents the migration of people to these empty areas. It is lack of communications, lack of educational facilities, and lack of detailed knowledge of local soil qualities and mineral resources that slow down these highly desirable transmigrations. Multispectral surveys from orbit and communications satellites can effectively remove the obstacles.

But the spiritual survival of mankind has also an aspect completely unrelated to "big government" or the limitations set by the earth's resources. It is more fundamental. In discussing the motivation for scientific research I said that the mainspring of science is curiosity. But curiosity has also been the driving force behind man's great exploratory voyages. We may well doubt whether Columbus, on the quarterdeck of the Santa Maria, was animated by a burning desire to reduce the freight rates on Indian tea when he sought a new route to Cathay and found America athwart his hawse.

What drives man to explore the unknown? Why are we flying to the moon? What is our purpose? What is the essential justification of the exploration of space? The answer, I am convinced, lies rooted not in whimsy but in the nature of man. Let me give you my personal view.

Man as a biological species is a rather anomalous animal. Whereas all other animals establish a place for themselves in nature's highly cooperative and competitive ecological system, man has established his place in nature by altering his natural environment through such actions as practicing agriculture rather than eating the natural fruits of the trees and the plants, and clearing forests to build cities.

Whereas all other living beings seem to find their places in the natural order and fulfill their role in life with a kind of calm acceptance, man clearly exhibits confusion. Why the anxiety? Why the storm and stress? Man really seems to be the only living thing uncertain of his role in the universe, and in his uncertainty he has been calling since time immemorial upon the stars and the heavens for salvation and for answers to his eternal questions: Who am I? Why am I here?

Wherever he fought, he invoked the stars for help. Wherever he loved, he invoked the moon. And all great religions hold out eternal life and salvation as man's reward for his good deeds here on earth. Whereas most animals follow, for their survival, certain telltale scents which are too refined for human perception, man seems to be uniquely equipped to perceive certain vibrations emanating from the celestial environment. As a result astronomy is the oldest science; it existed for thousands of years as the only science, and is to this day considered the uncrowned queen of the sciences. Although man lacks the eye of the night owl, the scent of the fox, or the hearing of the deer, he has an uncanny ability to learn about abstruse things like the motions of the planets, the cradle-to-grave cycle of the stars, and the distances between the galaxies.

Whereas all other species seem resigned to the environments in which they have been born, man clearly does not. Since his early beginning he has wanted to fly, and today he does fly. What is man's motivation? Why does he always want to explore what is outside his abode? Why is he so eager to pioneer activities beyond his natural endowments?

I guess it is all just in the basic makeup of man as God wanted him to be. And it explains why, now that all the white spots have been removed from our maps and nothing seems to be left to discover on the surface of the earth, for the first time in his long history man has developed the uneasy feeling that there are no more frontiers—forever.

Behind all the talk about "zero growth" is really the fear that the species of man is heading for the fate of a domesticated animal confined to the fences of its pasture. Moreover, as our numbers keep increasing and less and less elbowroom is left for the individual, there looms the dreadful idea that we may ultimately be reduced to mere numbers in a coercive and tightly regimented society like that of the honeybee. There would be no spiritual survival, and personal freedom would be dead.

This horrible outlook of the doomsday prophets for our long-range future leads me smoothly back to my favored subject, space flight. I happen to be convinced that man's newly acquired capability to travel through outer space provides us with a way out of our evolutionary dead alley. It takes, as it were, the lid off the pressure cooker called earth. Who can honestly claim that the earth is the only place where man can live? Our astronauts ran around happily on the moon, and whenever the distances they had to travel on the lunar surfaces became too great for walking, they even used a rental car they had brought along. When they became uncomfortably hot or cold, they just made a slight adjustment in the thermostat setting of their pressure suits.

If someone asked Mr. Hilton to build a hotel on the moon, offering the same comforts as his earthly inns, we could give him the technology to do it. We could even feed his guests with food grown in pressurized greenhouses and chicken farms adjacent to his hotel. Creating permanent habitats on the moon is no longer a question of science or technology, it is merely a question of our will and determination to do it.

As long as the flame of man's innate urge to extend his arena of activities and his knowledge is not extinguished, there is no reason why we could not extend our domain beyond the earth to the entire solar system. Of course, we do not have the technology to do all of it at once, but we can start slowly and implement the program gradually during the remainder of the five billion years the planet earth is expected to remain climatically inhabitable.

We hear the argument that on the moon there is no breathable atmosphere. Well, there is none in Los Angeles either, yet people still manage to live there, and many live there very well indeed. Mars's atmosphere, we are told, is too thin for human habitation. So what? People could live and work on Mars in pressurized, climate-controlled buildings as they do in Alaska or Siberia today. Venus is too hot! Well, suggestions have been made to inject loads of a suitable breed of algae, carried there by a fleet of rockets, into the higher, cooler, and water-vapor-containing layers of the Venus atmosphere. The algae, the originators of this scheme claim, would multiply by leaps and bounds and through photosynthesis would soon convert Venus's carbon dioxide atmosphere into one containing oxygen. The removal of the carbon dioxide would destroy the greenhouse effect with the result that the surface temperature of Venus would cool down to a level that would make the planet habitable for man.

Now I do not think that at this moment anyone can vouch for

the practicability of this concept, but then, who can predict what man will be able to accomplish in the next five billion years? With unlimited solar and thermonuclear energy at our disposal, we may learn to reengineer even some of the many moons of Jupiter and Saturn and make them fit for human habitation.

For the more immediate future, the twenty-first century, another concept for an unlimited growth of humanity has recently drawn much serious attention. Professor Gerald K. O'Neill of Princeton University has suggested the building of huge manmade habitats orbiting the earth at the so-called Libration or Lagrange points, which are equidistant from the earth and moon. A typical habitat may be a hollow pressurized cylinder nineteen miles long and four miles in diameter which would accommodate ten thousand people. It would rotate slowly about its axis to generate earth-normal gravity through centrifugal acceleration. The cylinder mantle would consist of alternate bands of glass and materials supporting interior land areas. The land areas, totaling about one hundred square miles, would provide housing for the inhabitants in surroundings more desirable than most inhabited places on earth. They would be covered with soil supporting the growth of trees, lawns, and gardens. From those land areas a resident would see a reflected image of the disc of the sun in the sky, and the sun's image would move from dawn to dusk within the time span of a day just as on earth.

Agriculture and poultry farming to support the space colony would be carried out in one or several separate cylinders nearby with climate control for optimum growth. Industrial activities, which provide employment for the colony, would likewise be conducted in several independent modules in order to avoid any kind of industrial pollution problems. Much of the industrial processing would be done taking full advantage of zero gravity. The main industrial products of a colony would be other habitats for future generations of space colonists. Rough estimates indicate that a population of ten thousand could manufacture about one new colony of equal size every two years. In addition, it could build two orbital solar power stations of 5000 megawatts each to beam badly needed energy to the earth. This could easily become the most attractive way to raise more money on earth for additional expansion in space.

Thus a mechanism can be generated through which the goal of further unmanageable population growth on the limited Earth is actually reconciled with the concept of "humanity unlimited."

Professor O'Neill suggests building the first habitats from lunar material launched to the Lagrange points with an electromagnetic launching device located on the moon. Powered by a nuclear reactor, this "mass driver"—in essence a recirculating linear electric motor—can accelerate a big bucketful of unprocessed lunar surface material every 150 seconds to the relatively low lunar escape speed required to reach the Lagrange point. A typical Apollo sample of lunar soil contains about forty percent oxygen, thirty percent metals and about twenty percent silicon, which is just about the right mix for the metal, glass, soil, and atmosphere required to establish a habitat. Calculations show that it is more cost-effective to process the lunar raw material in the zero-gravity environment at the habitat site itself rather than on the lunar surface.

Once, many millenia from now, we have run out of usable lunar material, Professor O'Neill proposes to bring the material in from the asteroid belt. The total quantity of material within only three of the largest asteroids is quite enough to permit building space colonies with a total land area more than ten thousand times that of the earth! With the inexhaustible sources of raw material from the asteroid belt and of energy from the sun, it seems that all that has to be added is human will and brainpower to assure humanity virtually unlimited growth.

I stated a little earlier in my paper that I believe that the mere fact that something is scientifically possible does not necessarily make it permissible. Are we possibly stepping beyond the bounds of human destiny by setting out to populate the vast empty spaces outside of the earth? I do not think we are, and I offer you three reasons.

First, nobody gets hurt in the process, but hundreds of millions would either starve to death, never be born, or live under unbearable regimentation if we decided not to pursue the option of a mass exodus into space.

Second, I think the concept of multiple space colonies can relieve us of a lot of problems here on earth. Since the beginning of recorded history man has conducted all sorts of social experiments. Time and again we see the spectacle of a charismatic leader arousing millions for some political, racial, economic, religious, or nationalistic cause which subsequently is pursued and defended in bloody wars. In the age of space habitats this permanent danger source could be removed from the earth. Anyone with a sufficiently large following could henceforth open up his own habitat where his group could lead the kind of life it prefers, without outside interference or the urge or means to impress its own lifestyle on others.

Do not think that this is in the realm of utopia. Right here in the United States a development took place along quite a similar pattern. Large affinity groups of people who had been persecuted in Europe for any number of reasons came to America with the sole motivation and hope of being able to continue the kind of life they preferred—the Puritans, the Amish, the Mormons, the Hugenots, the German democrats of 1848, to name just a few. The vastness of America provided adequate isolation between these groups which prevented them from promptly getting into each other's hair. In outer space, the separation between the habitats will have pretty much the same effect. Travel between the various habitats, however, should be easy, speedy, and cheap, as all of them will circle the earth at the same orbital altitude and speed; thus very little energy must be expended to go from one to another. Cultural and social exchange between habitats should therefore be easier than between different nations today. Any attempt of the population of a single habitat to build up the capability for acting against one of its neighbors could be easily nipped in the bud by a roving international police force.

Third, I strongly believe in what Immanuel Kant would have called the *cosmic categoric imperative.* I think a strong argument can be made that it is indeed the Creator's intent for man to use his intelligence to extend his domain beyond his home planet. Let me elaborate a bit.

Bioscientists have learned that for the most primitive forms of life to come into being anywhere, rather narrow constraints of physical conditions must prevail. For instance, there must be some water, temperatures must be within certain limits, and certain toxic substances must be absent. After under a conducive set of conditions simple life finally became entrenched, several billion years of a reasonably stable environment were required for the further evolution of intelligent life.

Astronomical and exobiological research during the past twenty-five years, aided by a fleet of unmanned planetary spacecraft, has led many to the conclusion that the necessary suitable environmental conditions prevailing over a sufficient time span to spawn intelligent life probably exist only on a relatively small percentage of the planets in our galaxy. But as we behold the immense machinery of the cosmos with its inexhaustible sources of energy and raw material, one thought is irrepressible: Could it be one of the fundamental concepts of the entire creation, that wherever in spite of these odds the evolution of higher intelligence has been successful, the Creator expects that form of higher intelligence to expand its activities from its home planet to its cosmic neighborhood?

As the great Russian space flight pioneer Edward Ziolkowsky put it, three-quarters of a century ago, "The earth is the cradle of man. But who wants to stay in the cradle forever?"

Nuclear Survival

In the field of nuclear strategic capability the two main adversaries, the United States and the U.S.S.R., now clearly possess the capability of multiple overkill. The destructive power has become so immense that in any all-out nuclear exchange both sides would perish. The situation has been called a "balance of terror." In spite of one or two uneasy confrontations and several nonnuclear wars (in which both sides were deeply or at least peripherally involved) that balance so far has proven to be remarkably stable.

One is reminded of that famous animal behavior experiment which showed that two male scorpions locked in a bottle will not harm each other, although in the open they are known to engage in combat ending invariably in the death of one of them. In the confinement of the bottle neither scorpion will attack, as each seems to be aware of the fact that even if it struck first there would be enough fight left in the dying opponent to retaliate against its trapped attacker with a deadly sting.

However, soon after the public had begun to draw a degree of comfort from the idea that nuclear double suicide was simply too terrible to be even thinkable, there were signs of possible destabilizing effects in the uneasy balance of terror. Suppose one side "hardened" (missile jargon for strengthening against near-misses of atomic bombs) its missile sites while the other did not? Or suppose only one party acquired an antimissile system that could reliably protect its missile sites as well as its cities and industrial complexes?

When the cold war showed signs of thawing in the late sixties, the United States and the Soviet Union decided to talk things over. Both sides readily agreed that an unchecked nuclear missile race was fraught with enormous dangers and painfully drained the economies of both countries. But from an agreement on a basic truth that was so obvious that it almost became a platitude to an ironclad and cheat-proof arms-control agreement was—and is—a difficult and rocky road. Delicate questions such as mutual inspections of top-secret missile sites arose. What good was an agreement on missile numbers if both sides were free to increase the "bang" delivered by the warheads or to place several warheads into the nose of a single rocket? Suppose that these multiple warheads could even be independently targeted and were maneuverable to evade antimissile missiles? If one of the two sides decided not to keep up this endless race, would it become a "sick scorpion," possibly tempting its bottle-mate to use the opportunity to strike for fear that it might one day become sick itself and an opportune victim of the other?

This is the eerie backdrop of the SALT (Strategic Arms Limitations Treaty) meetings, possibly the most fateful peace-seeking gatherings in which man has ever engaged. For the moment it looks as if the huge rockets with their awesome hydrogen warheads are keeping the big powers at peace in spite of their many disagreements and conflicting interests. Only the future can tell whether, as we all hope and pray, the age of the great world wars will be a thing of the past—forever.

We have a dramatic example here of how intricately science, technology, military policies, and national resolve to survive are interwoven. Clearly, life-and-death questions involving the fate of our nation—any nation—cannot be answered by scientists and technologists alone; they will always be taken up at the highest policy-making level of a country.

However, it was the international fraternity of nuclear Prometheuses—some of the brilliant scientists of our age—who had handed their respective national leaders the hot potato of that new unprecedented atomic fire with all its attendant hazards. The nuclear scientists and the rocket scientists who furnished them with the means of transporting their atomic fire to distant targets must leave no stone unturned to now also help their national leaders harness that fire.

The value of any existing and future SALT agreements is directly related to the ability of each side to monitor the other side's adherence to the agreements. This is an area where rocket and space technology at this very time is making a vital contribution to mankind's military survival. Without the capability of United States and Soviet reconnaisance satellites to keep an alert eye on activities on both sides of the Iron Curtain—such as new missile-launching sites, construction of missile-carrying submarines, or massive troop movements—any past and future SALT agreements would lack credibility to the two parties to the treaties and would not be worth the paper they are written on. Both sides see eye to eye that agreements involving their military survival must be cheat-proof. It is significant that the SALT 1 Treaty contains an explicit provision that neither side shall tamper or interfere with the other side's inspection satellites. This is a clear expression from both sides that all scientific and technological efforts aimed at improving the mutual inspection capability will greatly contribute to a safer world.

Nuclear survival also depends on our ability to learn to control the proliferation of nuclear fuel. All industrialized nations (and those who want to become industrialized) have an insatiable appetite for energy. If they have no reliable access to coal or oil, they want nuclear electrical power. But every nuclear reactor, whether of the conventional "light water" type or the futuristic "fast breeder," creates as a byproduct plutonium which can be extracted and fashioned into atomic bombs.

According to projections by the International Atomic Energy Agency in Vienna, Austria, the worldwide total of nuclear power reactors will quadruple to eight hundred over the next ten years. Studies estimate that by 1990 nuclear reactors of less developed countries will generate thirty thousand pounds of plutonium yearly. That is enough to make three thousand small atomic bombs. In a recent Senate hearing it was revealed that by mid-1974 the United States, which supplies about seventy percent of the world market in this field, had exported $3.9 billion in nuclear materials and equipment. Current exports were estimated at $1 billion a year and rising sharply.

The United States sells nuclear fuel "rods" to foreign countries only with the stipulation that the "irridiated rods" must be returned to the United States. As they are highly radioactive after several years of neutron bombardment in the reactor, it is impossible for a country without very sophisticated equipment to extract the plutonium which has formed in the rods during the activation stage of the reactor. But we are not the only supplier in this field, and others have more lenient rules for their sales.

It is hardly surprising that leading nuclear physicists are alarmed and recommended in congressional testimony a complete export ban on certain critical equipment such as plutonium extraction systems, isotope separation plants, or technology helpful in the perfection of the still highly experimental breeder reactors. The truly worrisome question is, of course, whether the horse isn't out of the barn already. The thought of nuclear bombs in the hands of terrorist groups or madmen is frightening indeed.

I believe the space program can offer a powerful tool to monitor and control the proliferation of nuclear fuel. A recent study proved the feasibility of establishing, for a fraction of the cost of our yearly nuclear exports, a satellite system that could identify and locate every nuclear fuel rod anywhere on earth.

Let me inject here a few technical details, so I can better explain the concept. A fuel rod is a long tube filled with pellets of metallic nuclear fuel. For a reactor to produce heat, it is loaded with a sizeable number of these rods, all separated from one another at carefully calculated distances. In a light water reactor the space between the rods is filled with water, which heats up when the reactor "goes critical." The heat extracted from this water then provides the power for the turbogenerators that produce electricity.

After several years of exposure to the intense neutron bombardment inside the reactor, the fuel rod contains such a high percentage of fission products that the nuclear chain reaction gets choked in its own nuclear waste. The highly radioactive rod must then be removed from the reactor and replaced by a new one. The "irridiated rod" can either be placed in a long-life coffin and buried (usually under water), or it can be sent, coffin and all, to a remote-controlled chemical facility, where the fission products are extracted. It is in this extraction process that the plutonium accrues.

Coming back now to the space monitoring concept, the idea is to attach to each fuel rod, while it is outside of the reactor, a wristwatch-sized receiver/transmitter or "transponder," which, when interrogated by a powerful satellite transmitter, will return a signal revealing its precise location and serial number. If the device is removed from the rod or deactivated by anyone, the satellite's bookkeeping computer would at once record the tampering or the disappearance of the signal.

Such a satellite monitoring system can be built with existing technology. Of course, it would provide effective protection against uncontrolled proliferation of nuclear fuel only if the world's few manufacturers of nuclear fuel can be persuaded to participate in the program by labeling all the rods they sell. Knowledgeable people in this field have told me that the concern about worldwide uncontrolled proliferation of nuclear fuel is so universal, and just as serious to the Soviets as it is to us, that they thought it would not be difficult to conclude an international treaty on this subject patterned on the ban on atmospheric testing of nuclear bombs.

Any attempt to maintain peace with a strong adversary who is in an expansionist mood can be successful only if the negotiations are conducted from a basis of strength. I am still convinced that World War II could have been avoided if in 1939 Great Britain had sent a man of Churchill's bent, escorted by some British and Allied military leaders, to Munich instead of a man with an umbrella willing to settle for what he called "peace in our time."

American SALT negotiators should be armed with better weapons than umbrellas. Their opposite numbers should know, for instance, that we are building up an effective globe-girdling system to monitor the movement of Soviet missile-carrying submarines, that we have a new breed of fighter aircraft that can quickly gain and maintain air superiority in any area of confrontation, or that we are making effective preparations to be able to stop a massive nonnuclear armored onslaught of the Warsaw Pact powers against the NATO forces without being forced into immediate nuclear retaliation.

The contributions required from science and technology to protect our pillar of nuclear survival are manifold indeed. In the wake of the unfortunate Vietnam War scientists and engineers working in the field of advanced weaponry were subjected to much harsh criticism. They found their moral standards questioned and were actively encouraged to discontinue work in these fields. In the last analysis, of course, each individual must settle such questions with his own conscience and I would not label a person a traitor who feels he must refuse to work on anything involving weapons of war. Speaking for myself, I hold to the conservative belief that until that day when all people have become saints and all swords have been beaten into plowshares, the risk of a nuclear Armageddon will be greatly reduced as long as Americans keep their armed forces the most advanced in the world.

Scientific Survival

There can be no doubt that the present mood of many Americans is antiscientific and antitechnological. Science and technology, they seem to feel, have brought us more problems than blessings. By the same token they realize that a return to the simple life, the "good old days," is not possible either. The family-owned farm, for instance, nostalgically remembered by many a city-dweller as the place where he was born and raised, may have been absorbed by a giant "agrobusiness," where on an immense spread huge crops are harvested with a handful of people operating expensive machinery.

Thus, with the retreat to their rustic past blocked and life in the cities getting less and less pleasant, many Americans view the future with dismay. But while they continue to blame science and technology for many of the ills that have befallen our society, they grudgingly concede that probably only more science and technology can get them out of the mess they feel they are in.

I am certain that the tide of antiscience sentiments is about to turn, and that, as it surges back, ever stronger demands will be heard for constructive contributions of science and technology to the world's down-to-earth problems. The near-simultaneous creation of the Energy Research and Development Agency and the Environmental Protection Agency, both at a time when everybody is complaining about the never-ending growth of "big government," is a pretty convincing indication of the reversal of the tide.

Like the magician in the vaudeville show, the scientist is once again expected to pull the white rabbit out of the hat and cure our ills by working another of his miracles. But before you can pull a white rabbit out of a hat someone first has to place the rabbit into the hat. This is the function of basic science.

In assessing the merits of any proposed experiment in basic as contrasted to applied science, one must carefully avoid the criterion of immediate payoff. You probably know the famous story of the British prime minister visiting Michael Faraday in his laboratory. As Faraday explained his exepriment on electromagnetic induction, the prime minister demanded what practical benefits one could ever expect from this eerie sort of thing. Faraday replied: "I do not know, sir, but I am sure that you will find a way to tax it." A century later, a worldwide electrical industry had grown on the foundation laid by Faraday's work.

Looking around at the many facets of scientific pursuit in 1976, I can discern many opportunities just as promising as Faraday's work. We touched already on the field of marine biology and its crucial importance for our environmental survival. We mentioned nuclear fusion research as the great hope to satisfy mankind's insatiable appetite for energy without the risks of nuclear fuel proliferation. We have seen how in recent years solid-state physicis has revolutionized the field of electronics and global communications, and we realize that we have only taken a glimpse at the fantastic future world of microminiaturization. We watched the fabulous successes of medical researchers who virtually eradicated most of the contagious diseases and mass epidemics of the past, while we are still witnessing their frontal assault against a few remaining and stubbornly resisting killers such as cancer and heart failure. And we have seen how through the "green revolution," the breeding of hardier and superior species of crops, the desperate need of the growing population for food has been alleviated in many parts of the world.

These examples should remind us that science is indeed helping mankind in many ways. But there is no denying that the same scientific accomplishment that helps mankind in such a large measure often also causes great harm. Take DDT, the pesticide widely used in agriculture the world over. Ecologists tell us that as the rains wash DDT from the fields it is supposed to protect into brooks and rivers, it creates havoc with the entire complicated food chain of marine organisms. Moreover, it decimates many bird species feeding on the crop-endangering insects dead or dying from DDT.

Shall we then, as many voices demand, simply ban DDT? It has been estimated that if India imposed such a ban, the crop losses due to insect infestation would lead to the starvation of many millions of people every year. A better solution, and from what I hear one we can realistically expect in the very near future, is for science to come up with a DDT replacement that decomposes after a few months when dry and at once when diluted with water.

Even people with an antiscientific bend will probably agree with this kind of scientific effort, but they still get up in arms when they hear that some of their tax money is being spent on science objectives that they are unable to relate at all to the benefit of man. As an example let us take planetary research with unmanned spacecraft. People know that this program costs many millions of dollars, and they wonder whether there are not other scientific objectives that should be accorded a much higher priority.

Unmanned spacecraft have now visited Mercury, Venus, Mars, and Jupiter, and one is on its way to Saturn, the planet with the mysterious ring. The scientists found the four planets these spacecrafts have already surveyed not only very different from the earth but very different from one another. The surface pressure of Venus's carbon dioxide atmosphere, for instance, was found to be about a hundred times as high as that of the earth. Mars's atmosphere, by contrast, turned out to be so tenuous that its surface pressure is only about one percent of ours. Giant Jupiter's atmosphere was found to be about 1000 kilometers thick and covering a storm-whipped ocean of liquid hydrogen.

The atmospheres of each of these three planets also displayed extremely interesting and quite unique meteorological phenomena. Their systematic observation will tell meteorologists a great deal about some of the fundamental laws that make different types of atmospheres tick, our own as well as exotically different ones. This broadening of their understanding of meterological processes in general is bound to improve their long-term weather forecasting ability. This, in turn, is of immense value to sea and air navigation, the tourist industry, and, most importantly, to agriculture. In India alone, a substantial portion of the yearly rice harvest is lost every year due to the inability of meteorologists to precisely predict the arrival day of the monsoon rains for a given region of the vast subcontinent.

Science may be motivated by man's innate curiosity, and it most certainly provides us with the most reliable set of answers to Pontius Pilate's skeptical question, "What is truth?" But in our fast-moving world, scientific survival is also a vital fifth support pillar of the dome representing the all-encompassing objective of "mankind's survival as a species."

Science and Religion

This symposium has been sponsored by the Lutheran Church in America, and my presentation would be incomplete if it failed to address the potential of the powerful forces of religion to help protect us from ourselves. I said earlier in my paper that neither science nor technology has a moral dimension. Can religion or its human institutions, the churches, give us the moral and ethical guidance we so desperately need to protect us from the genie that science has allowed to escape from the bottle?

In the Middle Ages, Western man lived under stern ethical directives from the all-powerful Catholic Church, and there was little room or reason left for doubt. Its old ramparts of faith provided the believers with a feeling of protection, comfort, and oneness with God. But ever since the Reformation and the Renaissance the Christian churches, already divided among themselves, have been battered by a relentelss onslaught of scientific skepticism. Faith in the Holy Scriptures gave way to unfettered curiosity, and doubt was raised about things hitherto accepted as unquestioned truths. This has led many of our contemporaries to believe that science and religion are not compatible, that "knowing" and "believing" cannot live side by side.

Nothing could be further from the truth. Science and religion are not antagonists. On the contrary, they are sisters. While science tries to learn more about the creation, religion tries to better understand the Creator. While through science man tries to harness the forces of nature around him, through religion he tries to harness the forces of nature within him.

Some people say that science has been unable to prove the existence of God. They admit that many of the miracles in the world around us are hard to understand, and they do not deny that the universe, as modern science sees it, is indeed a far more wondrous thing than the creation which medieval man could perceive. But they still maintain that, since science has provided us with so many answers, the day will soon arrive when we will be able to understand even the creation of the fundamental laws of nature without assuming a divine intent. They challenge science to prove the existence of God. But must we really light a candle to see the sun?

Many people who are intelligent and of good faith say they cannot visualize God. Well, can a physicist visualize an electron? The electron is materially inconceivable, and yet it is so perfectly known through its effects that we use it to illuminate our cities, guide our airliners through the night skies, and take the most accurate measurements. What strange rationale makes some physicists accept the inconceivable electron as real, while refusing to accept the reality of God on the ground that they cannot conceive of him? Being a physicist myself, I strongly suspect that, although we really do not understand the electron either, we are ready to accept it because we managed to produce a rather clumsy mechanical model of the atom consisting of electrons and other equally inconceivable subatomic particles, but we just wouldn't know how to begin building a model of God.

For me the idea of a creation is not conceivable without invoking the necessity for God. One cannot be exposed to the law and order of the universe without concluding that there must be a divine intent behind it all.

Many modern evolutionists believe that the creation is the

arbitrary result of random arrangements and rearrangements of uncounted atoms and molecules over billions of years. But when you consider the development of the human brain within a time span of less than a million years, statistical studies cast grave doubt on the question of whether this relatively short time span just was really long enough for random processes to produce the brain whose tremendous complexity we are only now beginning to understand. Or take the evolution of the eye in the animal world. What random process could possibly explain the simultaneous evolution of the eye's optical system, the nervous conductors of the optical signals from the eye to the brain, and the optical nerve center in the brain itself where the incoming light impulses are converted to an image the conscious mind can comprehend?

Then there is the even more mysterious interaction between animals and plants. We know that the eye of the honeybee cannot see red, but is sensitive to a band of ultraviolet light which the human eye cannot discern. Flowers, depending on visits by bees for their pollination, have developed intricate ultraviolet patterns designed to attract the bee's attention. Did the flowers fashion the bee's eye, or did the bees, through limiting their visits to a few flowers which through random mutation happened to have these attractive ultraviolet patterns, ensure their survival as the fittest for bees?

Let us be honest and let us be humble. Can all this really be explained without the notion of a divine intent, without a creator? It is one thing to accept natural order as a way of life, but the minute one asks "Why?" then again enters God and all his glory.

Our space ventures have been only the smallest of steps in the vast reaches of the universe and have introduced more mysteries than they have solved. Speaking for myself, I can only say that the grandeur of the cosmos serves only to confirm my belief in the certainty of a creator. Finite man cannot begin to comprehend an omnipresent, omniscient, omnipotent, and infinite God. In the final analysis, any effort to reduce God to comprehensible proportions beggars his greatness. I find it best to accept God, through faith, as an intelligent will, perfect in goodness, revealing himself through his creation—the world in which we live.

Science has taught us one most important lesson about God that we should never forget. We have learned that God does not interfere in the free order of life and nature which he created. If we do not accept this, we must abandon the entire concept of freedom. The discoveries in astronomy, biology, physics, and even in psychology have shown that we also have to enlarge the medieval image of God. If there is to be a mind behind the immense complexities of the multitude of phenomena which man, through the tools of science, can now observe, then it is that of a Being tremendous in power and wisdom. But we should not be dismayed by the relative insignificance of our own planet in the vast universe as modern science now sees it. For it is perfectly conceivable that such a divine being has a moral purpose which is being worked out on the stage of this insignificant planet.

When man, almost two thousand years ago, was given the opportunity to know Jesus Christ, to know God who had decided to live for a while as man amongst fellow men on this little planet, our world was turned upside down through the widespread witness of those who heard and understood him. The same thing can happen again today. I am not in despair about the discordant conditions of our social environment. In spite of all the temporary setbacks that humanity has suffered through the centuries, and the terrible things that have happened in our times, I strongly believe that God, in the same personal relationships he established through Jesus Christ, will see to it that man's path continues upward, leading toward gradual improvement.

Jesus greatly expanded the basic moral laws of Judaism which formed the foundation of his teachings. His commandment to "love thy neighbor as thyself" established the unselfish attitude that enables human beings to live peaceably together. It is also the basis of our present foreign aid program. Even more revolutionary was his commandment to "love thine enemies." Although it is all too rarely followed, it has left an indelible and unforgettable imprint on the person-to-person relationships among people everywhere on our globe.

I am also confident that, as we learn more and more about nature through science, we shall not only arrive at universally accepted scientific findings, but also at a universally accepted set of ethical standards for human behavior. This may sound like a highly optimistic statement in view of all the atrocities and acts of terror committed in our time. All right, so maybe I am an optimist. I am convinced that in spite of all temporary setbacks there is a slow but steady upward trend in mankind's universal standard of ethics.

Take the case of slavery. In antiquity, slavery was considered a perfectly normal thing. For the Greek and Roman civilizations it was an essential element in their way of life. The idea of developing a civilization without some people having to do the dirty work so others could write their poetry was considered absurd. Even during the early nineteenth century the thought of operating a cotton plantation in the southern United States without slaves was considered impractical. Yet today the very concept of slavery is universally condemned and labeled as repulsive, even in totalitarian countries.

Science and technology undoubtedly made decisive contributions to the abolition of slavery. They have provided everyone with a wide assortment of electrically- and gasoline-powered slaves which have once and for all done away with the need for any human slaves.

I am certain that this, too, was a part of the master plan of our Maker. In the world around us we can behold the obvious manifestations of his divine plan wherever we look. We can see the will of the species to live and propagate. We behold the gift of love. And we are humbled by the powerful forces at work on a galactic scale, and the purposeful orderliness of nature that endows a tiny and ungainly seed with the ability to develop into a beautiful flower. The better we understand the intricacies of the universe and all it harbors, the more reason we have found to marvel at God's creation.

Some of my scientific colleagues seem to have serious difficulties tying together certain biblical passages with the reality of science, such as the story of creation given by Genesis, or the account of Joshua's poetic appeal for the sun to stand still while the Israelites avenged themselves on their enemies. The interpretation of biblical passages has been the subject of argument among wiser people than myself for centuries. My own views on the delicate topic are that it helps to bridge the gap between the Bible and modern scientific thought if we remember that the Bible deals with man as well as God, and most of the people of whom the Bible speaks suffered from the same human frailties that we experience today.

In my opinion, (and let me emphasize here that I fully respect and honor different views), insistence on an inflexible type of religion, holding to a literal interpretation of every word of the Bible as ultimate truth, will tragically delay reconciling some of the biblical references to scientific interpretation. But I believe with all my heart that religion, like science, is evolutionary, growing and changing in the light of further revelations by God. While the Bible is the best preserved account that we have of the revelations of God's nature and love, we should recognize that particularly the early books such as Genesis were not written by scientific observers and witnesses, but by scribes who recorded ancient shepherd songs and tales because of their allegorical beauty.

A scientist who discovers a new bit of knowledge does not tear down his model of reality, but merely changes it to agree with a new set of observations and experiences. By doing so, he admits he has no claim on ultimate truth. His laws are simply observations of reality, which he is always ready to update as his enlightenment grows. And so I think it should be with the Christian religion. While preserving the ethical, moral, and spiritual meaning of the scriptures, the Christian churches should become a little more flexible with regard to various interpretations of the Bible as a historical account. We can still love and have faith in the words of the Bible as they reveal so effectively so many time-honored truths.

The Christian churches cannot hope to reassume their rightful responsibility for ethical guidance with irrelevant debates concerning science versus religion.

Genetic engineering may serve as an example of a controversial and urgent issue about which many scientists would gratefully accept categorical guidance from the church. The feasibility of man-made mutations by tampering with the famous double-helix-shaped genes which are imbedded in the chromosomes and determine the inheritable features of plants and animals, has already been repeatedly demonstrated. This capability opens the door to unfathomable opportunities for the breeding of high-yield strains of crops, straighter trees, or superior cattle, and we can expect to hear a lot of praise for all these potential benefits. But it seems that we are just one step away from being able to also tamper with the features of man.

Such a capability not only raises gruesome visions of future dictators and madmen breeding fearless soldiers or submissive citizens, it also touches on the fundamental issue of the dignity of man. It is here that in my opinion the church should step in. It seems to me that agreement among churchpeople should be readily obtainable, as the Bible provides a clear and unambiguous answer. Man is a creation of God, who wanted him the way he is—with all his good and bad characteristics—and he wanted each of us as a responsible and distinct individual. He has permitted man to probe God's creation to his heart's content, but he never gave him the right to permanently deform or modify man, either as an individual or as a species.

But in imposing categorical guidance of this kind the churches must be careful not to endanger the freedom of scientific pursuit. Although I know of no reference in which Christ ever commented on scientific work, I do know that he said, "You will know the truth, and the truth will make you free (John 8:32). Thus I am certain that were he among us today, Christ would encourage scientific research as modern man's most noble striving to comprehend and admire his Father's handiwork. I am certain that the leaders of our Christian churches know full well that they must come to grips with the world of twentieth-century realities which constitute the main concern of contemporary man.

The fresh wind which is blowing through most of the world's Christian institutions and meetings like the one we are attending here are sure indicators that the churches are indeed responding to the new and unprecedented demands placed on them by the space age. Ecumenical Council meetings in Rome and interdenominational and Judeo-Christian conferences in the United States, are strong evidence of a growing realization among church leaders that the most important criteria for the future of our religious institutions and the guiding role of Judeo-Christian ethics in these troubled times is emphasis on the crucial issues of right and wrong selections in this complex scientific and technical world that offers us more golden opportunities and more roads to disaster than any previous period in human history.

I am quite confident that the great majority of Christian church leaders know in their hearts that this united front can best be presented by a common faith of all Christians in the basic teachings of Jesus Christ. But it means learning to live with the findings of Copernicus, of Galileo, and of Darwin. This front requires an emphasis on the essentials of spiritual life as identified by Jesus Christ rather than on trivia. It requires the acceptance of change and the discarding of antiquated or downright erroneous ideas, no matter how painful.

Personally, I noticed with deep regret the rejection by the Catholic Church of the ideas presented in *The Phenomenon of Man* and some of his other books by Teilhard de Chardin, the French Jesuit paleontologist who died about twenty years ago. I think Teilhard's books made an immense contribution to the reconciliation of scientific facts with religious beliefs.

His concept of a "convergent cosmogenesis" builds a solid bridge between Darwin's random evolution and survival of the fittest (both of which Teilhard accepts as elementary working mechanisms in God's workshop) and the obvious evidence of a unifying consolidation of the cosmos under the influence of the same supreme unity that laid down the basic, universal, and all-embracing laws of nature. Teilhard's identification of the powers of love as the driving force behind this auto-convergence offers a beautiful explanation for the paradox that any upward development of the creation is in direct violation of the Second Law of Thermodynamics. This pitiless but all-embracing law of physics decrees that all random processes in nature lead from more order to more chaos; from states of lower probability (for instance a higher degree of sophistication) to states of higher probability (for instance, a lower degree of sophistication); from a mountainous geography supporting a swift, energy-releasing stream to a sluggish river, incapable of giving off energy as it moves through the flat silt beds formed by water erosion of the same mountains that gave birth to the river. Since Darwin, who never heard about mutations, we have learned that the vast majority of mutations of the genes of plant, animal, and human life tend to deteriorate rather than improve a species. It's hard to see how, with mutations, random evolution, and survival of the fittest alone, the living Word on earth could have progressed the way it did. But that doesn't mean we should throw Darwin's books out of the window.

The power of love, the most precious gift with which God endowed his creation, adds a new element to the dreadful probability statistics which, while still valid in the world of physics and in Darwin's evolutionary mechanism, all by themselves can never account for the marvels of the world in which we live. Teilhard de Chardin tells us to view the universe as both lovable and loving. In so doing, he also interprets Christ's teachings on the overriding importance of love and charity as not just desirable virtues but as fundamental forces in the nature of the creation.

Sigmund Freud once remarked, "Since Galileo, in the eyes of science, man has continuously lost, one after another, the privileges that had previously made him unique in the world. Astronomically . . . biologically . . . psychologically . . . " Now paradoxically Teilhard de Chardin finds that "this same man is in the process of re-emerging from his return to the crucible, more than ever at the head of nature; since his very melting back into the general current of convergent cosmogenesis, he is acquiring in our eyes the possibility and power of forming in the hearts of space and time, a single point of universalization for the very stuff of the world."

To me, Teilhard de Chardin's ideas offer the most promising bridge between science and religion, and his formulations should be most satisfying to modern man. The rejection of his work was a particularly hard blow to Catholic scientists, but it hurt other believing scientists as well. I understand that the church rejected Teilhard because he left no place in his system for original sin. Now while I am ready to confess that I am a sinner, and worse still, that I sometimes even enjoy being one, I must also confess that I have a hard time myself accepting the concept of original sin. None of us will probably live long enough to see it happen, but I am sure that Teilhard de Chardin will either be rehabilitated by the Catholic Church or go down in history as another Galileo.

In this reaching of the new millennium through faith in the words of Jesus Christ, science can be a valuable tool rather than an impediment. The universe as revealed through scientific inquiry is the living witness that God has indeed been at work. Understanding the nature of the creation provides a substantive basis for the faith by which we attempt to know the nature of the Creator.

After Frank Borman returned from his unforgettable Christmas 1968 flight around the moon with Apollo 8, he was told that a Soviet cosmonaut recently returned from a space flight had commented that he had seen neither God nor angels on his flight. Had Borman seen God? the reporter inquired. Frank Borman replied, "No, I did not see him either, but I saw his evidence."

Response

Krister Stendahl

We all regret deeply that Dr. von Braun is not with us here today, and I invite you first to join with me in asking God to assist and sustain Wernher von Braun with His grace and His healing powers.

Dr. von Braun's absence will also deprive you and me of a competent summary of his chapter in the volume we all have before us. As I have been asked even so, to give a summary, I do so hesitantly and with much trepidation. Partly because I am totally incompetent in his fields of expertise and partly because he has given us, as the happy warrior of space research that he has been through his life, a comprehensive and thoughtful text. But I must try.

He starts with a quotation from Emerson: "Men—and I take it also women—love to wonder and that is the seed of science." Science as grounded in wonder and curiosity is the basis for the scientific urge. Thus von Braun pleads for such education and such attitudes, such mental habits as can strengthen a genuine curiosity in both young and old, and which leads to the internalizing of the fundamental principles of science. While his point here is rather general, I am eager to stress that it is far from being trivial or self-evident. It is important, not least for the churches to ponder his plea, both for its colleges and for parish education. The urge toward scientific curiosity and the "internalizing of scientific principles" should not be muted by premature or nervous apologetics. I think that is his blunt point.

In his second section, "Science, Technology, Morality and the Question of Taboos," Dr. von Braun stresses that both science and technology have in themselves no moral dimensions, they are amoral. However, the decisions as to what to pursue and at what cost, and with what speed, and where to set the taboos, is a human question of high moral importance. Here Dr. von Braun sides with Prometheus against Zeus and says that if a committee had been appointed on Olympus to decide whether one should let Prometheus go ahead with his fire experiment, presumably the committee would have voted against it, and, according to Dr. von Braun, we are all fortunate that Prometheus broke the taboos of the committee of the Olympians. In a later part, toward the very end of his paper, it is interesting to note that there is, however, one specific area of scientific investigation about which Dr. von Braun voices serious and lasting personal fears and trepidations. That is in the field of genetic research, manipulation, and experimentation. Even so, he has great faith in the capacities and wisdoms of more enlightened committees than those of the Olympians, as, for example, the National Food and Drug Administration, the Department of Agriculture and the Environmental Protection Agency. He trusts that somehow they will come up with the protection and the wisdom necessary. On the whole, von Braun does believe that technology can solve the problems that technology has created, and science can solve the problems that science has created. Thus he defends the principle that there should be little interference and much encouragement at the early stages of any scientific pursuit. And then, once that scientific pursuit has been carried out to a certain level so that one can better estimate the pros and the cons, only then should the taboos be applied. He is willing to take the risk of that momentum which no doubt has been built up by then. He is not blind to the problems with this position and he knows how foundations or Congress will be eager to get their money's worth for primary investigations once they are launched.

The third section is the crucial one in von Braun's presentation. He lists "the five pillars supporting the dome" of "Survival of Mankind as a Species" as humankind's most pressing problems. He consciously limits himself from considering other problems of high priority in the world, and he gives his reasons for not taking up the question of "the painful evolution of democracy," as he calls it, in areas such as some Latin American countries, or the immensely complex Middle East problems. His task is scientific, and requires sharp focus.

The five pillars of the dome for the survival of humankind as a species are: (1) Resources survival, (2) Environmental survival, (3) Spiritual survival, (4) Nuclear survival, and (5) Scientific survival.

As to resources survival, he gives positive reports on the Energy Research and Development Administration's programs and work, he discusses the possibilities of atomic power already here, and takes it up of course again in the fourth section on nuclear survival. He mentions the problem of the increase of plutonium produced by reactors. He puts much emphasis on the literacy programs, which he claims are indispensable for both resources and environmental survival. This is so since there is no possibility of applying resources programs on a global level without eradicating illiteracy in its traditional sense of reading ability, and even more illiteracy in the basics of technology.

As to environmental survival his main emphasis falls on a substantial strengthening in the area of marine biology and he is anxious to remind us, as he often does in this article, that when we face all of these problems some of the gains that have already occurred should not be forgotten. Let me quote an example: The chief killer in pre-automobile days was the common housefly. The automobile "thus surely made the cities healthier. True, we traded this gain for the health-impairing effects of smog, but that will probably be a temporary nuisance . . ."

Being a clergyman I reserve Dr. von Braun's discussion of spiritual survival until I come to my own comments.

On nuclear survival he outlines in positive terms the various hopes and possibilities for international controls, greatly increased by the possibilities of surviellance from space. On scientific survival his comments add up to a further plea for a strong posture in terms of scientific research as well as its base in education at all levels.

His fourth main section is entitled "Science and Religion." Here he presents in his own terms a way in which he finds it not only possible but meaningful to combine a scientific world view with a faith in God; he pleads with the Lutheran Church in America and with all communities of faith to eradicate such types of biblical and theological interpretations that create unnecessary and erroneous tension between science and theology. He calls upon the churches to provide the Bible's clear and unambiguous answers to moral questions. He confesses his attraction to the Roman Catholic scientist and theologian, Teilhard de Chardin, with his cosmic and scientific optimism. He expresses his regrets that Roman Catholic theologians criticized Teilhard de Chardin, and especially that they did so by pointing out that his system had no place for "original sin," a concept with which von Braun admits his difficulties.

This is not the place to discuss the concept of original sin, but it is part of our summary to note that as the chapter ends with that discussion, it is clear that Dr. von Braun's presentation is rooted in an impressive optimism, one that his life's work made contagious and productive.

In attempting this summary, I have tried to give you a feel of the structure of Dr. von Braun's presentation and I regret even more now than when I began that he is not here with us today.

Let me concentrate my own comments at a few points. I was very interested in what Dr. von Braun means by *spiritual survival,* which is one of the five pillars of the dome for the survival of mankind as a species. In that passage we find a type of thinking, a thoughtful and competent type of thinking, which I think is at the center of any discussion, any critique, any evaluation and any search for bearings, for where we go from here.

The term *spiritual survival* in Dr. von Braun's presentation refers to the important task of creating a technological society without drifting into a regimented and coercive society. He recognizes the risks and affirms the need to restore and protect inalienable personal freedom. There must be elbowroom for the individual. This requires a reversal of the trend toward urbanization. Thus spiritual survival is described primarily in terms of freedom for the individual to expand.

The ultimate suggestion of Dr. von Braun's at this point is his reporting, and apparently with approval, on an ambitious scheme of Professor Gerald K. O'Neil of Princeton University. He envisages the creation of *habitats*—cylinders four miles in diameter capable of accommodating 10,000 people—orbiting the earth at the libration or Lagrangian (that is where the pull between the moon and the pull between the earth cancel out). From these cylinders it would be possible to build other cylinders ad infinitum from material coming from the moon rather than from earth. Life in these cylinders for human living conditions, these habitats, would open up the possibility of counteracting the overcrowding of the earth, producing food, and finding energy.

I have chosen that example—given in the section on spiritual survival—in order to test for myself the style and pattern of thinking of this paper. To most of us flat-footed earth dwellers it seems pretty far out—in all respects. For somebody who has fought with architects at Harvard University for retaining the possibility of opening windows in our dormitories instead of having sealed air-conditioning, this scheme is not very attractive. I am not trying to be funny or condescending. Rather, what interests me in this pattern of thinking is that it is an extreme case of problem solving by expansion.

This is very American if I may say so. Expansion is our glory, not least in the bicentennial year. The whole thinking of this nation and also its highest level intellectuals is and was conditioned by the frontier, by the possibility of new and untried opportunities. And I am struck by the fact that the legislation even in matters of race and sex discrimination has always been coined in the terms of opportunity, "equal opportunity." I don't know if it is as obvious to you as it seems to me, that all equal opportunity solutions of our questions—be they scientific or be they social and economic—require a frontier or require fast growth of society and the economy. If there are no opportunities and unemployment increases, it doesn't help the poor much that the opportunity is equal—for there is no opportunity. Equal-opportunity thinking requires growth, substantial growth. And the pain of our present situation in all respects is that even with equal opportunity ideology, the rich are getting richer, the poor are getting poorer, and the jobs are getting fewer.

And so, the radical solution to keep up the momentum of growth of the new frontier is, of course, going into space. And the self-evidence with which this suggestion is appealing to Wernher von Braun as he argues the case of scientific growth implies and demonstrates a whole view of growth at almost any cost as a self-evident good and certainly as a necessity. Last summer, as I was thinking toward this event here today, I found in the *New York Times*, an extreme example of that thinking where growth is taken for granted as an unambiguous value. As you know, the Mobil Oil Company is using its resources in order to balance editorial opinion by placing ads on the OP-ED page and they had this wonderful ad:

> You Ain't Seen Nothin' Yet!
>
> Even though the tools of projection have become more sophisticated, it remains fashionable to peer into the future with dismay. When programmed with a doomsday bias, computers can now tell us at what point in the future we will run out of natural resources for food and energy, or when a proliferating human race will pollute itself out of existence.
>
> Happily, there are some who peer at the future in a brighter light. One of these is Stephen Rosen, whose book "Future Facts," points to some ways in which the quality of life will be markedly improved by the turn of the century.
>
> He tells us, for instance, that research already in progress may make it possible for people to grow new limbs by electric stimulation; that productivity may be enhanced by machines that are activated by the operator's eye movements; that the golden age of transportation is yet to come, including a 21-minute subway ride between New York and Los Angeles. He sees electronic communication substituting for face-to-face meetings so people can live and work in rural areas without losing any of the benefits of today's urban centers.
>
> Scanning the lighter side of future lifestyles, Dr. Rosen visualizes an ultrasonic home sewing machine that welds fabric seams; TV sets that automatically record your bowling score; even a scientific measurement for romantic love.
>
> And there is nothing even remotely pessimistic about the future envisioned by the Hudson Institute, one of the nation's most respected "think tanks." The Institute looks ahead to an era of economic abundance sparked, surprisingly, by the very gap that now separates the "haves" from the "have-nots" among nations. The larger the gap, the Institute says, the stronger the stimulus toward a higher standard of living for everyone.

> We share with Dr. Rosen and the Hudson Institute the belief that people can take these great changes in stride. After all, the jet plane became commonplace within the lifetimes of many who remembered the first flight at Kitty Hawk. People not only adapt to change, they eventually embrace it.
>
> And so we're with those who look to the future with more than a dash of optimism, clinging firmly to the belief that we "ain't seen nothin' yet."[1]

But some of us think that we have seen enough. And this is a serious question. And what I would like to ask you about is the mind-set behind this way of thinking and solving problems by expansion. There may be limits for growth and there may be limits that we have not thought about. If, when I was a kid, someone had said, "Be careful so that you do not pollute the ocean," I would have taken it to be a joke. It may be that technology can solve the problems that technology has created, but there seem to be limits.

I have lifted up this "growth pattern" since I believe that our habit of solving our problems by expansion is sometimes an excuse from considering the other alternative. If there are limits to safe and sound growth, then the alternative is redistribution of resources and recasting of priorities and timetables. Then the key to spiritual survival is not unlimited individual expansion, but new ways for individuals and communities to see that the available and safely increased resources are shared with maximum distributive justice. The solution by expansion often blinds us to that alternative which is far more ascetic for the haves and beneficial for the have-nots. Spiritual survival in a limited world calls for other models than those suggested by Dr. von Braun, and they also call for our listening with more respect to the common sense of nonspecialists.

In the recent election in Sweden, the Socialists finally lost out after forty-four years. The tip of the balance was really the question of nuclear energy, the Socialist government having gone in favor of substantial increase of nuclear power plants. But the population at large said no, because on a common-sense level it

1. *New York Times,* 12 August 1976. Used by permission.

seemed clear that before one really knows whether he or she has the know-how of what to do with the waste, one does not have the right to expand in that area. The issue is not "no growth," the issue is how to grow, where to grow, and at what pace. The timetable, the speed of application is what is at hand and at stake. It has always been so. I think it is true to say that the space program about which Dr. von Braun writes would have neither been authorized nor founded at the level it was, had it not had military implications and Russian-American competitive dimensions. Did we really need to go that fast—in order to beat the Russians to the moon while our cities decayed and the black ghettos were burning out of despair and unemployment?

Even more important than the question of timing and speed is the question of "where to grow," that is, how the areas of priorities for technological efforts are chosen. It is fair to say that technological expansion in our society often tends toward areas which profit the few rather than the many. Dr. von Braun mentions this problem when he raises but does not pursue the question "If we can go to the moon and walk on the moon why can we not solve our housing, why can we not solve our health programs, why can we not solve some of the problems in the cities, and why can we not solve the question of public transportation?" It was an interesting moment in the history of this nation when Congress voted against the supersonic transport, and I think the determinant for that decision was the growing awareness that the SST would be to the advantage of such a small group of the jet set that it was almost obscene to put money into that area when we have momentous transportation problems much closer at hand. Thus, we must ask toward what questions engineers and technologists at all levels are gravitating. Or, to move to the other extreme, the electric toothbrush is a silly symbol for technological expansion without reasonable priorities, or with priorities guided by affluent consumerism.

I was very much struck by the statement on sexism that came before the World Council of Churches in Nairobi in 1975. One of the first items listed as a must toward overcoming sexism in the world was technological research and implementation of water-delivery systems—because in most parts of the world it is the women who draw the water. Such a priority may have less glamour, and I think also the women of the world are right in their suspicion that technology comes late to the problems felt most by women.

Thus, I am struck by the fact that there is often so little attention, so little pressure on steering technology toward the problems that hurt closer at hand in our communities. And I have the suspicion that perhaps it appears not as intellectually fascinating, interesting or glamorous. Yet, it stands to reason that both primary and applied research, if good, should have possibilities of coming to grips with problems closer at hand than on the moon or in capsules circling the earth, where some get away from that place where those who are the wounded and the losers will have to remain.

Both primary and applied science require that curiosity—that playful imagination of which Dr. von Braun speaks so well. Primary science cannot be done well if asked to produce specific answers to predetermined questions and problems. But I believe that the interplay between science, the individual scientist, and society is more complex than von Braun's model suggests. For is it not true that our imagination and the imagination of the scientists are influenced by their total perception of the world of which they are a part? Is it not true that each of us has a conscious and unconscious set of priorities and scale of urgencies? It would surprise me if the very imagination of the individual scientist is not influenced, prodded, enlivened or dulled by that set of priorities and scale of urgencies—not to speak of the pressure of the self-interest of the profession.

Furthermore, the distinction between a primary science "beyond good and evil," morally neutral, is increasingly difficult to maintain. As Professor Hans Jonas has demonstrated so well "moral and legal issues arise in the inner workings of science long before the question of application arises—issues that crash through the territorial barriers of science and present themselves before the general court of ethics and law. To the public authority of that court even the vaunted freedom of inquiry must bow."[2]

2. Hans Jonas, "Freedom of Scientific Inquiry and the Public Interest" in *The Hastings Center Report*, August, 1976.

As Jonas sees it, I believe rightly, most primary research is far from premodern "pure science." It lives on the intellectual feedback of advanced technology, it requires increasingly expensive tools, and thus the priority of funding enters the very choice of primary scientific projects. Thus, "the alibi of pure, disinterested theory has been destroyed" and science has been put squarely in the realms of social action where every agent is accountable for his deeds."

Thus, it seems clear to me that we must ask more forcefully that the scientific and technological community become increasingly sensitive to the needs of humankind, and that the built-in tendencies toward the glamorous and the spectacular be counteracted by the needs of the many, not least, the many outside the Western orbit.

Here it is important to watch how we use the pronoun *we*. Whom do we think of when we say "we"? In the United States it has become wise and increasingly natural to think about the year 1976 not so much as a year for declaration of independence but declaration of *inter*dependence. Two declarations have been properly promulgated in this very city of Philadelphia: the Women's Coalition for the Third Century's Declaration on Interdependence, and the World Affairs Council's declaration, written by Henry Steele Commager.

Both of these are very congenial to the church. I think I do not overstate the case if I say that the Christian churches in this country are perhaps the only grass-roots organizations which have relatively strong international connections. The American labor movement is a totally American movement, different from the labor movements in most Western countries which have a high degree of international consciousness—after all, their old battle hymn is still the "International." To be sure, the scientists and the learned community, and the business community have very strong international ties, but as grass-roots organizations, the churches have a special gift and challenge through their international network in Jesus Christ. And hence we Christians are increasingly aware that the abbreviation *U.S.* for the United States should be read *us* in the sense of us Americans, a relatively small part of the world in which there are many other "we's." In the article by Dr. von Braun, it seems to be taken for granted that if we, the United States, give attention to certain things or solve certain problems, then thereby we speak and think and act for the world. The shape of this self-aggrandizement can be seen on page 90 where we read: "Scientific survival. Unless the United States retains leadership in the natural sciences and in technology, [the other] support pillars for the dome we called 'Survival of Mankind as a Species' are bound to erode and collapse."

Now, it is true that in many areas we have both the know-how and the resources, but I think it is important to note that when it comes to world survival, we must recognize that the old slogan What Is Good for General Motors Is Good for the Country is not a very sound slogan, nor is it so obvious that what seems good for the United States is good for the world. The question is rather how our limited role can find its place in a world of growing interdependence. Because we live in a world of interdependence. It is true that the mass education in India by electronic devices from satellites is a possibility, but I am far from sure as to how Indians would see and implement such a scheme. It is true that the Landsat satellites have an uncanny ability of detecting the resources and the unused resources of the globe. It is also true that the quick introduction of Western modes of agriculture was one of the chief reasons for the hunger and the famine and the drought in the Sahel and the calamities in the misdirection of the agricultural economy of Zaire. We have to become much more aware that different parts of the world are different and that *we* cannot solve the problems of the world by saying "we" and pretending that we think and act for everybody. The many "we's" must be heard in a new order of interdependence.

Finally, let me turn to the relation between science and religion. Personally, I do not believe in any conflict between science and religion. Here, I agree with Dr. von Braun. I base this conviction on my studies as a reader of the Bible and thinking about religious movements in general. I would venture the suggestion that there has never been a single religious leader, a single religious genius in the world that has not taken the scientific world view of his own time for granted. This is true about Jesus, true about Moses, it's true about Muhammad, it's true about Luther, it's true about them all. They just took for granted the scientific knowledge, and the world view of their time. I never read of a great originator of religious tradition who said: "Science says so and so, but I say unto you. . . ." The scientific *Readers Digest* level, commonsense views are taken for granted and form the basis on which they speak. If that has been true through the ages, there is no reason to believe that it shouldn't be true now. Therefore, conflicts between science and religion occur when a religious tradition becomes wedded to and a defender of outdated scientific views. It is as simple as that.

This can be demonstrated throughout the history of the church. The pattern repeats itself. In the first round the church tends to oppose new scientific ideas; in the second, it says that it doesn't matter since religion and science are on different levels; and in the third round, hymns are written on the basis of that new scientific understanding. The church has changed world views in a major fashion at least three times in its history. It started with a Near Eastern biblical world view, with the heaven up there and the flat earth here, and then you had the underneath, this pancake earth floating on the oceans of the chaos waters. Then came the Ptolemaic world view with its circles within circles and everything had to be circular because it was God's creation and God was perfect and according to this classical way of thinking there was only one perfect form and that was the circle, and so, of course, everything was circular and also, of course, we humans were in the center. Then came the Copernican revolution. It took a while before we could write hymns in Copernican language, but we did:

> The day thou gavest, Lord, is ended . . .
> . . . .
> The sun that bids us rest is waking,
> Our brethren neath the western sky,
> And hour by hour fresh lips are making
> Thy wondrous doings heard on high.

The so-called conflict between science and theology is always just a question of the world and the church being on different timetables, a question of scientific lag in the churches. Thus, I join with Dr. von Braun in urging the church to overcome that lag, and I would suggest that one decisive element of such a resolution of the spurious conflict between science and religion is to recognize the symbolic and even the "playful" nature of theological language. If we truly are children of God, then the only appropriate language should have an element of playfulness. The Jewish tradition has known this much better than we Christians. They have always done theology by telling funny stories, thereby indicating that it is improper for human beings to behave as if they had been up to Heaven with polaroid cameras. Religious language is obviously symbolical, but the question is whether that symbol has power, meaning, and truth.

Therefore, I was a little surprised when Arthur Schlesinger said that the religious instinct has died out and none of "these melodramas," as he called the religious views, have any meaning anymore except as symbols. I always thought that when Jesus spoke about these things he did so in parables and symbols. From Jesus to the Johannine Apocalypse we are given powerful symbols. You may ask, Is it all just poetry? Why *just* poetry? Is not poetic (which means "creative") language the very means by which human beings speak about that which is most important? The language of symbols is the language about meaning, transcendence—that wholeness which cannot be spoken of in any other way. If it were otherwise, we would be able to control God instead of finding ourselves in our finitude under God in his infinite and eternal glory.

This perspective is the more important when we recognize that biblical theology has always been "Copernican" in the sense that not we but God is the center. That is what the first commandment, what biblical monotheism is about. To be a Christian is to see the world as having its center in God, and not to allow anything but God to be thought of or dealt with as ultimate. When we reflect upon "the nature of a humane society" and when we reflect upon the survival of the human species, even then, especially then, the first thing to remember is that God is God and that we are in the hands of God as part of his creation.

The discussion of ecology can help to clarify the point I am trying to make. There are those who argue ecology on the basis that unless we behave, *we* will not have clean water to drink, we will not have clean air to breath, and so forth. It does not seem to matter much what happens to the animals except that they belong to the ecological system on which *we* depend. And nature is there "for us." I don't know if you understand what I mean, but I think that the self-evidency with which everything is seen from the point of view of "us" is a break against the first commandment. There is a wonderful Norwegian hymn that says, "God is God even if all men were dead, God is God even if all lands were waste." That is the other perspective. . . . It says something about where the center is, and I happen to believe that for us to live fully as human beings *that* center, rather than the center of humaneness as such, is necessary. Human dignity does not require self-aggrandizement. It rather suffers from such tendencies. With our center in God, the Creator, Redeemer, and Giver of Life, we must more humbly seek our place within God's whole creation, animate and inanimate, on the tiny spaceship, Earth, in the vast cosmos. Also, here we seek a smaller "we" in the hands of a greater God.

Before I close, I must add this: What may be missing in the ways of thinking that I have criticized is the dimension of tragedy which is also to say the dimension of original sin. The concept of original sin has its difficulties, and I remember the preacher who said "I don't see why they have difficulties with original sin. I never understood what was so original about it." That is not only a joke, for the meaning of original sin is exactly to come to grips with the tragedy of life, and that tragedy is there. The question is how we live with it. There is no sense of tragedy in the essay we are discussing, and that scares me, especially since contemporary science and technology has such enormous tragic dimensions in terms of atom bombs and the way in which so many inventions have been both fostered and used by evil causes. It strikes me that Dr. von Braun refers to the Vietnam

War as "the unfortunate Vietnam War." If one does not have any way of coping with tragedy, then the Vietnam War perhaps was just "unfortunate." But to many of us, it seems to have been a grave tragedy. Now, how does one live with tragedy? How does one live with original sin? One should not wallow in it, one should not wallow in guilt as we sometimes do since we get so angry with the happy-go-lucky, operation-bootstrap superficial view of human beings. But that does not help anyone. It might even be positively dangerous, since we can hold on to that guilt only so long, and then we get tired of it and try to take it out on others. How does one live with tragedy? The church has an answer. The dignity of human beings does not lie in our successfulness or our goodness. It lies in the hands of God whatever happens—beyond optimism and pessimism. There is the perspective, the faith without which I do not think that we can move safely, nor have the climate in which the right priorities come out in scientific and technological developments.

Limits to Growth

Jonas E. Salk

This meeting has afforded a unique experience by providing an opportunity to gain insights from realms other than those we normally inhabit.

First, I would like to explain that the title "Limits to Growth" was originally assigned to Gunnar Myrdal and I had been asked to comment on the text he would have produced. Regretfully, he could not be here. He would have expounded on this subject differently than I. I believe that I was asked to be a commentator because of the point of view expressed in my book *The Survival of the Wisest*, and Dr. Aldrich now has the assignment to comment upon what I have to say.

Since I could not prepare a paper in advance, I have used the theme of my book as the basis for my remarks; I will introduce my viewpoint about growth and how I perceive it, from material contained in the book.[1]

As a logical overture, let us look at the growth of the human population on the face of the earth and the present reasonable projection over the next few decades to the year 2000. It raises vast and complex implications for the character and quality of human life that concern relationships as well as resources for the present and the future. It raises questions as to the means that Man or Nature will invoke to deal with the excesses that have developed and the insufficiencies that persist. Will Man

1. Adapted and excerpted from Jonas E. Salk, *The Survival of the Wisest* (New York: Harper & Row, 1973). Copyright © 1973 by Jonas E. Salk. Reprinted by permission of the publisher.

create his own procedures to deal with them or will Nature's simple ways come into play, some of which may prove quite undesirable from Man's point of view? This, in fact, may already be occurring. Before turning our attention to the questions and consequences of the rapidly mounting curve of population increase as drawn in Figure 1, or to the implications of its curtailment or of its continuation, let us look at patterns of growth in other living systems. For example, Figure 2 shows the growth curve of a fruit-fly population in a closed system as observed by Raymond Pearl in 1925.

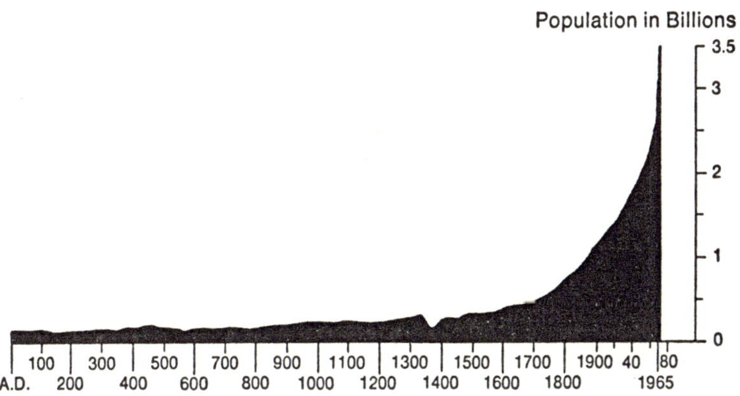

Figure 1. World population estimates, A.D. 0-1965. Adapted from *World Facts and Trends,* by John McHale.

The S-shaped, or sigmoid, curve that describes the growth of fruit flies is also seen in curves of growth of micro-organisms and of cells or molecules. Since the planet earth can be considered a closed system and *since the sigmoid curve reflects the operation of control and regulatory mechanisms that appear to be associated with survival of the individual or of the species* it would seem reasonable to expect that the pattern of future population growth in Man will tend to stabilize at an optimal level described by an S-shaped curve. It is possible, of course, that an alternative pattern might resemble that of the lemmings (Figure 3), in which periodic catastrophe occurs with enormous loss of life. However, Man's attitude toward human life would have to alter significantly for such patterns to be endured; he is more likely to choose *other ways than catastrophe for maintaining optimal numbers on the face of the earth while remaining within the limit of available resources.*

As Man has still to complete a cycle of growth on this planet, he has not yet fully revealed the pattern biologically programmed in him, or the way it will be influenced by factors he is responsible for, or by natural forces beyond his control. Therefore we are unable to know the pattern of his trajectory in the short-

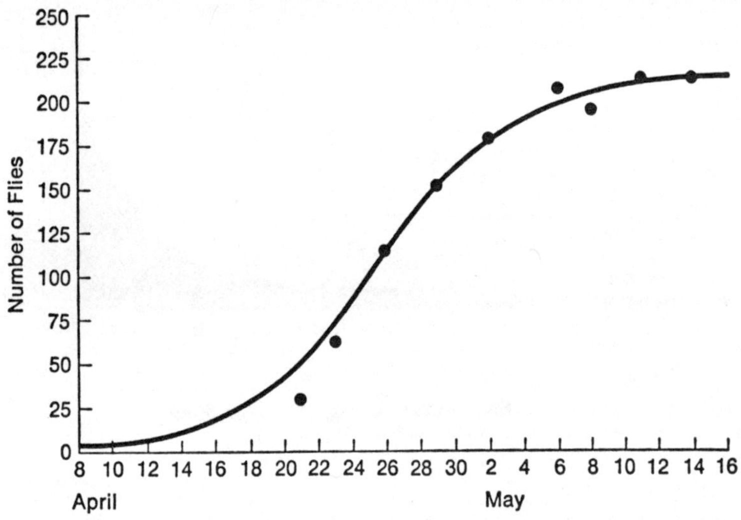

Figure 2. Growth of fruit-fly population. From *The Biology of Population Growth*, by Raymond Pearl. Copyright 1925 by A. A. Knopf, Inc. and renewed 1953 by Maude de Witt Pearl. Reprinted by permission of the publisher.

or longer-term future. The "catastrophists" and harbingers of doom *are in themselves evidence that Man possesses a signaling mechanism for sounding warnings* of danger, sensed more acutely and more clearly by some who alarmingly represent the problem of population increase as shown in Figure 1.

If we assume, however, that Man has the power of choice and can influence the course of his growth curve on this planet,

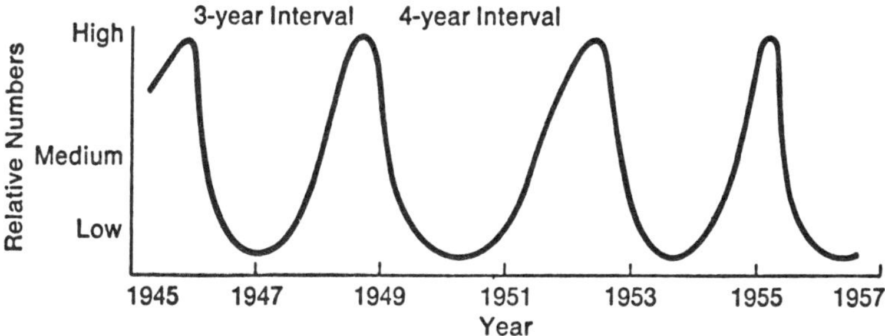

Figure 3. Generalized curve of the three-to-four-year cycle of the brown lemming population. From CRM Books, *Biology: An Appreciation of Life*, © 1972 by Communications Research Machines, Inc.

then it is of special interest to look carefully at the sigmoid curve in terms meaningful for him. Since our deeper purpose is to try to discern the nature of order in the human realm in relation to the nature of order in the realm of life in general, it is interesting to explore the possible meaning of the similarities observed in the human population growth curve as manifested thus far, and the first portion of the growth curve of the fruit-fly population and similar curves in the subsystems of other living systems.

My purpose is to elucidate the factors and forces affecting the quality of human life through ideas that emerge while "playing with" the growth curve and reflecting upon the developmental and evolutionary processes of Man in the critical stage in which we seem to be at this point in time.

As we study the curve in Figure 4 consideration of the lower portion only gives the impression of continuous, even explosive expansion, whereas consideration of the upper portion gives the impression of modulation and control of this expansion, so that finally a limit is established. At the junction of the lower and upper portions of the curve is a region of inflection at which there is a change *from progressive acceleration to progressive deceleration* and at which the influence of the controlling processes is clearly visible. The break apparent in this region suggests that a "signaling" mechanism of some kind must operate to bring about this change, producing an effect that, judging from the shape of the curve, indicates the existence of a uniform

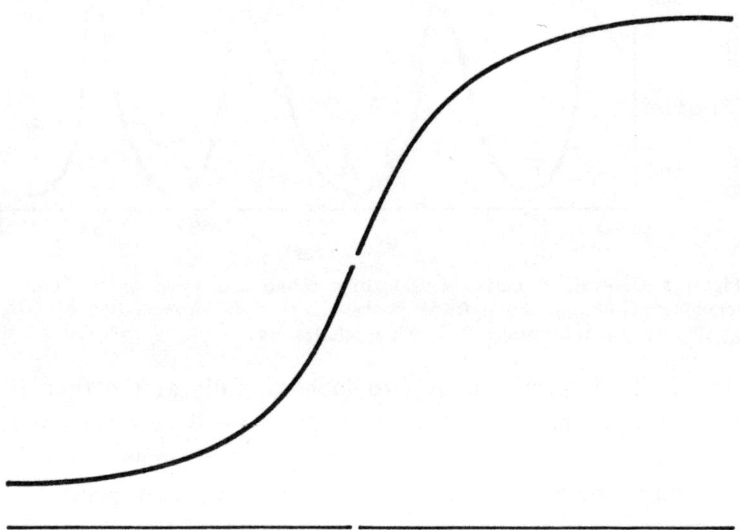

Figure 4.

process, reflecting the operation of some kind of ordering principle in response to "signals" both from the environment and from within the organisms themselves. At different points in time along the curve, latent qualities and reactions are evoked appropriate to survival, the program for which is coded in the germ plasm, which also contains an accumulation of control and regulatory factors essential thereto.

At the plateau stage of numbers, the individuals in the fly population would be expected to "behave" differently as compared with those alive earlier in the growth curve, *i.e.*, before the zone of inflection when different "problems" prevailed. The extent to which circumstances differ, at different points in time along the curve, is graphically suggested in Figure 5 by breaking the continuity at the point of inflection so as to create two curves, A and B.

These curves are intended to emphasize the difference in attitude and outlook in the two periods and help create a visual image of what can be sensed "intuitively." They also convey concretely what might be appreciated "cognitively" by means of

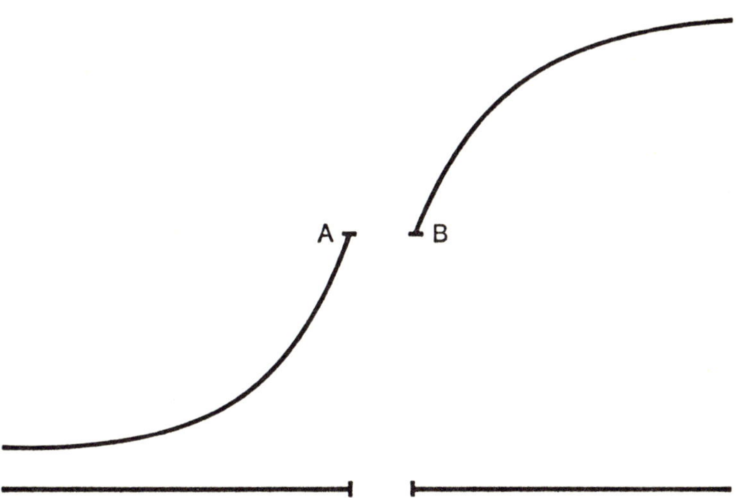

Figure 5.

an objective analysis of the increasingly complex problems generated by the growing numbers of individuals. In the discussion to follow, curves A and B will be used as symbols of the "shape" of the past and of the future, as we attempt to characterize each.

Man differs from other living organisms in possessing another "control and regulatory" system, for response to environmental and other changes, in addition to that genetically coded and automatically operative as in the fruit fly, which has been tested and selected in the course of its evolutionary history. Man is able to exercise learned behavior. He also possesses individual will, which can be either in accord or in conflict with genetically coded patterns of response. In this sense Man is more complex and more unpredictable than the fruit fly. He can learn to behave in ways that are anti-life as well as pro-life, anti-evolution as well as pro-evolution. He remains to be tested for this pattern of response to all that is implied in the need for changing values to make the transition from Epoch A to Epoch B. In view of the greed and ideologies of Man as causes of his conflicts, attitudes as well as values will be put to test in the transition from Epoch A to Epoch B.

Genetic programming does not change as rapidly as the attitudes and values that also guide human behavior. Since genetically as well as culturally determined responses are "environmentally" linked, the circumstantial differences implied by the dissimilar "shapes" of the curves symbolizing Epoch A and Epoch B will be expected to evoke different sets of genetic as well as cultural potentialities. In Epoch B those attitudes and attributes which are of the greatest value will determine the "real" and not merely the "presumed" shape of the population growth curve and the quality of life. Value systems such as prevailed in Epoch A will, of necessity, have to be replaced by those appropriate for Epoch B, and new concepts will emerge about the nature of Man and his relationship to all parts of the cosmos.

TABLE I

Epoch A	*Epoch B*
Anti-Death	Pro-Life
Anti-Disease	Pro-Health
Death Control	Birth Control
Self-Repression	Self-Expression
External Restraint	Self-Restraint
Competition	Cooperation
Power	Influence
Win-Lose	Double-Win

Table I indicates the changing trends and values, with reconciliation of the complementary patterns that are now converging and intertwining in a mutually reinforcing way.

The fork-in-the-road at which Man *now* stands offers either a path toward the development of ways and means for maximizing self-expression *and* self-restraint, by means of external restraints that are not suppressive or oppressive, or an alternative path of limitless license which would unleash destructive and pathological greed at the expense of constructive and creative individuals. In the latter case, a strong reaction can be expected to develop in response to the sense of order upon which their survival is based. The challenge is to establish an equilibrium between *self-expression with self-restraint* on the one hand and *self-protection with self-restraint* on the other. If Man is to take advantage of opportunities to remedy difficulties that have arisen as a result of his evolution, then he needs to understand his relationship to the evolutionary process which plays with and upon him.

An unprecedented explosion of interest and movements concerned with the survival of the species is now taking place. The idea of the extermination, by Man, of various forms of life on the planet, and the danger to human life, induces a fear that preoccupies increasing numbers of individuals, especially of the generations now maturing. Those who are ecologically oriented and those who are profoundly concerned about the quality of life for the species as well as for the individual appear to stand in opposition to others less aware of such problems, who are more concerned with themselves in their own life spans. The fundamental difference between these two attitudes is that the first expresses concern for *the individual and the species;* the second reveals principally, and perhaps exclusively, an interest in the *individual* and the *particular group* of which he is a part. The more broadly concerned *(i.e., with the species and the individual)* fall into two categories. One consists of those born after such threats came into full evidence; the other, of those born earlier but who, having witnessed the change, are now reacting to previously prophesied dangers which have become realities. Those preoccupied only with their own problems are either unaware or unperturbed in the face of a process in human evolution to which others are sensitive and, if aware, feel frustrated, helpless, or apathetic.

In the course of evolution many more species have become extinct than have survived, each perhaps for particular causes very different from those which might cause the extinction of Man. For in Man's case, at this point in his evolution, his extinction might well arise for internal reasons. The way he deals with unresolved conflicts within himself individually and collectively might lead to his own destruction. The process of natural selection has developed survivors resistant to various infectious diseases and to some of the vicissitudes of the environment. It has also led to the selection for survival of those successful in escaping the ravages of war and those ingenious enough to escape human tyranny. Thus until now the qualities that have been selected for survival reflect the conditions and circumstances that have prevailed as much as the potentialities that exist in Man. As Nature continues its game of biological mutation and selection, and as Man plays his own games of selection of ideas and of cultural innovations, Nature will have the last word. Therefore it is up to Man to look closely and deeply into Nature's workings, not only at the molecular and cellular levels but also at the consequences of advancing knowledge and cultural practices as these bear on the question of survival and the quality of life. It is in this respect that wisdom will be required for which a balanced creative center for judgment is needed.

If human life is to express as much harmony, constructiveness, and creativity as are possible for fulfilling the purpose *of* life, as "required" by Nature, and the purposes *in* life, as "chosen" by Man, an attitude will be needed, not of Man "against" Nature, but of Man "inclusive with" Nature. A more reasonable attitude would be for Man to "serve Nature" in order to serve himself, rather than to "serve himself" without regard for, or at the expense of, Nature and others. By recognizing and respecting the natural "hierarchies of purpose" Man would be better able to gauge his latitude to select and pursue his own "chosen purposes" without coming into conflict with the "purpose of Nature," which appears to be the continuation of life as long as conditions on the planet permit.

I am convinced that, although we cannot predict the future, with understanding Man can, to a considerable degree, influence the course of coming events in his favor. This is based upon the evidence that a new transformation is occurring in the circumstances of human life—new in the history of Man and of the planet—to suggest that Man's past performance should not be taken as the *only* basis for judging his future.

Because of the inevitability of the evolutionary process, the present must be viewed from a perspective of the future, as well as of the past. From the past, we can learn in part *how to* and *how not to* conduct ourselves; and from imagining some of the elements which are likely to combine in shaping the future, we might learn how to behave not merely in terms of the past but in consideration of the effect of alternatives from which we might choose, based upon our knowledge of the "way," or the "wisdom," of Nature.

Response

Human Life-Span Development
A Life Science for Epoch B

Robert A. Aldrich

It is with immense pleasure that I accept the privilege of responding to Dr. Salk's remarks before this Symposium as well as to the more comprehensive treatment of the topic in his most recent book.[1] We have found that periodically our paths meet at an intellectual crossroads like this one where "taking stock" of the human predicament is the major concern and where approaches to solving the many kinds of problems that make up the predicament must be sought. This sort of thing is both optimistic in tone and likely to be helpful in inching human beings toward a better future.

A primary assumption that I must expose now is that a humane society requires humane people. We must learn how to raise humane adults in our next hundred years. It is not my generation that will make the difference in that time, nor do I believe that it will be the present child-bearing generation now in their twenties and thirties. It is the offspring that these young people are producing who will determine the nature of our next century. These new citizens will be the ones who *should* be educated about the full nature of human beings as

1. Jonas E. Salk, *The Survival of the Wisest* (New York: Harper & Row, 1973).

they live over the trajectory of the life span, they are the population of the future who can create and maintain the new kinds of institutions that *should* either arise de novo or evolve from those in existence that are capable of change, and they will have in their hands the knowledge and the resources to restore and prosper very fundamental elements of society such as the family.[2] I recognize that taking what many would call "the long view" is just a part of this whole approach. There are a great many specific moves that we can make today, moves that prepare and set the stage for the transitions expressed by Dr. Salk.

How *do* we raise humane adults? How and where do processes of human life-span development go astray? Where does the pathology lie? What are the points where intervention is preventative thus permitting normal processes to continue? These are only a sample of the questions uppermost in my mind today, the remainder of my comments will address some ways by which all of us can start answering these queries:

1. Greatly expanded public education is needed for adults and right on down to the preschool child. We should be presenting what we know about human beings to the young parents of the generation that will make a difference. Those in their twenties and thirties know little about child rearing (or raising adults—as I prefer to call it) except what they themselves have experienced or received secondhand a long time ago. There must be a reexamination of parental child rearing concepts as well as reeducation of *both* sexes for parenthood. Life span developments of the male and female *are* distinctly different and ought to be emphasized early in our education for their social, behavioral, and biological implications.

It is quite evident that the complicated new knowledge gained by science can quickly be fed into the organized body of useful knowledge nurturing young minds. I want to emphasize *young minds.* The same young minds are seeking today to understand man. How do we build bridges between these young minds and those of us who are concerned with the development of human

2. Victor C. Vaughan, III and T. Berry Brazelton, eds., "The Family—Can It Be Saved," The Year Book Medical Publishers (1976).

beings? We carry a tremendous burden as well as a challenge in surmounting the difficulties of transmitting knowledge between the generations.

2. We are witnessing today a convergence of major movements of public interests in several important ways. Very specific areas of knowledge are becoming related so that general forms and larger strategies are coming under consideration. Nowhere is this more evident and more exciting than in the life span studies of the fundamental interdependency between human beings, their society and their "habitats" or environment.

The impacts of habitat at various times in the life span are known to be both positive and negative in their influences on the processes of growth and development of individual human beings and of families. Serious scientific investigations along these lines are relatively new, but their significance for human beings can hardly be overemphasized.

Synthesis of knowledge regarding the processes of growth and development of individuals is moving at a tremendous rate and bringing together scholars from the social sciences, biomedical sciences, environmental sciences and humanistic studies in an effort to understand the human trajectory throughout life. We are learning about the effects of inhibiting these processes at critical times, and about opportunities for preventive intervention when sequences are going astray. For example, as health moves closer to the values of "well-being" and "quality of life," medicine is seen by the public as only a modest section of the much larger concept of health.

Above all, we are facing the most basic relationship of all—that between the human species and the planetary ecosystem. There may be an analogy between the discovery of the deoxyribonucleic acid (DNA) code for human beings and a possible discovery of an environmental code for humankind's continuation.

In the face of growing scarcity of planetary resources, the challenge to our institutions of higher learning is clear. Sharing of knowledge and concepts between disciplines and professions is one important response. Synthesis can be achieved better through interdisciplinary efforts. Universities can take leadership in the directions just proposed through providing for students and faculty new ways of working together across disciplines and professions.

3. Science and technology underlie a great many of the prominent characteristics of modern American society. All of us are familiar with the qualitative and quantitative changes brought about by urbanization. We are presently engaged in heavy national and local controversy over the selection of fuels for future energy with far-reaching implications stretching ahead for many generations and with decisions made that those most likely to be affected will have had no share in. Values must be part of human life span development. How do values become a part of us? How do they change during our lives? How is ethical behavior related to one's values, and Why?

I believe that we should reconsider the values we hold *before* assigning technology to a task. Very often when new technology is developed to a point where it can be put to use, the decision is made to go ahead because it is possible, not because it is a part of the value system of the individuals or community that is directly affected.

There are four E's that should be satisfied before undertaking civic or national projects because they are part of understanding how to enter Epoch-B concepts with life-span development principles. First of all is *E*conomics of the project. Is it economically feasible or possible? Second is *E*ngineering. Is the project engineered for practical effectiveness and safety? Third, *E*sthetics is sometimes considered but not always. Is the project tasteful, harmonious and beautiful? Fourth is *E*thics. This is the most troublesome. It is usually the one left out and yet it should be given the most thought. Is the project within the values and ethics of a humane society?

One Approach to Human Life Span Development

The search for the laws of human growth and development seems likely to provide us with clues to the future evolution of human beings and human society. Certainly, the improvement of the character of the American people is a desirable goal for which there is both evidence that it is occurring and hope that it will continue.

In view of the complicated nature of this task it is helpful to reread Warren Weaver, who, in a profound essay set forth the essential features of "organized complexity" in contrast to "disorganized complexity."[3] The former relates to problems involving a considerable number of variables but showing the distinctive feature of organization, while the latter, disorganized complexity featuring millions or billions of variables, must be handled by statistical mechanics and probability theory, life insurance statistics, the motion of atoms, laws of heredity, and the like. His strong exposition of approaches to the solution of problems of organized complexity stressed operations analysis utilizing interdisciplinary teams mixing physical sciences with biomedical and social-behavioral sciences. Among the problems he pointed to for analysis by these techniques was the "incredibly complicated story of the biochemistry of the aging organism."[4]

Emboldened by Albert Rosenfeld's essays on "The Doctor as Biophilosopher"[5] and by Salk's book,[6] my colleague[7] and I have undertaken to describe the human life cycle in qualitative and quantitative terms that analyze the situations in which human beings live and conduct their affairs in human settlements. This model was offered to undergraduate baccalaureate students at the University of Colorado's Denver Campus as an effort "to put man back together again" in the context of the different kinds of human settlements where human beings dwell.

The Life Cycle Model

The human life cycle can be compared to the trajectory of an airplane or a missile. It has a take-off point and a landing point with distances in between that are measured in terms of time

3. Warren Weaver, "Science and Complexity," *The American Scientist* (6 October 1948) 6:536–44.

4. Ibid.

5. Albert Rosenfeld, "The Doctor as Biophilosopher," *Modern Medicine* (N.Y. Times Media Co., 1975).

6. See above, note 1.

7. Lorna Grindlay Moore, Ph.D., Assistant Professor, Department of Anthropology, University of Colorado.

rather than miles and are subject to the characteristics of the individual and the situation in which he or she lives. During the life span there occur a continuous series of critical periods and important life events. The critical periods are usually viewed as a time in the life cycle when there is change taking place at a rapid rate or on a very large scale. Examples of critical periods would be conception (when the chromosomes are being sorted out), the generation of form (embryogenesis), birth, puberty, and so forth. At each of these critical periods there are things that can go wrong and sometimes it is possible to intervene and prevent undesirable events. Life events, on the other hand, can be characterized by such things as infant-mother bonding, the first day at school, the first date, marriage, loss of one's job, the "empty nest," retirement. Dr. Thomas Holmes at the University of Washington has developed a sophisticated scoring system for life events or "life change" as he calls it, which has some capability to predict illness when the scores are too high.[8] His material was developed for application to adults and so far a comparable investigation has not been completed that will apply to the period of childhood and youth. It is diffi-

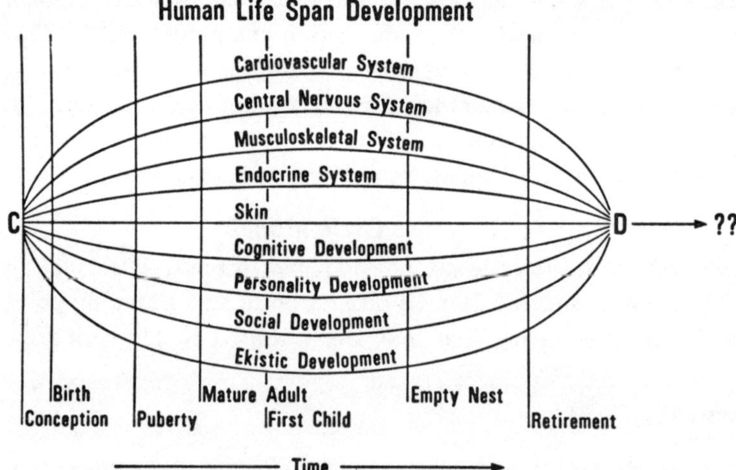

Figure I.

8. Thomas H. Holmes and M. Masuda, "Life Change and Illness Susceptibility," *Separation and Depression*, AAAS (1973), pp. 161–86.

cult not to be drawn into speculation regarding the relationships that may exist between life events in the adult years and important life events in the years of prematurity.

The life cycle model (Figure I) that we have been using can be pictured as a long oval that is three-dimensional. It looks for all the world like an elongated watermelon. On this eliptical model with stripes running from one end to the other are represented organ systems, social processes, and behavioral processes. The purpose of this model is to portray biomedical organ systems like the cardiovascular or the central nervous system, alongside social and behavioral processes like personality development, social development, cognitive development, and so forth. Since all of these must operate in direct relationship to each other if the organism as a whole is to function effectively through the life span, this manner of representing these interdependencies against time has a good deal of practical value.

The critical periods and the life events are depicted on this model by perpendicular lines that cut across the ellipse at appropriate intervals in time. The drawing illustrates the life-span model with a selected group of critical periods and life events placed upon it. Using this device we have had considerable success in expressing the nature of the human life cycle to baccalaureate college and university students as well as to graduate and professional students. The model lends itself particularly well to courses in medical anthropology; it is flexible enough to be applied to any kind of culture and it is very helpful in separating out the differences in the life span of the male as compared to the female. In our teaching activities during the last year we have placed special emphasis on four aspects of each critical period—lifestyle, genetics, education, and environment. It is important to emphasize that this particular approach assists greatly in identifying things that can go wrong at each critical period and what possible remedies are available to prevent them from going wrong. Here, basically, we are able to synthesize the mainstream of anthropological and biomedical thinking which is the history of man and the life cycle of man with unavoidable questions arising about the future of the species. It is of some interest that students usually perceive this approach as an excellent way to understand the origin of values and the process by which values are translated into ethical behavior.

Human beings have always devised their own human settlements as far back in time as we are able to go. Very ancient settlements had to be on a human scale so that they met the limitations of human beings of the time. With the arrival of technical inventions leading to the high technology of today, human settlements have left behind some of these basic human values and the human scale to which man as a species was able to adapt. The modern metropolis exceeds the capability of human beings to adapt in an almost limitless variety of ways. Noise, vehicular traffic, air pollution, limitations of movement, water pollution, and many other features of today's cities are posing very serious problems to mankind at all ages.

In a remarkable book by C. A. Doxiadis one can find an exceedingly illuminating analysis of the relationships between the growing human being at different stages of life and the kinds of human settlement environment which would indeed prosper

Anthropos	1
Room	2
House	5
Housegroup	40
Small neighborhood	250
Neighborhood	1,500
Small polis	10,000
Polis	75,000
Small metropolis	500,000
Metropolis	4 million
Small megalopolis	25 million
Megalopolis	150 million
Small eperopolis	1,000 million
Eperopolis	7,500 million
Ecumenopolis	50,000 million

Figure II.

growth and development from both a biological and social and behavioral standpoint.[9] The development of the basic theories of ekistics by Doxiadis[10] across the human life span is in my view a singular achievement because it provides both a qualitative and a quantitative methodology for examining the needs of human beings in each of the types of situations in which they live and conduct their lives. Using the techniques of Doxiadis, one can readily place a person in any one of the fifteen ekistic units (Figure II) and knowing a great deal about the individual at that point in his or her life (what the requirements are for growth and development), one can analyze that particular ekistic unit to see if it does indeed contain the elements necessary for optimum growth and development of the individual under study.

In each of the fifteen ekistic units one observes five elements (Figure III). These are nature, man, society, shells, and networks. From these five elements it is possible to make a synthesis of the situation and draw some conclusions that connect the particular individual or group of individuals under study with a specific ekistic unit. In studying an individual such as a thirteen-year-old male at the onset of puberty, it would be apparent that the second ekistic unit, a room in a house, is not going to provide the sorts of things that a boy at this age requires, while it might be quite adequate for a newborn baby. Therefore, one needs to examine each ekistic unit from one to fifteen in terms of the individual under study and hopefully arrive at an appropriate type of situation for that particular individual. There is a very helpful matrix that has been developed by the scholars at the Athens Center of Ekistics and this depicts in a visual manner the relationship between an individual at a particular point in the life cycle and each ekistic unit. The volume, *Anthropopolis—A City for Human Development,* provides scores of illustrations of these relationships.[11]

9. Constantinos A. Doxiadis, *Anthropopolis—City for Human Development* (Athens, Greece: Athens Publishing Center, 1974).

10. Constantinos A. Doxiadis, *Ekistics—An Introduction to the Science of Human Settlements* (London: Hutchinson & Co., Ltd., 1968).

11. See above, note 9.

NATURE(N)
1. Environmental analysis
2. Resource utilization
3. Land use; landscape
4. Recreation areas

ANTHROPOS(A)
1. Physiological needs
2. Safety, security
3. Affection, belonging, esteem
4. Self-realization, knowledge, esthetics

SOCIETY(S)
1. Public administration, participation and law
2. Social relations, population trends, cultural patterns
3. Urban systems and urban change
4. Economics

SHELLS(Sh)
1. Housing
2. Service facilities: hospitals, fire stations, etc.
3. Shops, offices, factories
4. Cultural and educational units

NETWORKS(Ne)
1. Public utility systems: water, power, sewerage
2. Transportation systems: road, rail, air
3. Personal and mass communication systems
4. Computer and information technology

SYNTHESIS: HUMAN SETTLEMENTS(HS)
1. Physical planning
2. Ekistic theory

Figure III.

My major point here is that a synthesis of the life cycle with the principles of ekistics (ekistic development) offer a very good method for studying man holistically within the environmental circumstances in which he finds himself. It draws conceptually from Warren Weaver's exposition of "organized complexity" and, in my opinion, provides an enormous area for both qualitative and quantitative research enlisting the minds and vigor of a very much wider constellation of disciplines than we customarily encounter in the study of human development. This is necessary if man is to continue to survive as a species and to evolve as a species and a society. He must take his dual role seriously for he is both guinea pig and research director on this planet. Man is not infinitely adaptable as René Jules Dubos has so eloquently described. We must return to human scale and values that prosper human development as man moves ahead toward the future.

Middle Aging (Mediatrics) and Aging

Part of "taking stock" is to single out areas where more attention is desirable. In the broad sweep of life-span development the place of much ignorance is middle age. It is a time of life that contains so many life events of significance and "bunching" of them with a resultant capability for overriding adaptive mechanisms. It is well for us to look at current demographic trends in the United States for implications.

A recent special study by the Bureau of the Census gives in many details the demography of the older population in the United States.[12] I highly commend this report. It shows that the population over age sixty-five will continue to grow and number in the vicinity of thirty million by the year 2000. This will be between 10.7 and 12.5 percent of the United States population in that same year. Projections further into the next century show continuing growth in number with a probable peak in the year 2030 between 12.8 and 20.9 percent. With this large elderly population one cannot avoid speculating about the other end of the age spectrum and whether or not the population of younger people will be adequate in numbers to conduct the affairs of the nation and also provide for the retirement and other needs of the elder population. The possibilities are high for critical public issues to arise as a result of these forces. For instance, if the younger population were insufficient in number to man the business of the country, it might be necessary for the elder population to take a later retirement and to remain in the work force for longer periods. One cannot know what will happen to the fertility of the nation in subsequent years for this is a highly variable phenomenon. However, those reaching elder years in the remainder of this century and the first few decades thereafter, are already on this planet so that this end of the

12. *Demographic Aspects of Aging and the Older Population in the United States.* Current Population Reports, Special Studies Series 59 (May 1976), p. 23.

demographic chart is relatively predictable. Further breakthroughs in medical care may further reduce the mortality rate in the elder years which would add to the relative increase in numbers of individuals in the older age-bracket.

We know very little about the long-term effects of child development. The correlations between the physiology and behavior of children and youth with those of the middle aged and the elderly are poorly described. There remain huge areas of ignorance that will require vigorous recombinations of scientific disciplines with new perspectives if we are to understand the life span of the human being and the process we call "aging." Some years ago I had an opportunity to present some ideas on how this could be done.[13] It was pointed out that a primary justification of pediatric and child development programs has been that a healthier, better developed child would lead to healthier adults. This hypothesis remains to be placed under rigorous testing although there can be no doubt whatsoever that better child development and better child health has been achieved. The subspecialization and fragmentation of science have their own laudable goals but there is much more to the study of man as a whole. Human development, the study of man as a whole, appears to be best able to facilitate the unification of the sciences and the humanities, and to open up the perspectives we need to view the past as well as the future evolution of ourselves and our society. In recent years there is now useful knowledge about the growth and development of values during early life and the manner in which values become expressed as ethical behavior. Great interest is focused today on changing values in our society, particularly the differences in value systems between different age generations who live together in the same society.

Better understanding of the whole life span and the aging

13. Robert A. Aldrich, "Pediatrics, Mediatrics and Geriatrics," Proceedings of the International Congress of Pediatrics, Mexico City (2 December 1968); and *Issues in Human Development*, ed. Victor C. Vaughan, III, M.D. A Symposium sponsored by Temple University, St. Christopher's Hospital for Children, The National Institute of Child Health and Human Development (Washington: U.S. Government Printing Office, 1967).

process is not only desirable, but in all probability is absolutely essential if we are to be able to give reasonable guidance to future generations. In the world of nature we learned as children that everything is interrelated. There is the familiar relationship between human beings and plants, we give off carbon dioxide needed by plants and the plants give off oxygen which we need. As adults, we have also learned that you cannot upset natural systems without changing the relationship among things which may bring unintentional damage no matter how beneficial in their intent we believed our actions to have been. There seem always to be unexpected and unforeseen consequences of interventions into natural systems. In our society today we are seeing "the law of unforeseen consequences" working in our cities where there is *urban renewal.* We are seeing the same law operating as those supposed to be benefited by social actions are resisting them because of the unexpected and adverse impact these actions have had. Thus, human development as a life-span subject does offer the potential for understanding ourselves and our interrelationship with the environment—both built and natural—and ought to be a means by which we can reach our humane ends.

Attitudes are extremely fundamental. I refer to the attitudes that we acquire regarding both the aging process and the elderly. Presently we are suffering from a taboo. The attitude not infrequently implied or even stated is that old people are expendable and it is all right to isolate them from the mainstream of social activities. I believe that this widespread negative attitude toward aging as a phenomenon and the elderly as a part of our American society actually contributes to the rate of aging of many individuals. Certainly, it is an added stress factor which one hears articulated particularly clearly by those reaching middle age and passing through nodal birthdays such as forty, fifty, sixty. One must ask why and how these attitudes are acquired and why they are based upon a negative value in our society. In all probability this particular value is developed in children starting before their fifth or sixth birthdays as is the case with many other values. The reinforcement of this negative value is so powerful during the school years that it would be a great surprise if this negative value was not present in nearly everyone by the time he or she reached puberty. Aside from "catching" this cultural value within the family, it is widely present in books for children as well as in nearly all other media. Even greeting cards and birthday cards as well as other popular media present the negative value of being old or of getting old.

Not every culture takes the same point of view toward being old or getting old. Painters, sculptors and other artists have set forth the very lovely relationship which so often exists between very young children at the early run-about age (two, three, and four) and their grandparent generation. Artists seem to recognize that there is some curious affinity between this very young child and the generation just older than his or her parents. One can only speculate about it but it may be that children at that age have not yet developed the negative attitudes described earlier. Grandparents, on the other hand, take these little ones very seriously indeed, so there may be a natural affinity between the two generations.

Earlier in this essay reference was made to the demographic changes taking place in American society. There is an issue here that is of strategic grade, namely, that after the turn of the century, if the young population remains at a low birthrate and the elder population is as large as projected, the younger generation may become much more dependent upon the elder generation—joining the work force and helping to conduct the affairs of the nation. In the event that the negative attitudes toward aging persist in the younger generations, there could be a significant and possibly damaging confrontation based solely upon attitudes. I am firmly convinced that we must begin to apply what we know about changing attitudes and see if we cannot overcome the negative attitudes abroad today, and through our knowledge of human development, prevent negative attitudes of this kind from appearing as early and widely in our population. Here is a task for collaboration between educators, biomedical and social scientists, and the public and private media.

Simultaneously, by changing this attitude we can achieve much less stress and the concomitant acceleration of aging while also reducing the potential for social confrontation in the future between the young and the old.

In conclusion, I have considered human life-span development as both a theoretical and practical endeavor that can help us to move through the huge transitions implied in Dr. Salk's presentation. Paramount among these considerations are a focus on new institutions devoted to the subject of life span human development, much greater public education, inclusion of the role of habitat in human development, and more emphasis on the segment of the life cycle represented by aging—particularly middle aging.

The attitudes of the scientific community and its structure may be decisive in determining whether this new life science will emerge in time. May I remind you of the immortal words of Pogo, the eminent observer, who once said, "We have met the enemy, and they are us."

Toward Women As Equal and Essential Participants

Matina S. Horner

We hold these truths to be self-evident: that all men and women are created equal.

Seneca Falls, 1848

The anxiety of mankind to interfere in behalf of nature, for fear lest nature should not succeed in effecting its purpose, is an altogether unnecessary solicitude. What women by nature cannot do, it is quite superfluous to forbid them from doing. What they can do but not so well as the men who are their competitors, competition suffices to exclude them from. . . . If women have a greater natural inclination for some things than for others, there is no need of laws or social inculcation to make the majority of them do the former in preference of the latter.

J. S. Mill, *Subjection of Women*, 1869

One's freedom is a void in the absence of a place for one in the culture or a firm set of alternatives.

Kate Chopin, *The Awakening*, 1899

Equality is not when a female Einstein gets promoted to assistant professor; equality is when a female schlemiel moves ahead as fast as a male schlemiel.

Ewald Nyquist, deploring the fact that there is not a single female school superintendent in 758 upstate districts, *New York Times*, October 8, 1975

The position of women is one of many important and sensitive indices of a society's basic character and fundamental value system. It seems, therefore, vitally important at the dawning of America's third century that we pause to reflect on this particular index of our national character, and that we do so both prospectively and retrospectively. Otherwise, we may once again be guilty of confirming Thomas Paine's lament that "in the progress of politics, as in the common occurrences in life, we are not only apt to forget the ground we have traveled over but frequently neglect to gather up experience (and wisdom) as we go." If, on the other hand, we are armed with an understanding of the advances achieved and the setbacks confronted by women during the two centuries just past and of the family, social and economic contexts within which these occurred, we will be much better prepared to evaluate meaningfully the experiences and traditions of the past and, even more importantly, to assess the changing trends of the present and their implications for the future.

Toward Women As Equal and Essential Participants

We celebrate this year the Bicentennial of the American Revolution, reaffirming the principles of freedom and equality which inspired it, but aware that the process of implementing these principles has been a slow and uneven one. For women and other groups, the promise of this nation has yet to be fulfilled. Only two years ago, during the House Judiciary Committee hearings on "Watergate," which profoundly tested the value and strength of the Constitution of our nation, the wisdom of its laws and the ultimate safeguards its processes provide, we heard Barbara Jordan movingly testify that when that Constitution was written, she *as a black and as a woman* was not included in the phrase, "we the people." It gave us pause, or should have, for we were reminded once again that equality is and must be treated as a matter of ethics and not one of genetics.

Nineteen hundred seventy-six also marked the beginning of the United Nations' designated "Decade for Women" (1976–1985). There is a strong sense that "equality of justice and opportunity before the law"—a fundamental principle of democracy and one of the major goals of the nation's founding fathers—is an idea whose time has finally come; and we feel a compelling need to identify and eliminate as quickly as possible whatever barriers remain which prevent women from sharing equally in and contributing freely to our society, each in her own way. Not until the gap that currently exists between women's current roles and the opportunity for them to be, feel, and be recognized as "equal and essential participants in" and "contributors to" modern American life and society has been bridged, can we hope to even approximate, let alone fulfill the American dream.

The revitalization of the women's movement in the second half of the 1960s increased significantly the level of public awareness and concern about the new needs and changing aspirations, values, expectations, status and achievement potential of women in our society. There has been considerable debate about how far and how fast we have come—how long we can stay—and whether we will continue to progress or have already begun to regress.

During the past ten years considerable progress has certainly been made in documenting the existence of sex-based inequalities (not always synonymous with discrimination) in many important aspects of life in this society: in the law, in education, in employment, in the political arena and in the family. In each area, the higher one looks, the fewer the women and the greater the inequality. There has also been substantial progress in verifying the existence of discrimination by sex and, more importantly, in attempting corrective action through legislation, executive orders, and the establishment of several remedial programs and services. Clearly, a hitherto nonexistent set of options and opportunities has been created, and the direction of many lives has been altered in profound and intangible ways, perhaps difficult yet to measure and define.

Nevertheless, much remains to be done, for paralleling these positive developments there has been a growing recognition that traditional stereotypic assumptions about innate differences between men and women in physical, emotional, intellectual and moral development, in ability, interests, motivation and values are deeply rooted and particularly resilient to change (Katz, 1976; Gallup poll, 1976). Despite advances in legislation (Title IX, affirmative action, ERA) and considerable scholarly evidence to the contrary, these assumptions persist and have repeatedly thwarted efforts directed toward eliminating existing undesirable, often inadvertent, patterns of inequality, sexism and discrimination. It is this phenomenon that led Elizabeth Reid of Australia to comment during the International Woman's Year Conference (June, 1975) in Mexico City that the "world's women do not stand to benefit so much from economic or political revolution as from 'revolution in the heads of people,' "—a considerably more complex mission.

The problem is exacerbated, moreover, because despite stated institutional goals to the contrary and changes in the culture at large, more often than not, many of our institutions have changed little if at all. Government agencies, educational institutions and social structures continue to mirror in both their traditions and practices the ambivalent attitudes and implicit values that exist toward women. They have frequently, though inadvertently perhaps, reinforced many existing myths and assumptions about women and the roles for which they are believed in our society to be by nature best suited and qualified.

Thus the women's movement has in a sense reemphasized and sensitized us to the point J. S. Mill made one hundred years before (1869): "What is now called the nature of women is an eminently artificial thing . . . the result of forced repression in some directions, unnatural stimulation in others." Considerable attention has been directed to a new vision of the benefits that could accrue to individuals and society if, for example, a more androgynous pattern of life were adopted and the hitherto repressed achievement potential of women and the repressed expressiveness of men were freed from existing constraints and socialized inhibitions.

Much has been written recently about the inappropriateness of the traditional socialization of men and women at a time when the nature of current social contingencies has so dramatically changed the incentive value of various achievement and affiliation goals. For most young people of *both* sexes, there is today, at least consciously, a much greater parity between the two goals and considerably less difference between the sexes with respect to which goal is valued most highly. As Margaret Mead has suggested, both dependence and autonomy enter into all *human* relations. Cherishing, care, competence and responsibility are *human,* not sex-linked responsibilities and attributes, and neither expressive nor instrumental competence is a sex-linked trait by biological predetermination even though both have been treated as such. Intragender pluralism is certainly as great, if not greater than differences between the sexes. Given that people tend to differ from each other as individuals, perhaps more than men and women do as groups, to imply or attribute sex differences in areas where one's gender is an irrelevant variable or criterion, as is commonly done, is not only damaging and unethical, but is now as it has been in the past very wasteful of a vast reservoir of human talent and resources.

As an integral part of any period of transition in society from one set of significant social norms and preferred lifestyles to another, there are many practical and psychological Mount Everests that must be scaled. During the current transitional process, men and women are being called upon to exercise many previously unpracticed skills in all aspects of their lives—interpersonal, sexual, social, psychological, professional—for which neither tradition nor education have prepared them. As age-old assumptions are challenged and new criteria for personal and professional fulfillment are established—are publicly endorsed and, are ultimately at least consciously adopted—there is a growing need for considerably greater understanding of the problems of readjustment to be faced, and potential coping strategies needed for dealing with them. The new options for both men and women must be understood in terms of both the advantages they offer and the personal costs they may entail, so that each may choose freely according to his or her own sense of priorities.

Whenever change is proposed, many are frightened by its

implications though aware of the need for change; and yet, without change the cost in human terms would be considerably greater. There is increasing evidence that for men and women alike the genuine experiences of equality and self-worth depend not only on the opportunities and barriers the educational process and society provide, but also, and perhaps more importantly, on the reactions and beliefs those involved have about themselves and each other—rooted in prior socialization and in current social and economic conditions and future prospects. Currently, considerable attention has been directed to the profound impact recent changes in women's roles and expectations have had on the behavior, attitudes, feelings and self-esteem of men. How women will interpret and respond to these reactions is a matter of considerable interest and importance for predicting future patterns of education, employment, marriage and fertility in our society.

The self-confidence of a "salient man" has certainly proven to be a key factor enabling highly trained or accomplished women to actualize their potential (Successful Women, and Analysis of Determinants, New York Academy of Sciences, 1973). Given the evidence (Haug, 1973) that most men marry "down" and women, "up" with respect to educational level and economic status as well as with respect to age, height and weight, as gaps in the relative proportion of educated men and women, for instance, decrease (Tables III and IV), women will face a cohort problem in finding similarly trained and confident partners. Haug (1973) reports that three out of four postgraduate men had higher education than their wives, and one out of four had the same. Among college educated men, 55% were better educated than their wives and 36% were at the same level. Sixty-three per cent of the men with a partial college education had more education than their wives and 25% had the same. At lower levels, women often had the same or higher education than their husbands but the level was so low that no advantage for the women was evident. These figures are of course only suggestive but do raise many interesting questions. Judith Stiehm (1976) summarizes the phenomenon in this way: "There are tall, mature, educated, high income, high status women in this society. Conventionally, they ally themselves with taller, older, more educated, wealthier, higher status men. Thus, what may be absolute excellence is regularly experienced by these women as relatively ordinary." It is not surprising, then, to find suggestive evidence that the courage to assert one's full humanity appears to be more readily and clearly manifested by those who, armed with knowledge and mutual understanding, have been able in one way or another to resolve doubts about their own manhood or womanhood (Pleck and Sawyer, 1974; Hoffman, 1976). Furthermore, the capacity for cooperation, mutual support and interdependence appears, more often than not, to be a sign of strength, self-confidence, knowledge, maturity and realism. This is not unrelated to the need recently identified for further inquiry into the nature of the personal and social consequences for men and women in our society of both inter- and intragender cooperative and competitive behavior.

Consistent with the above and in many ways closely associated with the fundamental issues and concerns of the women's movement has been the recent surge of interest and emphasis on the importance of enhancing the "quality of life" in our society, to be measured 'how' one is not sure, but clearly not by the conventional yardstick of consumer goods and materialistic gains. Disappointment with the consequences of the economic growth of the fifties and sixties has stimulated in recent years the recognition that though competitive striving, greater affluence and material wealth heighten aspirations, they do not fulfill them nor automatically provide for either social harmony or a sense of personal well-being and fulfillment. In "Second Thoughts on the Human Prospect," Heilbroner (1975) points out that:

> Economic growth and technical achievement, the greatest triumphs of our epoch of history, have shown themselves to be inadequate sources for collective contentment and hope . . . unable to satisfy the human spirit.

Bardwick (1970) argues that:

> Like many women, many men are not happy. As affluence burdens

> us with the task of finding new goals and as technology deprives more people of a self-sufficient self-esteem and as more people are made aware of the costs to their humanity of an achievement-circumscribed life, then men, like women, will have to redefine their sexual identity within a less rigid idea of human identity.

And Holloman (cited in Bardwick, 1970, p. 99) points out that:

> We seek a new way which includes in our values the early ideas of human concern, a respect for reason, the sensing of beauty, the humane use of technology, a respect for human life, a rebirth of the sense of interdependence and community.

Though many now talk about the need for a higher quality of life, few know how precisely to define it, and fewer still, what to do to achieve it and what, if any, minimal consensus can be found. In a recent national survey Campbell et al. (1976) found a widespread need among people for a "wider and more satisfying life experience" which included needs for a sense of equity, recognition and self-actualization, and a move away from emphasis on "consumer values" and materialism.

From all that has already been said, it is obvious that we face today many compelling and complexly interrelated social, economic, demographic, psychological and political realities. Our moment in history is probably unprecedented in the complexity, depth and rapidity with which fundamental social changes are being sought and are occurring. In some areas of our lives (technology, sex and race role stereotyping, for example) the pace of change has been so rapid and dramatic that, as a student recently said to me, "You get the sense that the future becomes the past before you can even have a chance to identify and assess the nature of the change or understand its implications." Clearly, at such times setting priorities and making choices are difficult, conflict is inevitable; the need for foresight is great. As quickly as new opportunities emerge and beckon, new sets of problems appear, escalating the challenges and putting a heavier burden on the intelligence and moral fiber of all concerned. We are all familiar with the new moral dilemmas that recent advances in medical technology have created, and Florence Howe (1975) reminds us of the private costs of public success and of the new strains that have been created for women attempting to integrate full personal and professional lives. Howe argues: "For academic women feminism raises more problems and conflicts than it currently offers solutions. The retiring or invisible woman in academe (of the past) has been replaced by a person too busy for her own life. Indeed she may have little life beyond her work." In several other current surveys of women in different careers and professions, the women report working 80–120 hours per week, confirming Howe's sense that the "New Woman" is generally overcommitted and raising several questions with regard to the "quality of life." If we are to enrich and enlarge our lives and enhance the lives of those around us, to change our institutions and not merely the gender of their participants and leaders, intelligence, creative social energy, vigilance, maintenance of a sense of proportion, humor and flexibility will all be more essential than ever before. We want to insure that our behavior does not run ahead of our psychological capacity to cope.

If, furthermore, in this period of rapid social change and shifting expectations, we are to plan creatively and prepare actively for the inevitable changes ahead, our knowledge needs are great. There is, to begin with, an urgent need for more research of the kind that will enable us to distinguish more effectively between short-run trends or temporary changes and those that are long-term trends and reflect enduring basic dynamics and human needs. It is a difficult task. As Ruth Ginsberg has indicated: "Realizing the equality principle will require a long and persistent effort, after the artificial barriers are removed to prevent perpetuation of the effects of past discrimination (and inequalities) long into the future. . . ."

Our success in translating these valued principles into reality will depend on how effective we are in finding alternatives for which there have been no viable precedents in history and which can and will challenge myths and laws that have kept women in their place, and will transcend if not dismantle current anachronistic sex-related barriers to self-actualization of both the intrapsychic and environmental variety for both men and women. There is within our "knowledge need" a need for considerably more research on the "problems faced" and "coping strategies" used by achievement-oriented and achieving women living within various family and economic contexts.

In this, the Bicentennial, year of the American Revolution, a time of reassessment and review of the 200-year history of this nation, it has become clear that education was a key factor underlying the hope of actually realizing the principles and dreams of a "more perfect union" which motivated that revolution and established our Constitution. Education was considered not only "our best hope for a better day" but also as a personally and collectively liberating force. For Horace Mann, it was the great equalizer and balance wheel of society, and for Jefferson, it was the "keystone of the arch of government, which should therefore be readily accessible to all young people regardless of parental background." Jefferson believed strongly that democracy depended on the integrity of an educational system and its capacity to produce what he called an "aristocracy of talent." Thus with firm conviction that education is an essential foundation for freedom and equality, that ignorance and slavery are synonymous, the early leadership of the nation was committed to broadening the base of literacy among its people and to developing thereby an educated electorate which would understand, protect and monitor the democratic principles for which they had fought so hard. It is worth noting that the extension of suffrage to a broader constituency which included women in the twentieth century was not unrelated to the growth of literacy and higher education for women in the late nineteenth century.

As the nation grew socially and technologically more complex, education became increasingly central as a vehicle for gaining access to most of her valued opportunities. It became in fact the ultimate sine qua non for the fulfillment of many of our national goals as well as personal aspirations for status, power, respect, social mobility and employment. (Although the nature of the relationship has been very different for men and women, education, employment, lifetime earnings have been closely correlated for both sexes. The participation of women in the work force in general and in high level careers in particular is strongly related with the level of education attained, as is long-term persistence at a career. In their recent national survey Campbell et al (1976) find that although not all women want to work, level of education especially college education makes an important difference in whether or not one is happy or satisfied if not working. Table I shows the relationship of income earned and level of schooling attained and provides evidence of the fact that women have not been paid equitably—a college educated woman earns about the same as a high-school educated black male, both considerably below their white male counterparts.

TABLE I

MEAN INCOME BY SCHOOLING, RACE, AND SEX

	Years of Schooling					
	7 or less	*8*	*9-11*	*12*	*13-14*	*16+*
White males	$4,651	6,143	7,902	9,389	11,081	14,640
Black males	3,671	4,633	5,704	6,523	7,579	10,155
White females	1,947	2,360	2,938	3,752	4,334	6,340
Black females	1,629	2,088	2,717	3,706	4,692	7,284

SOURCE: *The 1974 World Almanac*, (New York: Newspaper Enterprise Assoc., 1974).

Statistics from the 1973 U.S. Department of Labor show very clearly that the more education a woman has the more likely she is to be in the Labor Force. More than two out of three or 69% of those with five years or more of college were workers, compared with less than 30% of those with only elementary education, about 50% of those with high school education, and 58% of those with four years of college behind them.

The educational community plays a critically important part in the socialization and channeling of our youth. Therefore, how institutions behave, what they stress, what they ignore and how their professed values match their way of life is an important set of issues. Currently, the question of how well they have served, in Veblen's terms, as "corporations for the cultivation of the community's highest ideals and aspirations" is a relevant issue of considerable interest and debate, particularly with regard to questions of equal opportunity and access. The educational system has played a critical role both directly and indirectly in shaping the goals and expectations men and women have for themselves and those around them, and in "channeling" them by both training and contacts into certain patterns of life and work. Several studies (Campbell et al., 1976; Feldman, 1974; Gallup poll, March 1976) have shown that among women educational level is a very mportant determinant and predictor of some of our most basic social indicators, including family and employment patterns, career persistence, family size and fertility rate. For all these reasons it seemed valuable to approach this topic by considering the role education and, later, educational institutions have played in forming (or precluding) a "more perfect union" in which men and women could be accepted as "equal and essential participants."

It is not difficult to see why the participation of women at various levels of the educational system can in many ways be a sensitive index of the position and value women have in the society. Their role in the system is very closely associated with the expectations held for and ultimately by them, and reflects closely the roles they are called upon to play in the home, in the family, in the political arena, in the paid work force and in the broader community. It is not an altogether encouraging picture, for despite the fact that in studies as far back as 1929, women have had consistently better academic records at each level of the educational system than men, at each step a decreasing proportion of women go on to the next higher level in the system.[1]

1. Komisar (1972) reports an interesting pattern. More girls than boys actually finish high school, and they do so with a higher percentage of honors. Among the 1960 Project Talent seniors, for instance, 51% of the girls and 39% of the boys reported high-school averages of mostly As and Bs or above (Cross, 1971). Yet, as Komisar and others report, only about 40% of the college population is female. Of those women that actually get to college, 68%

Hence it seemed particularly appropriate and useful before trying any further prospective analysis on women's potential for greater participation in the mainstream of our society: (1) to examine the nature and scope of their participation in the educational system thus far; (2) to consider the impact this has had on their lives, on that of their families and on the economy; (3) to pay particular attention to the nature of the incentives and barriers for the participation of women in higher education during the century just past; and (4) to identify the context within which these developed.

The historical era into which we are born and during which we develop, greatly influences the pattern of our expectations, our values and behavior, the options available to us, and the ways in which we utilize both our natural and human resources. In order to understand how the next century will shape the experience of women, it is important to understand the patterns and changes of the past and the context in which they occurred. In the words of Justice Holmes, "a page of history is worth a volume of logic."

The history of higher education for women is a fascinating story with many important implications about the present and future prospects for women and their lives in our society. It is a story of achievement in the face of protest, active resistance, subtle and not-so-subtle social, political, psychological and economic dissuasion that came in many forms from many different sources for many different reasons. Most influential and damaging of all were, of course, the dire predictions of the clergy and many in the medical profession about the extensive physical

---

get Bs or better as average grades whereas only 54% of the men do. Yet again, the representation of women in programs of higher degrees does not reflect their academic performance. Only 35% of the master's degree candidates are women; 13% of the doctoral candidates are women and 5% of professional degree candidates are women. These latter figures in no way have any relationship to measured aptitude and potential of the two sexes. For instance, whereas 40% of those who show aptitude in engineering are women, only 2% of the engineers are women. A similar pattern occurs at the faculty and administrative levels as many studies have shown repeatedly (Kilson, 1976; Feldman, 1974; Carnegie Commission on Higher Education, 1973).

and moral disintegration as well as social ostracism that awaited women who dared enter a life of learning.

During the colonial period—a period of "self-sufficient households" where women played very central, productive though subordinate roles—formal education for women was virtually nonexistent and the rate of illiteracy was very high. [The institutions of higher education at that time like Harvard and Yale were essentially training grounds for the colonial ministry and clearly off limits to women.] Those women who did manage to become "educated" somehow and who, even more so, dared publicly to manifest their learning were severely chastised. John Winthrop is said to have maintained the view that intellectual exertion could rot the female mind and blamed the madness of Ann Hopkins[2] on her intellectual curiosity. "If she had attended her household affairs and such things as are proper for women," he said, "she'd have kept her wits and might have improved them usefully" (Ryan, 1975, p. 70).

At the turn of the century, as the individualistic ambition among men to acquire greater parcels of land increased, there was a call for increasing the educational level of women by giving them some instruction in history, geography, politics and religion. There were two main reasons for this change: (1) to enable women to be wise stewards and guardians of their husband's property; and (2) so that American mothers could populate the new republic with wise leaders and patriotic citizens.

By the second half of the nineteenth century, the industrialization process and Victorian era were in full bloom. Hindsight reinforces the idea, suggested in the Plan of Action for the United Nations "Decade for Women," that: "women are usually affected to a greater extent than men by the social problems caused by rapid modernization and industrialization: and that such events have generally created problems that required remedial action [at a later stage]." With a growing recognition of the implications and potential negative consequences for women in lifestyle, status, self-esteem, as a result of changes in the functional

2. Wife of the governor of Connecticut.

utility of the family and the productive interdependence of its members and changes in demography necessitated by the industrializing process, the "Woman Question" came to a head and opportunity for higher education for women seemed to some an attractive way to help rectify the situation.

This period is worthy of a moment's pause, for it depicts clearly the complex interrelationship between family patterns, the economy, employment patterns and education that are very much a part of today's concerns. With the expansion of the railroad, the development of such machinery as the sewing machine and typewriter, there was migration out of rural settings and into urban factories and bureaucracies. The economic role of women was greatly diminished as many of her previous creative and productive functions were removed from the family milieu to garment and goods-processing factories. The individual wage soon replaced what had until then been a "family income" reflecting the labor of the entire family. All skilled and decently paying employment went to men—stronger, better-trained and better-educated. That left married women of the middle and upper classes with what some viewed as a life of leisure and consumerism (a symbol of their husbands' success, functionally not unlike the binding of women's feet in China). [It was in many ways an earlier version of the materialism, suburbanization, economic expansion and loneliness characteristic of the 1950s and early 1960s.] On the other hand, single women (and as many married women in the lower class as could get them) were left with the opportunity to work for low salaries under deplorable conditions in unskilled or semi-skilled jobs in the factories. In both tradition and practice most societies have developed an elaborate and segregated network of roles for each sex with little interaction or exchange between the two, and most prefer to retain these traditional definitions of male and female spheres even when modifying the content of the spheres in practice. As the society over the years became more industrialized, these basic differences intensified, often in unanticipated ways, with unexpected and unstudied consequences. Increasingly after the industrial revolution, society was segmented into distinct domains and activities considered appropriate for an individual as a function of age, race, wealth, but most forcefully as a function of sex. In the process, women's activities were devalued, with prestige and high status accorded to those activities pursued and attained primarily by men.

Disenchanted by a process that had removed them from the "flow of adult life" and separated them from close association with work—which had been an important part of the prior bond between men and women in the society—some brave women with their pens, others with their purses and a few from their platforms, responded to the frustrations of women and stubbornly sought to gain recognition and understanding, if not total respect, for the intellectual, political and economic rights of their sisters. Gradually they were able to win support and overcome such formal barriers to women's equality as votelessness and *overt* educational and occupational neglect and discrimination, while at the same time attracting for themselves considerable mistrust, hatred, disdain and unfounded suspicion that they were "man haters."

Several separate factors at that time, including passage of the Land Grant Act in the 1860s, combined to stimulate access to higher education for women and to counteract the opposition. To begin with, the Civil War brought women into the foreground as nurses and volunteers. This new public visibility generated a new interest in the potential availability of higher education for women. Many believed that given a fine education, women could "have their wrongs redressed, their wages adjusted, and the weight of their influence in reforming the evils of society greatly increased."[3] There was at this time great concern that the moral fiber of the nation was in difficulty and that such valued institutions as the family, the village community and the church were eroding.

A second key factor was the fact that financial exigencies plagued most of the nation's colleges at this time. A number of the better-endowed institutions made efforts to revise their

3. From the will of Sophia Smith, the founder of Smith College.

curriculum in innovative ways (the elective system was introduced at Harvard) or they created "feeder" schools so as to increase the number of tuition-paying students. Institutions less well-endowed were forced to resort to more daring and desperate measures such as the admission of women, for example, the University of Michigan's "Dangerous Experiment." Concerns that the introduction of coeducation would have a serious debilitating or feminizing influence proved to be unfounded and coeducation in fact saved many former men's colleges from financial disaster. Clearly, though unfortunately (with one clear exception—namely, Oberlin which had opened its doors to women much earlier—in 1837), the decision to become coeducational following the Civil War, as in many instances within the past decade, had considerably less to do with women's education than the institution's financial plight and, as in some recent cases, with the impending threat of no longer being able to attract enough male students of sufficiently high quality to the institution.

After a half century of coeducation, reassuring those who had been greatly concerned, Arthur Calhoun (1919) reported that rather than blurring sex roles—masculinizing females, feminizing males—as had been feared, coeducation had actually visibly strengthened women's sense of "maternal and marital responsibility." Regardless of their feelings about the relative merits of single-sex and coeducational systems, many have asked whether the ultimate effect of the new wave of coeducation and co-residency, especially within the prestigious, formerly single-sex institutions of our country will be comparable. In other words, whether, despite newly expressed interest in a more androgynous society, we will witness a strengthening of interest in and reinforcement of more traditional roles and relationships for the sake of "social harmony"? It is of interest that in response to the women's movement and consistent with the goals of "equal opportunity," we have observed in recent years both a rapid expansion of coeducation and a reaffirmation of the importance of single-sex education for women.

Earlier, it was indicated that financial difficulties were a key factor in opening the doors to a college education for women. There were some, however, in the late nineteenth and twentieth centuries, who did recognize the implications of industralism for women and the importance of educating women quite apart from any financial considerations about the survival of existing male institutions. Women were for them the top priority. It is they who, within a decade of the nation's centennial, were in large part responsible for the founding and development of many of our distinguished women's colleges. Those who founded women's colleges, especially the "Seven Sisters," saw them as a way to provide women with the means of "usefulness, happiness, and honor" in a new, uncertain and continually evolving social and economic milieu. They had great faith in the intellectual ability of their sex, and the standards they imposed on the curriculum were meant to disabuse the popular mind of the impression that women's colleges would be inferior. Their standards were to be a visible sign that such schools were neither sanitariums nor sanctuaries, and that women could meet the highest standards of scholarship without any obvious, negative impact on their health, reproductive organs, winsomeness, marriage or morals—or any other negative consequences that so many feared would occur.

By the end of the 1870s, the early graduates of these colleges (whether working within the family, as paid professional workers, or as agents of charitable work) were, by their efforts and through the quality of their intellectual, social and moral attainments, challenging existing assumptions and "authoritative evidence" about the mental inferiority of women—that is, that women's brains weighed less than men's and that women's head bone-structure was less mature than men's. It is worth noting that modern day versions of these ideas can be found a century later: "Their (women's) physical and psychological disabilities render them unfit to make important decisions or hold positions of power" (Dr. Edgar Berman, Fall, 1970). "And it is highly probable that the undoubted, superiority of the male sex in intellectual and creative achievement is related to their greater endowment of aggression. . . . The hypothesis that women, if only given the opportunity and encouragement, would equal or surpass the creative achievements of men is hardly defensible." (Anthony Storr, *Human Aggression* [1970], p. 68).

Be that as it may, the early graduates provided ample evidence that they had not only the physical stamina and energy to compete successfully with men and master the same or comparable curricula, but also that they had the resourcefulness and "creative aggressiveness" to overcome some existing barriers and to find ways to improve the quality of life (the health, education, and welfare) of their sex and of the community about them even if it meant the creation of whole new professions such as social work. Employment opportunities for the early female college-graduates were by and large restricted primarily to the service professions (teaching, nursing and social work), where wages were low, where work was considered appropriately feminine and was seen as complementing or supplementing men's work and not conflicting nor competing with it. These jobs were filled either with spinsters or with graduates who intended to marry but who were using the five to ten year average interim between graduation and marriage to put their education to use. Making use of one's education to contribute to society had a very high value and coincidentally gave ample opportunity for educated young men to establish themselves as "eligible suitors." Only about fifty percent of college educated women at that time chose or were chosen for marriage (a figure that rose to 90% in the late fifties and early sixties). The rest resolved their marriage-career conflict by repressing or sublimating their emotional and personal drives for the sake of public service. Those like Jane Addams who dedicated themselves to this kind of work exemplified new roles that offered "dignified and valued alternatives to marriage in the early part of the twentieth century.

Thus, because of the successful efforts of the early graduates, the resistance and forebodings about educating women like men turned of necessity from fundamental questions about whether women could do the work, to what the consequences of educating women would be for society. As Victorian prohibitions and prudery lifted, the vague allusions to the "results we all know" were replaced with quite vivid and explicit medical-scientific portrayals of the gynecological dangers (damage to the reproductive organs) awaiting college- or universty-educated women because of prolonged or intensive mental work. One very damaging but highly influential book in this area was *Sex in Education* (1873) by Dr. Edward Clarke of Harvard. Women, recalls M. Carey Thomas (in Rossi, 1974), were haunted by "that gloomy little spectre (Clarke's book), and we did not know when we began whether women's health could stand the strain of college education. The strict schedules set up in all educational institutions to safeguard the health and well-being of their women students were almost an obsessional response to these dire warnings. Nevertheless, in the first fifty years of higher education for women, there was a very rapid growth in women's enrollments. Whereas in 1870, women represented 21% of all undergraduates (59% of these in women's colleges), by 1920, women represented 47% of all undergraduates (19% of these in women's colleges), a level not yet achieved since the precipitous decline of the 1950s.

TABLE II

Male/Female Enrollment Patterns at 4-Year Colleges

	Percentage	
Year	*Male*	*Female*
1870	79%	21%
1920	53%	47%
1950	69%	31%
1960	63%	37%
1965	61%	39%
1970	58%	42%
1974	55%	45%

Recent figures reflect in part removal of the draft, emergence of the women's movement and perhaps for men the fact that the value of a liberal arts education has been called into question.

Given the forebodings of the times, it is easy to understand why those who opened the doors of higher education for women did so with considerable trepidation. Speaking at Smith College's first commencement in 1879, President Eliot of Harvard highlighted the fact that:

> The college education of young women is an experiment, the issue of which can be completely revealed only after the lapse of many years or even generations. . . . There are, however, dubitable dangers besetting the experiment. . . . The chief danger to be dreaded is the danger to health.

By 1918 it was evident that great progress had been made, for President Eliot, speaking once again at Smith College seemed convinced that:

> It is no longer necessary to provide proof that young women in good health can take a four-year college course without impairing their physical vigor or that women can excel in the studies which formerly made up the prescribed course in colleges for men, or that separate colleges for women are to be preferred to colleges for men and women together, or that a broad elective system is even more advantageous to young women than to young men. These questions are settled now and are no longer discussed. . . .

Going on to speak of the role of women in his talk, President Eliot indicated that:

> [The] College sends year by year into American society a stream of young women well-fitted to be the equal mates and effective comrades of pure, vigorous, courageous, reasoning, and aspiring young men. The future of the American state depends on the future of the American family.

During the next several decades much of the controversy about educating and employing women centered precisely on this latter issue. Just what impact educating women woud have on the American family was a matter of considerable consternation. Education for women had to be justified on the grounds that it would make women better homemakers, better mothers, and more intelligent companions for their husbands. If time permitted, they could be "moral crusaders" as well. The growth of educational opportunity had indeed broadened the outlook and possibilities and changed the attitudes of women toward their position in society; and yet, the expectations of the majority about the basic pattern of their lives did NOT change. Although the census data of the time questions the realism of their expectation, most women expected to marry. Once married, they did not expect to enter or stay in the labor market UNLESS their husbands failed to support them or they were widowed (not an inconsiderable number, given the mortality rates of the time). This same issue is closely related to questions asked in the recent postwar years with regard to what impact women's increased participation in the work force would have on the women themselves, on their husbands and on their families. Even more recently the concern centered on the impact women's increased interest in high-level careers might have.

In the early 1900s there was an increasing concentration of effort directed toward some resolution of the marriage-career/child-producing/child-rearing dilemmas faced by women, men and society, but faced most directly by women. From existing statistics, it soon became clear that educational and occupational achievement exposed women to risks of nonmarriage and childlessness. Exacerbating these risks was the fact that the occupations available to them were "not so fulfilling, so remunerative, or so prestigious" as to make taking the risk of impairing already-limited marital opportunities worthwhile. A serious setback for higher education for women came with the evidence in the early twentieth century of a serious decline in the birthrate, particularly among intelligent, college-educated women (most of whom were members of elite families). Considerable fear and concern was raised at the thought of greater fertility among the new immigrant families from southeastern Europe than among the nation's college-educated women. At a time when the heredity component of intelligence was considered to be of paramount importance, great concern was raised in many circles that educating women could well be the quickest path to "racial suicide."[4] How different the issues were then compared to the overriding concern in recent years with overpopu-

4. Currently there are mumblings about potential "intellectual suicide" because of the recent "birth dearth" especially among college-educated women who are particularly responsive to the issues and importance of population control and to new opportunities in society.

lation and the need to find for women attractive alternatives to motherhood as a source of self-esteem such as access to educational opportunities at the highest levels and thence to meaningful, personally rewarding careers as opposed to merely "jobs."

In an interesting article in *Scientific American* (1973) Ryder anticipates a broader version of the concern expressed: "Individuals," he says, "will show their intention and ability to prevent the birth of too many children, and societies will respond by subsidizing the reproductive endeavor, to prevent the birth of too few children. Because society needs it and because the individual needs it, the family will survive." With the threat of potential racial suicide, society did respond. Former arguments that too much brainwork was the greatest danger to women and that it was unwise, therefore, to encourage girls to endanger their true avocation of motherhood by attending college" were revived and had the sophisticated support and endorsement of such eminent scholars as psychologist G. Stanley Hall (also president of Clark University). As a result, quotas for admission of women to coeducational schools like the University of Michigan were introduced, deans of women were appointed to be sure women understood the true meaning of their education, and a new crusade for "moral purity" got underway.

At about this time, suffrage became an issue. President Wilson appealed to the Senate in 1918 to support suffrage for women which was vital to the winning of the war and essential to implementing democracy. "The executive tasks of this war rest on me. I ask that you lighten them and place in my hands instruments . . . which I do not now have, which I sorely need and which I have daily to apologize for not being able to employ" (Chafe, 1972, p.1). The enactment of the nineteenth Amendment to the Constitution was for women a significant turning point in the struggle for equality and owed much to the efforts of the educated women we have been talking about until now. Although hindsight suggests that the optimism felt by the suffragists—that suffrage would take care of most of women's problems in society—was misplaced or premature, it was how-

TABLE III

Proportion of Doctorates Earned by Women 1920–1972

	Number of Doctorates		
	Women	*Men*	*Proportion*
1970-1972			15%
1960-1969	18,986	144,959	11%
1950-1959	8,214	75,333	9.5%
1940-1949	4,101	26,204	13%
1930-1939	3,763	21,823	14.5%
1920-1929	1,816	11,458	16%

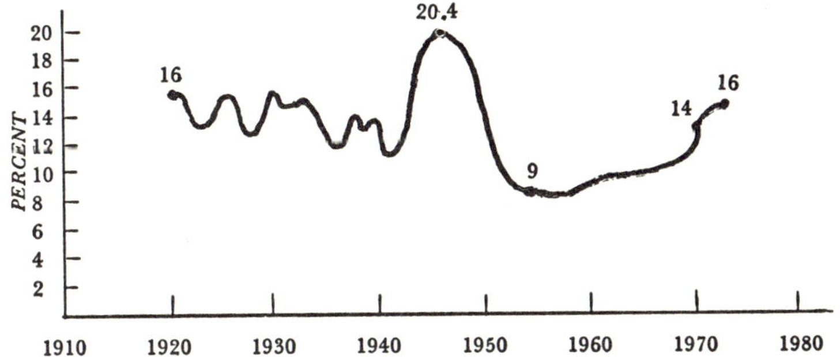

Sources: 1. Rossi and Calderwood, *Academic Women on the Move* (Russell Sage Foundation Press, 1973), chaps. 2, 21.

2. *1975 Handbook on Women Workers,* bulletin no. 297 (U.S. Dept. of Labor, 1975), pp. 205-206.

ever a vital step. Exhausted by their efforts, many relaxed their vigilance and gave in to the "roaring twenties."

The second quarter of the twentieth century is a particularly interesting and informative period, encompassing the end of the "roaring twenties," the Great Depression of the thirties, the Second World War in the forties, all of which had a tremendous effect on the role and function of both undergraduate and of graduate and professional education for women. By 1930 women had progressed enough to make up 45% of professional

TABLE IV

WOMEN PHYSICIANS IN BOSTON

Year	*Number of Physicians*	*Proportion of Physicians*
1880	132	14.9%
1890	210	18.0%
1900	330	18.1%
1910	258	13.7%
1920-1940	166-142	~9%
1950	140	8.3%
1960	200	5.8%
1970	325	8.1%
1973	527	11.7%

Mary Walsh, "Doctors Wanted: No Women Need Apply," in *Sexual Barriers in the Medical Profession 1835–1975* (Yale Press, 1976).

and semiprofessional workers, a level that has yet to be repeated. In education, women at that time represented 32% of the nation's college administrators and professors; but with the Great Depression, the economy contracted and married women, in particular, were discouraged from "taking jobs away from men." Their participation in graduate study was severely slowed down, especially at the end of World War II and has not yet again reached the level of doctoral degrees granted to women in the 1930s and 1940s.

As a result women lost considerable ground in many fields and professions as is evident in Table IV with regard to women physicians.

In 1950, with the postwar surge of education for men associated with "sputnik" and the great expansion of scientific and technical fields at the universities, the percentage of all degrees awarded to women graduates and undergraduates dropped precipitously. A not-insignificant factor is the fact that these were areas in which women were considered to be by nature unmotivated and definitely untalented and many women believed this of themselves.

Paralleling these shifts in higher education and employment were shifts in 'attitudes toward' and 'value of' the family. To quote Caroline Bird (1969): "The 1950s saw an unprecedented return to family life. Never had husbands, home and children been more sentimentalized. Never had so many girls married so young. Not for fifty years had American women been so fertile nor defined themselves so exclusively as mother." There was a great influx at the time of "how-to" books relating to child care and other aspects of family life. (Perhaps it was a sign of just how affluent society was becoming that so many well-trained individuals could be spared and remain unrepresented at the upper levels of the work force.) Another major change was reflected in the number of married women now in the work force. Most of these young women found jobs that would support husbands through graduate school, most of them at levels significantly below their training or capabilities. Employers hired more and more married women because there simply weren't enough single ones left to hire to maintain productivity. Despite these changes, the notion that there are two groups of women—married and career—persisted and still does, even though about forty percent of working Americans are women and about one out of every two married women work outside the home:

Six out of ten new additions to the labor force in the past ten years have been women.

Forty-three percent of all working-age women are in the labor force and three out of five (58%) of them are married and living with their husbands. One third of these women have children under six.

Because we continue to assume the "married or career woman" distinction, little has been done to change the nature of the work place or to bring the work place or work schedules in line with reality (for example, environmental health hazzards for pregnant women). As Keller (1972) suggests "The working woman is one of America's best kept secrets" (in Van Dusen and Sheldon, 1976).

> Generally speaking, frontier conditions—war, revolutions, and feverish boom times which provide urgent work for all hands—have motivated men and women to similar or androgynous goals. By contrast periods of slow or orderly economic growth such as the first and fifth decades of this century have cultivated masculinity or femininity as goals in themselves. . . .
> Androgynous periods are often marked by feminist movements which assert the right of women to independent action. Male-dominated or masculinist periods, on the other hand, encourage women to define themselves in terms of their relationships to men. The two philosophies have altered just frequently enough to keep every generation of American women from using their mothers as models. (Bird, 1969, p. 18).

These two philosophies have altered just frequently enough to intermittently reinforce the notion that achievement outside the home and femininity are not always consistent. What has emerged is that work outside the home is acceptable for women provided it is done in a period of financial need or national crisis; for example, World War II or the felt need as in the 1950s to maintain or enhance the standard of living of the family that requires two incomes. Even with that, it was and is considered important that the relative status, prestige, and earning power of the women remain below that of the men.

It seems perfectly clear, however, that "no society can boast of democratic ideals if it utilizes women power in crisis and neglects it in peace" (Women's Advisory Committee, in Chafe, 1972).

With the publication of Betty Friedan's book, *The Feminine Mystique,* in the mid-1960s came a new wave of feminism, one with which we are all familiar and on which, therefore, I need not dwell. Clearly the specific concerns and issues focused upon by the women's movement at the end of the nineteenth century were quite different than those focused on by today's movement. Yet, both were consciousness-raising efforts highlighting new possibilities to which women might aspire and from which society might benefit. The "woman question" today is a HUMAN question involving the quality of life of both sexes and calls into question the way we have organized society with men immersed for longer than they would wish in remunerative work, with too little time for their families and poor consequences for their health, and women striving for an equal chance to become immersed with their ambitions outside the home, at levels comparable to their abilities, interests and training. The changes called for have profound implications for the structures of society to which we have become accustomed, and for the patterns of life, work, education, recreation, and even health care that we have come to view as "traditional" even though most of them materialized in that unique period of the 1950s. The hope is that an increasing proportion of the population will find the work it does both within and outside the home intrinsically satisfying as well as necessary. There are many conscious and unconscious contradictions and conflicts inherent in modern social realities, and hence this is obviously easier said than done. Yet, it is probably the first time in history that we can even entertain the possibility of approximating our goals while realizing that there still exist many practical and psychological Mount Everests on the way as tangible as the economy and intangible as attitudes and concepts of femininity, masculinity, and justice.

All too often, throughout our history, as the proportion of men and women doing any particular thing reaches a certain indefinable point, there has been a tendency for statistical information to move from being descriptive to being *pre*scriptive or even *pro*scriptive. Certainly, structuring alternatives into all-work or all-home is neither realistic nor desirable for women or for men if it is a matter of rigid stereotypic prescription of how to be a woman or a man, and not a matter of free choice. As we have already noted both traditional roles and emerging lifestyles offer both fulfillment and frustration and as new and traditional values coexist, at least until there is greater harmony of adult sex roles with "socioeconomic and ideological characteristics of modern society, stress and some confusion will be inevitable.

In keeping with the Bicentennial spirit of review and evaluation, it is worthwhile to pause and reassess the validity of our current assumptions about just what the "new woman" and "new man" are doing, thinking and feeling, and how they are responding to some of the changes in expectations about their relative participation in the "mainstream of thought and achievement" in our society. Figures just released in the 1975 Handbook on Women Workers by the Department of Labor entail a threat as well as a promise for the future, and suggest that we may not have been as effective in taking down the hurdles, at least at top levels, as we have been assuming. Certainly there has been progress since 1970, and we have witnessed an amelioration of many unwarranted and undesirable differences. Laws have been enacted to provide for equal opportunity: (1) in training and employment, (2) in obtaining credit, and (3) in gaining access to educational programs and activities. Between 1969 and 1974 the proportion of employed women in professional and technical jobs increased from 14% to 16% and the proportion in managerial and administrative jobs, from 4% to 6%.

It is quite evident, however, that barriers remain. The report shows that the earnings gap between men and women continues to widen. As women's earnings improved, so did men's earnings —at a greater rate. In 1973, the earnings of women who worked full time during the year were only 57% of men's as compared with 61% in 1969 and 64% in 1955. The recent figures highlight the continued small number and, in some cases declining proportion of women professionals, managers, and entrepreneurs give a relatively conservative picture and challenge many widespread assumptions about what has occurred.

In her paper on the status of women in higher education, "Down the Up Staircase," Marion Kilson (1976) emphasizes that within higher education the number of top-level administrators who are women has declined, the proportion of tenured faculty who are women has declined, and the salary differential between men and women in colleges and universities has increased. Remembering that in 1930 women were 32% of the nation's college administrators and professors and that by 1960 this figure had plummeted to 19%, these trends are disconcerting and we can not be totally comforted by or complacent because of recent increases in the proportion of women enrolled in professional and graduate school programs, as gratifying as those figures may be. Under current economic conditions, the future is not bright within higher education. As Juanita Kreps observes, "If the number of additional professors required to staff universities and colleges in the 1970s is small, the probability of improving the lot of academic women is much lower than could occur in a high-growth period such as the 1960s, even if sex discrimination were discontinued."

Evidence of both progress made and distance yet to go is also found in a recently published Gallup Opinion Index on Women in America based on information gathered between September of 1975 and March of 1976. With regard to women's economic role or participation in the work force, we learn that whereas in 1938 only one in five Americans (22%) approved of a wife working, today 68% approve of working wives. Yet, three out of ten still believe that "married women who have husbands who can support them should *not* work." Furthermore, "by a nine to one margin most Americans would prefer to work for a man than for a woman if taking a new job, and their preferences have not changed "over the last quarter century." And across both age and sex, traditional stereotypes persisted when it came to the "perceived skills of men and women in various professions and jobs."

Several have observed that equality depends on the mutual perception of shared roles among men and women in a society. In a recent study on the evolving relationship between college women and men, Katz (1976) finds a high level of mutual endorsement for more equality, less sex-typing and more role-sharing in many sexual, domestic and occupational spheres; with substantial support from the men for the changed attitudes of women. For example, 90% of the women say and 76% of the men agree with them that young women today must make more independent plans for their lives than their mothers did. Eighty-six percent of the men and 92% of the women say that fathers should spend as much time as mothers in bringing up their children. In the same study, however, he finds that certain ambiguities remain and that certain conceptions of women's roles persist that are inconsistent with their newly asserted equality . . . and with their premium on cooperative versus competitive behavior. It is of interest to note that on the question of who earns the money, 76% of the women see it as a joint task and only 44% of the men do (but even that is a change).

Alice Rossi (1976) reports a functionally similar phenomenon among college students of both sexes who demand equality of opportunity-of work-and-of pay, but for whom there is considerable ambivalence toward, if not outright rejection of: (1) the idea of women as bosses and supervisors, and (2) the idea of a wife earning more than a husband. Several dual career studies have documented the extreme to which women will go to avoid this, to essentially protect the self-esteem and security of the spouse or person in private life who is salient, and to preserve the functional balance of their relationships.

Similarly in a study by Yorburg and Arafat in the spring and fall of 1973 on a sample of over 1,000 New York subjects, the majority of both sexes opted for more role-sharing and less sex-typing at home, at work, and in rearing children than traditionally expected. However, as one moved from the more theoretical to the more specific and concrete issues, very significant differences between the men and women emerged suggesting some roots of potential intrapersonal dissonance and ambivalence. Of particular interest in that study is the fact that 60.1% of the women versus 47.5% of the men felt that despite currently high levels of consciousness, marriage to a liberated woman would be a threat to the male ego. Several recent studies (Katz, 1976, Komarovsky, 1964) point to the problems created for men by the new demands for expressiveness placed on them by women in modern sexual relationships and within the new "companionship marriages." There are increasingly reports of feelings of sexual and psychological impotence among men in response to these new demands with resulting interpersonal role strain.

In recent years our awareness of the trade-offs between the

benevolent and problematic aspects of social change has been dramatically enhanced as have efforts to find ways to minimize social conflict resulting from the increasing overlap between "male and female spheres." The need to alter traditional assumptions and institutional structures in order to accommodate the parental and occupational roles of men and women has become a top priority if we are in fact to sustain the work and progress made thus far and meet the needs of the "baby boom cohort" in a tight economy for education, jobs, and social services.

In *The Awakening,* Kate Chopin reminds us that "one's freedom is a Void in the absence of a place for one in the culture or a firm set of (viable, or realistic) alternatives." For those forced to confront and cope with economic constraints and social realities which do not correspond with nor can accommodate their newly adopted (culturally and legally endorsed) personal and professional aspirations, "the absence of a place" is, as recent evidence makes clear, an inevitable source of frustration, confusion, anxiety, and dissatisfaction of enormous cost to both the individual and society. Several trends in the current social science literature and many formal as well as informal conversations with some of today's college men and women suggest many new sources of actual and potential interpersonal conflict, of profound intrapersonal ambivalence, and of role strain because of a lack of mutuality in role definitions and expectations between role partners in several aspects of their lives. We have, furthermore, only begun to think about the possible social-psychological ramifications of widespread underemployment of college-educated talent, if Labor Department predictions about the nature of the "marketplace" will be in the 1980s.

Until options now legally available are attainable in fact and barriers to their attainment (as tangible as the economy and as intangible as attitudes) are understood, if not removed, the great rift between possibility and actuality, between fact and aspiration will grin painfully at us. The new freedom will indeed be a void if the disturbing dissonance created because existing economic-intellectual-physical and emotional resources are inadequate for fulfilling the newly raised expectations of so many men and women for a better life.

Not long ago, Senator Muskie indicated that the future of America lies in the humanistic management of interdependency. It may seem iconoclastic to talk about interdependence as we pause as a nation to celebrate two centuries of progress and prosperity initiated by a Declaration of Independence. If, however, during the century ahead, we are to fulfill America's dream, an appreciation of our interdependence will be an essential prerequisite for elimination of sex-based inequalities that have for so long prevented women from participating in and contributing to our society in full measure, particularly when these have been exacerbated by age and racial factors. We are the poorer for it and the "quality of our lives" has suffered.

As Leo Kanowitz reminds us in *Women and the Law*:

> When men and women are prevented from recognizing one another's essential humanity by sexual prejudices nourished by legal as well as racial institutions, society as a whole remains less than it could otherwise become.

References

"Opportunities for Women in Higher Education," A Report of the Carnegie Commission on Higher Education, September 1973.

"Successful Women in the Sciences: An Analysis of Determinants," *Annals of the New York Academy of Sciences*, Vol. 208, 1973.

Gallup Poll Opinion Index, March 1976.

"Decade for Women," World Plan of Action, United Nations, 1976.

"The Educated Woman: Prospects and Problems," Report of a Committee of the Group for the Advancement of Psychiatry, 1975.

Astin *et al.*, "Some Action of Her Own: The Adult Woman and Higher Education," 1975.

Bardwick, J., "The New Psychology of Women" in McGuigan, D. (ed.), *New Research on Women*, University of Michigan Press, Ann Arbor.

Bird, Caroline, *Born Female*, 1969.

Blitz, R. C., "Women in the Professions, 1870-1970," *Monthly Labor Review*, May 1974.

Calhoun, A., *A Social History of the American Family, 1865-1919*, Vol. III, Barnes and Noble, Inc., New York, 1919, 1960.

Campbell, A., Converse, P. E., and Rodgers, W. L., *The Quality of*

American Life, Perceptions, Evaluations and Satisfactions, Russel Sage Foundation, New York, 1976.

Cohen, Audrey, "Women and a Full Employment Policy," speech to Free Employment Action Council, Commodore Hotel, May 7, 1976.

Feldman, S., "Escape from the Doll's House," A Report of the Carnegie Commission on Higher Education, 1974.

Fidell, L. S., "Empirical Verification of Sex Discrimination in Hiring Practices in Psychology," *American Psychologist*, 1970, Vol. 25, pp. 1094-1098.

Haug, Marie, "Social Class Measurement and Women's Occupational Roles," *Social Forces* 49, September 1973, p. 81.

Heilbroner, R., "Second Thoughts on the Human Prospect," *Challenge*, May-June, 1975.

Hoffman, L., "Fear of Success in 1965 and 1974: A Follow-up Study," prepublication draft, 1976.

Howe, F. (ed.), *Women and the Power to Change*, Carnegie Commission on Higher Education, McGraw-Hill, New York, 1975.

Kanowitz, Leo, *Women and the Law: The Unfinished Revolution*, Albuquerque, University of New Mexico Press, 1969.

Kilson, M., "The Status of Women in Higher Education: Down the Up Staircase," *Signs*, Summer 1976.

Komisar, L. *The New Feminism*. New York: Warner Paperback Library, 1971.

Mill, J. S., *The Subjection of Women*, 1869, in Rossi, *The Feminist Papers*, pp. 196-238.

Pleck, J., and Sawyer, J., *Men and Masculinity*, Prentice-Hall, Englewood Cliffs, 1974.

Rossi, A. (ed.), *The Feminist Papers*, Bantam Books, New York, 1974.

Ryan, M. P., *Womanhood in America, from Colonial Times to the Present*, New Viewpoints, New York, 1975.

Ryder, *Scientific American*, 1973.

Shinn, M. B., "Secondary School Coeducation and the Fears of Success and Failure," Unpublished Honors Thesis, Harvard University, 1973.

Stewart, A., "Longitudinal Prediction from Personality to Life Outcomes among College-educated Women," Unpublished Doctoral Dissertation, Harvard University, 1975.

Van Dusen, R., and Sheldon, E., "The Changing Status of American Women: A Life Cycle Perspective," *American Psychologist*, Vol. 31, #2, 1976.

Walsh, M., *Doctors Wanted: No Women Need Apply: Sexual Barriers in the Medical Profession, 1835-1975*, Yale University Press, 1976.

Response

Coretta Scott King

We are dealing with a "human question," as Dr. Horner says, rather than only a "woman question." Its dimensions are universal and they have everything to do with the *interdependent* network of society's institutional structure.

Dr. Horner approaches the topic through a consideration of the role of education and educational institutions in producing a society in which men and women are "equal and essential" participants. . . . The topic could be treated by examining the role of economic and political institutions; the legal structure; class, income, and ethnic group patterns; family structure; and structure of organized religious, social and cultural groups.

Educational institutions are indeed a most significant element . . . but the essential interdependence among human beings, of which Dr. Horner speaks, would perhaps be more fully illustrated by broadening the focus.

Toward that end I may contribute an additional element by dealing with the position of black women in society.

The problems of black women are perhaps the most complex of any of our sex in this society. To be a woman, as we know, is to be burdened and harassed by deeply rooted discrimination, having economic and social roots. To be black is to be doubly burdened and as if this were not enough, some observers have argued that black women dominate black men; that black society, unlike the larger society, is essentially matriarchal.

Volumes would be required adequately to exhaust this intricate phenomenon. I will have to narrow the inquiry to economic and family problems that impinge on black life in America today.

Since Dr. Horner does not deal with the position of the black woman specifically, I would like to examine that topic. It is the status in the human family I know most intimately. I will focus on the black woman's position in the economic and family spheres of the institutional structure.

One example of the interdependence between these two spheres and their ties with educational programs, is especially shattering in its implication for black women and their families. The current recession has predictably resulted in the "last hired" being "first fired." A large share of those last hired are women, blacks, and other minority-group members. Many of them are college graduates and holders of advanced degrees. Frequently they obtained their jobs and higher education because of the translation of an ideological position—equal opportunity for all—into political and legal action. The academy provided training that the labor market failed to utilize, and families have suffered severe strains.

This devastating syndrome is, of course, not unique to the United States, but it has a unique impact here—unique in the sense that expectations held by a majority of Americans center on opportunity to pursue work, education and training. By availing themselves of these opportunities, it is believed, they will gain access (unparalleled in other societies) to the "good life." This is the credo that brought millions of immigrants to the New World. Let us see how it applies to descendants of the New World's enslaved immigrants.

The American dream, the American promise of which Dr. Horner speaks, produced the American dilemma. America is the "New World" where life, liberty and the pursuit of happiness are the rights of all, regardless of race, creed, color or national origin.

And so enters the dilemma: reconciling this right to pursue life, liberty and happiness without regard to race, creed, color or national origin, in the face of the denial of this right to blacks. This is an old and familiar dilemma to blacks. But in contemporary America, it has been extended to many minority groups and particularly to women.

The arguments legitimizing the subjugation of American blacks have much in common with those justifying the status quo for women—placing the black woman, thus doubly abused, in a profoundly bleak position.

It has been said that intellectually and temperamentally blacks and women are not suited to high-level work responsibilities requiring abstract and rational thinking, or to administrative and supervisory roles—over whites or men. One consequence is that many blacks and women have become victims of a self-image of low self-esteem and are unmotivated to prepare for nontraditional occupations. Remember when the young blacks who did enter and remain in high school were counseled to study a "practical" field, and certainly *not* to pursue a college preparatory course? After all, who would hire them?

Young girls have been encouraged to be nurses rather than doctors, laboratory technicians rather than chemists, bookkeepers rather than accountants or mathematicians, or to be only mothers and wives.

While there have been changes—and this fixed response is no longer treated as an occupational law—we have far to go before either black or white women are treated on their individual merits without prejudice distorting attitudes and conclusions.

Aspirations to nontraditional careers, by blacks and women who somehow overcome these rigid biases, are still frequently met by discriminatory quotas or straightforward exclusions from educational institutions, and by employers. In the past, for both blacks and women, "separate but equal" facilities appeared and remain—Negro colleges: men's, women's and coeducational schools, and colleges for white women. And still persisting from the past into the present, for both groups the financial rewards of their education are proportionately less than those of their counterparts. That is, blacks earn less than whites of the same and even lower educational levels, and women earn less than men who have the same or less amount of education.

Where does this leave the black woman? A member of both minorities! First, most black women are not even part of the work force that is college-prepared and composed of nurses, M.D.'s, bookkeepers, accountants, technicians, and so on. The large majority—about 70 percent in 1969—worked in factories on assembly lines and as laborers, and as service employees. Thus, less than one-third (29 percent) of black women are employed in professional, managerial and clerical occupations. Hispanic and other minority women are in the same position in the labor market. In contrast, among white women over one-half (53 percent) work in these areas while the remaining 46 percent are employed in the factory, service and sales work.[1]

However, for both groups most of the women in the professional, managerial, and clerical category are working in the most menial white-collar jobs—telephone company operators, key-punch operators, and low-level clerical positions. Work conditions are frequently authoritarian, fringe benefits are minimal, and there are few opportunities for promotion and training. Similarly, women in the professions regardless of race, are concentrated in the lowest-paid professional occupations—teachers, social workers, librarians, and nurses—and usually not in administrative positions.

Second, for most black women, choices and options have very little to do with their occupation. A description of the minority worker in the study, *Work in America*, elaborates: "Many look for jobs—the only ones they are likely to get—that they know beforehand they will hate. In effect, minority workers are the unwilling monopolists of the worst jobs that our society has to offer."[2]

For the black woman, those jobs are principally in service positions and as unskilled and semiskilled workers. Forty-four percent of all working black women were employed in menial service occupations as late as 1969—a shockingly high proportion. Almost 18 percent were "operatives and kindred workers," that is, semiskilled factory workers.[3]

Let us look first at those in the service sector of the economy. Historically, it is more typical of black working women than of any other working women, to enter the labor market as domestic workers. Black women are unique among minorities in working-class occupations in having entered the labor market as domestic

1. Raymond S. Franklin and Solomon Resnik, *The Political Economy of Racism*. (New York: Holt, Rinehart & Winston, 1973), pp. 46–47.

2. *Work in America*, Report of a Special Task Force to the Secretary of Health, Education, and Welfare. (Cambridge: The M.I.T. Press, 1972), p. 52.

3. Franklin & Resnik, *Political Economy*, pp. 46–47.

servants rather than directly as factory laborers. Furthermore, it appears that many have remained in that work. Again, as recently as 1969, over four times as many black and other nonwhite women were employed as "private household workers" than were white women.[4]

What are the implications of this "unwilling monopoly" of one of the "worst jobs that our society has to offer"? As an occupation, private household work ranks seventh among eight occupations in which the median incomes for women are *below* the national median income.[5] Thus, first, the concentration of black women in domestic service means that they make up a disproportionately large share of the lowest income groups. Many black women provide either a significant portion of, or the sole support of their families. Yet their wages as domestic servants do not insure a minimally decent living for them and their families.

Nor do these jobs offer hope for a better or at least a more secure future. Their jobs are dead-end and without most fringe benefits. Aside from Social Security provisions, which are not consistently applied, there are no long-range benefits.

A less concrete but equally important implication of the monopoly black women have in domestic service stems from the *quality* of their working life. Their work is drudgery—stultifying and isolating. It lends itself readily to exploitation and above all is degrading. The "Hazel" of television land, presented as an equal in the family, was a cardboard character of preposterous dimensions—a Walt Disney-like view of domestic servantry. This is not to discount the atmosphere of decency and respect for domestic workers' dignity characterizing many private homes employing household workers.

This may be true because of an enlightened employer, or a strong personality of the employee—or both. But the predominant view of maid's work is that it is demeaning, requiring no particular aptitude or training. Tragically, this view is widely held, shared often by those who perform domestic work. The best expression of the impact this experience can have on black

4. Ibid., p. 47.
5. Ibid.

women workers was voiced by a paraprofessional teacher-aide. After she obtained employment in a Head-Start center, enabling her to leave domestic service, she said: "Now I can talk about my work—nobody wants to talk about being a maid. Head-Start work makes me respectable."

Paradoxically, performing the household work our Head-Start worker is ashamed of, has until recently been regarded as a major part of the fundamental and proper role for women who are wives or mothers. Perhaps consigning wives and mothers to this poorly regarded work reveals more about our real attitudes toward women and motherhood than we would openly profess.

The best illustration of our relegating wives or mothers to the boundless virtues of maintaining a clean bathroom and a white wash are the multitude of television commercials that appear as endless as the bacteria they would exterminate.

Once again, parallels between the inhibiting effect of stereotypes applied to women and to blacks come to mind. That which they are judged to be best suited to, by their endowed nature and temperament, is devalued. For the black woman this debasement, again, is a double curse.

Even when she has entered the labor force advancing from domestic service in private households, it usually has been in two fields: service, in jobs similar to household work, and as unskilled labor in factories and shops; once more, work near the bottom of the job hierarchy in almost every respect—salary, security, training required, prestige and so on. The salaries, although higher than for domestic service, are still not enough to provide the decent living this hard labor should afford. And, the quality of working life is barely improved.

Indeed, the legacy for many black women, from association with domestic service, resulted in employment in related capacities—no matter what the setting—as chambermaids and cleaning women certainly, but also in laundries; in maintenance and cleaning jobs in factories and shops; and as kitchen or service workers in hospitals and similar institutions.

In hospitals there has been a respectable amount of upgrading of black women to nurse's aide positions. In most of these work settings, however, another aspect of the legacy of domestic service is often a reluctance to train and promote black women. Parenthetically, unions have helped force management to advance minorities.

An additional consequence of the domestic service monopoly is that too many black women have little experience or contact with organized labor, or with formally organized work associations of any kind. When they do, principally in factory settings, it usually takes the form of relatively passive participation. Union membership is low among black women and there are less than a handful who are union officers at either local or national levels.

It is interesting to note that the occupational category composed principally of unskilled and semiskilled factory workers is that in which similar proportions of both the black female labor force and the white female labor force are employed. Seventeen percent of employed black women and fifteen percent of white working women labored as "operatives and kindred workers" in 1969.[6]

Here then is equality—equality in work settings often with wretched conditions. Yet, for the black women these jobs are a second step on the occupational ladder, after domestic service. For her white coworker, they are the bottom rung of entry. For white women in this society it is considered an advancement to go from factory work to white collar or managerial positions—that is, to get out of the factory. For black women to get out of the kitchen and into a factory is a social advance.

The other full-time occupation of fifty-eight percent of all black working-women in 1969 was as mothers of children under eighteen, in two-parent families. This is a substantially higher proportion than that of white working-mothers in two-parent families, of whom only forty percent had children under eighteen.[7] In a considerable search for statistics, I could find none on a comparison of black and white working-mothers living without a husband.

6. Ibid., p. 46.

7. U.S., Department of Labor, *Summary*, "Children of Working Mothers," Bureau of Labor Statistics, Special Labor Force Report, September 1973, p. 2.

It has been estimated that working women spend an average of forty hours per week on housework and child care.[8] Perhaps this excludes those working women able to afford a "private household worker." At any rate, it is not far from the truth to call the responsibilty of housework and child care of employed women, both black and white, a second occupation.

Black women, however, are much more apt to be working out of dire economic necessity. Most recent findings reveal blacks continuing to make up a grossly disproportionately large share of America's poor—thirty-one percent—while comprising less than twelve percent of all Americans.[9] Consistent with this condition, the official unemployment rate in May of 1975 among black workers (men and women), was almost double that of whites.[10]

Furthermore, the official unemployment rate does not take into account certain conditions which illuminate the problems of all women, and as usual, especially the problems of black women. As the important study *Work in America* has reported, they are "among the millions of people who answer no to the question 'are you seeking work?' but who would in fact desire a job if one were available under reasonably satisfactory conditions." They include: (1) the "millions of women who do not look for . . . employment because they know it is not available at all, or unavailable under conditions that would enable them to discharge their family responsibilities; (2) persons on welfare, many of whom are female heads-of-households, who cannot support their families by holding down the types of jobs available to them; and (3) young women for the most part in low-income families, who remain at home because they find it difficult to secure a suitable job."[11]

8. *Work in America*, p. 64.

9. U.S., Bureau of the Census, *Money Income and Poverty Status of Families and Persons in the United States, 1974–75*. Reported by Eileen Shanahan, "Poor in U.S. Rose by 2.5 Million in 1975 . . . ," *New York Times*, 26 September 1975, p. 1.

10. U.S., Department of Labor, Bureau of Labor Statistics, *Employment and Earnings*, vol. 22, no. 12, p. 27.

11. *Work in America*, pp. 155–56.

Consider these points, now, against the knowledge that black families make up a disproportionately large share of all poor families, and that at the same time a larger proportion of black women with children are employed than are white women with families. When these facts are considered, the unwilling monopoly by black women of "private household work" falls neatly into place.

In the land of the American promise, America's oppressed blacks have suffered in the context of one of the world's wealthiest and most economically developed nations.

Ten years ago Martin Luther King, Jr. said that "pervasive and persistent economic want" is "at the root of the difficulty in Negro life. . . . To grow from within," he said, "the Negro needs only fair opportunity for jobs, education, housing and access to culture. To be strengthened from the outside requires protection from the grim exploitation that has haunted Negro life for three hundred years."[12]

The strength from the outside, and the inner growth of which Martin Luther King, Jr. spoke, refer now—as they did ten years ago—to the need for further legislation and implementation of existing government policies. Legislative enactments and government regulations must continue to buttress the legal climate for the "equal and essential participation" of blacks and of women in American society.

Just as we have found that blacks and women share special oppression, it is equally a fact that certain solutions will apply to each equally. In the most immediate terms this means greater political power through increased voter registration and a federal program of guaranteed full employment.

I am tremendously awed by the strength of black women. The double token they represent in equal opportunity, affirmative action programs, symbolizes their plight. Jo Freeman's interpretation of comments made by Myrdal underlines this plight. "In

12. An Address by Dr. Martin Luther King, Jr., Abbot House, Westchester County, New York, 29 October 1965. In Lee Rainwater and William L. Yancey, *The Moynihan Report and the Politics of Controversy*. (Cambridge: The M.I.T. Press, 1967), p. 408.

a little noted appendix to his monumental study of the American Negro," she notes, "Myrdal wrote that when a legal status had to be found for Negro slaves in the seventeenth century, 'the nearest and most natural analogy was the status of women.' Both groups 'were placed under the jurisdiction of paternal power,' and their main function was defined as freeing the white male from menial concerns."[13]

And currently, Eleanor Holmes Norton has put the matter succinctly: "If women were suddenly to achieve equality with men tomorrow, black women would continue to carry the entire array of utterly oppressive handicaps associated with race."[14]

Many black women have been broken by a cruel society. Many live lives of tragic and hopeless desperation. Many are incredibly strong—stronger than they should have to be. On the basis of characteristics most basic to their personal identity—their sex and their race, physical characteristics with which they were born —black women have been the subject of the most vicious treatment, from benevolent condescension to economic exploitation and physical degradation.

It is remarkable that generations of black women have survived in America as well as they have. It is because of that endurance that their families have survived. Slavery, Reconstruction, migration to the North in the nineteenth and early twentieth centuries, the era of World War II and its aftermath of far-reaching consequences for race relations affecting us most strongly today—each of these periods has seen the black family struggle against incredible oppression and constraints. The specific form of oppression changes, progress is made, but there is *always struggle* against a debilitating array of racist beliefs and practices.

The statistics I have cited present a partial, factual picture of the consequences of these conditions for black women, their families, and thus all blacks. It is imperative to have data on income,

13. Joreen (Jo Freeman), "The 51 Percent Minority Group: A Statistical Essay," in Robin Morgan, ed., *Sisterhood Is Powerful.* (New York: Vintage Books, 1970), p. 44.

14. Eleanor Holmes Norton, "For Sadie and Maude," in R. Morgan, *Sisterhood Is Powerful*, p. 355.

occupation, family status. But my concern is to convey the anguish such figures represent, as much as to cite the figures themselves.

But there is more. As I think we have demonstrated, black women are at the bottom. If we would free all women, then in the struggle to free black women from their crushing burden we do more than simply lift blacks. In the process we are dismantling and dissolving discrimination against all women. There is an inseparability in discrimination—wipe it out for the "least of these" and you wipe it out for all.

As A. Philip Randolph has said, "If you raise those at the bottom of society to enlarge their civil and social rights, you raise everyone above them and the whole society is enriched."

In short, white women will be fighting for their own liberation when they fight for the liberation of black women. The struggle for democracy has always had its primary and derivative results. Hence the bond of solidarity between white women and black women should be the strongest of all components in the women's revolution. Unfortunately it is not yet so.

We still have to examine and strengthen our alliance because it should be evident we are positioned tragically far from the goal of "equal and essential" participants. This is not the era of equality; it is the era of a tumultuous struggle for equality, an equality that must be realized if our nation is to survive.

In Search of a Basis for Mutual Understanding and Racial Harmony

James Baldwin

The subject is terrifying in its elusive—and authoritative—simplicity: one wishes, nearly, to be attempting to decipher it out of the scratches made on some ancient, forgotten stone slab. What an idea, one might then say. And then: I wonder what happened to the poor guy who 'scratched' this! One would take it for granted that he could not have had a very ordinary or a very happy life.

Mutual understanding and racial harmony: one will find almost no one willing to declare himself or herself against it. On the other hand, not one of the presidential candidates, in this bicentennial year, appears to find the subject obsessive. They have another set of priorities—so they themselves would put it. The possibility of understanding and harmony does not appear to take priority anywhere in the world, be it Syria, Lebanon, Israel, Greece, or Africa. Yet one senses that these dreadful struggles are very deeply motivated by this hope—by the hope, at last, of peace—the imponderable question being on what *basis* to achieve it.

Human harmony—or more accurately, social harmony—resides still in the area of the possible, remains for the most part a hope, and is a matter of the most painful speculation. Human conflict is as universal as air, and would seem to be as necessary. And very probably it is, if we wish to stare the question in the face. It may be important to suggest that there is a distinction between *human* conflict and *social* conflict: these feed on and resemble each other, but they are not the same thing. One may even say that the social conflict reveals the failure, or the poverty, brought about by the human conflict.

I do not think that we can hope, ever, to eliminate human conflict, nor do I believe that we should. I think we should learn to use and trust it. Conflict does not necessarily imply murder or hatred or even hostility. Human conflict can be mightily productive—for example, the conflict in the mind which produces the idea, or the conflict in the soul which leads to revelation. The conflict between parent and child, between generations, must be considered as indispensable to the evolving maturity of both. There can be no life without conflict; were this not so, we would never need love, and there is no love without conflict.

This is carrying me somewhat ahead of myself. Our grandiose title is "A Basis for Mutual Understanding and Racial Harmony." Well, this is what the Christian church, to use but one social example, has always described itself as offering. This was the "good news" proclaimed by the gospel. Alas, the church begins with the crucifixion and has been forging nails and hammering these into human flesh every hour on the hour since that day. The "good news" was good news only to those who accepted this good news on the basis dictated by the church. But this basis was not acceptable to everyone. Not everyone wished, nor was able, to be transformed from Saul into Paul. And this is made absolutely clear from the mail we are presently receiving from, for example, Johannesburg, Dakar, Beirut, Dublin, London, and Boston—to say nothing, of course, of Rome.

It would appear that the basis on which the church intended or presumed to establish human harmony proved to be unable to serve this particular human need. The basis on which the fellowship of Christians was offered to the black slave, and then to the American black, was and remains intolerable. The basis for human harmony cannot be established by denying or forbidding to the human being the right to *be*—which means the right to discover—who he or she is. This being said, it must be added—a crucial matter—that people's *right* to be themselves does not necessarily imply that they have any *desire* to be themselves: the self is a journey which many, perhaps most, are reluctant to make. But no one knows enough about this mystery. Certainly I do not. When I was young I, like many others, battled on the side of labor unions and would never have dreamed of crossing a picket line. The hunted labor organizer of that hour has evolved into a fat, racist, neofascist bureaucrat, and the grateful rank and file are defending their rights against all comers, especially the niggers, and slobbering into their television sets. This is not exactly the result which many of us had in mind. But this may be and indeed must be accepted, at least provisionally, as a vivid illustration of human desire. I would like to think that this phenomenon illustrates *frustrated* human desire, but I certainly cannot prove this, and in any case it is probably the height of tragic folly to suppose that one can imagine what another person wants. Just the same, it is very vivid to me that millions of people in this country now cling, in a kind of infantile hysteria, to things they know they do not need and which they do not really want. But they do not let go of these things. They do not know how, do not dare to assume their freedom; the very suspicion of freedom fills them with a mortal dread, which makes them mortally dangerous.

Ancient maps of the world stated that the then unknown and unimaginable void in which America was to be discovered was infernally dangerous territory: "Here," the map says, "be dragons." Everyone believed them then, of course, and besides, as we are now (reluctantly) discovering, they were perfetcly right.

Here, indeed, be dragons: "We hold these truths to be self-evident—that all men are created equal, and are endowed by their Creator with certain inalienable rights." Swing low, sweet chariot! Consider the Dred Scott decision, which stated that a black person had no rights which a white person was bound to respect. Reconsider the so highly overrated Emancipation Proclamation, in which Lincoln freed those slaves he could not reach in order, hopefully, to "destabilize" the Confederate government. Consider that the "freed" slaves not only never received the promised "forty acres and a mule," but were murdered whenever and wherever they attempted to claim anything as their own; consider that this country has never honored a single treaty made with the American Indian; consider how many people were slaughtered by the doctrine of Manifest Destiny.

Consider the reasoned testimony of Frederick Douglass concerning the basis for mutual understanding and racial harmony: "Slave-holders have made it almost impossible for the slave to commit any crime, known either to the laws of God or to the laws of man. If he steals, he takes his own; if he kills his master, he imitates only the heroes of the revolution." (Booker T. Washington did not agree with this at all. He believed, or said that he believed, that in all things pertaining to the common good we could be as one as the hand, and in all things social, as separate as the fingers: but a grateful Republic fastened on the word *separate*. This is almost exactly what happened in our own day with Malcolm X and Martin Luther King, Jr., with the difference that in our day both men found themselves driven, by their common situation, closer and closer together, and also with the difference that whereas Frederick Douglass and Booker T. Washington both died natural deaths, Martin and Malcolm were assassinated.)

Consider that this tension, and Douglass's statement, are absolutely relevant today—in New York's garment center, for example. Douglass's book or its present day equivalent may be in the hip pocket of that boy over there, pushing the truck, and in Boston's Roxbury; in every ghetto, every city in this nation, every reservation within these continental limits and beyond; in every prison, every school; in the hearts of maids, porters, truckdrivers, taxidrivers, singers, comedians, actors, dancers; and in the hearts of brothers (face the meaning of the history of George and Jonathan Jackson!) sisters, sweethearts, mothers and fathers, and small children. Consider, to paraphrase the late Langston Hughes, that this country has always treated black people as "second-class fools"—and then ask yourself on what basis we are likely to arrive at mutual understanding and racial harmony.

I have tried to suggest that human conflict is a necessity which need not debase, which can be ennobling: it is out of this tension that we learn and grow. Everyone, for example, is born into a language: a *particular* language, there being no general ones. Languages are—or reveal—various ways of looking at the world. Language is the word made flesh, and reveals the root human necessity of ordering, or making coherent, the chaos of experience; language is a way of controlling the specific reality into which one is born.

Clearly, then, what is east for England cannot be east for China. Columbus, looking for a passage to India, discovered what is now called the West, and sometimes the Far West—or, depending on one's stars, the North. Well, we are certainly west of something; everybody is. We are also south, east, and north of something; everybody is. One is neither inferior nor superior to the compass: one knows that one must learn to read it, since all seas are rough. One is neither superior nor inferior to a language. One learns a language by exposing oneself to the assumptions of this language. These unspoken assumptions contain the key to the people who were born into this language, who live it, who form it every day and who are being formed by it every day; thus one begins to glimpse something of the way in which one is oneself endlessly forming and endlessly being formed.

There is no such thing as a "civilized" or an "uncivilized" language; the language *is* the civilization, or at the very least, reveals it. It may be an appalling civilization, from my point of view; but so is the civilization into which I was born, from another or from many other points of view—or indeed, from my own point of view, even though I was born into this particular civilization. There can exist no civilization which does not have its appalling, even barbaric aspects, but this does not mean that it is not a civilization any more than it means that the people who are creating it and who are being created by it are not people.

Some of the things I have seen in other countries appalled me. I am not accustomed to (physically) deformed children, one-eyed beggars, men amputated from the waist down, scavengers circling the city or the village streets. So I say; I am on far more dubious ground if I proclaim myself shocked by the sight of women as chattel, or when I imagine myself as being no longer accustomed to latrines. I, born a Christian, found myself offended by the sight and sound and smell of so much unregenerate flesh.

But this says far more about me than it says about the people I flattered myself as observing, and whom I failed to see. For the children of Sunset Boulevard are at least equally devastated, and I have encountered more than one blind and stinking beggar in the executive suites and mansions of my own country. They were, however dreadfully, my countrymen: I did not want to see what I saw. And they were not foreign. They were too familiar for me to take refuge in "observing" them. An observer is never touched or threatened, and can therefore produce volumes of authoritative detail concerning those others who, crucially, are not the observer. The details so authoritatively and painlessly amassed, as in political polls and public questionnaires, convey various reflexes (known as "facts") and have nothing whatever to do with the truth—the truth being contained in the point of view, and still more in the journey which creates the point of view. No matter, for example, how hostile or friendly the South Boston housewife or hardhat may be, neither she nor he can possibly convey the real reasons for their anguish and terror. The anguish and terror are real. They suppose, since they have no easy means of arriving at any other supposition, that they do not want their children to go to school with niggers, do not want their neighborhoods destroyed, do not want the government "interfering" in their lives. They were poor too, and never asked for anything, and anyone who really wants to can prosper in this country. These are "facts."

But the truth is that the point of view dictated by their unlearned history has precipitated these people into nothing less than paranoia. The truth is that the presence of the nigger has prevented them from realizing that they themselves are treated no better than niggers: if they had not forced themselves to forget the real reasons for their voyage, they might be better equipped to bear the promised land. The truth is that their neighborhoods are always being destroyed. The truth is that their government has deliberately placed them in their dreadful position, and manipulates every hour of every day they live. The truth is that the poor whites are absolutely indispensable for the maintainance of the status quo, and madly forge the chains which bind them, imagining that these chains are for blacks only. They, because they are white, can become anything at all—movie stars, labor leaders, president—and everything they see around them, God knows, would seem to prove it. They know that they are free, freedom being a matter of getting the other fellow before he gets you.

On what basis can this panic-stricken multitude conceive of mutual understanding and racial harmony?

Mutual understanding is possible only among people who accept that they have something in common, and when whatever they have in common does not menace them. Blacks and whites, in this country, and especially in the South, have a very great deal in common, but they can scarcely put this quantity to any affirmative use, since they are forced to approach it from such different points of view.

For example, both my father and Governor Wallace's father must have known something about cotton fields, but the fact that they held this knowledge in common did not create between them any possibility of mutual understanding. The cotton field had to represent to white people the possibility of freedom from toil, of power—however insanely occult this may sound—and their imaginations dared not allow them to assume for an instant that this same field of cotton could represent the same possibility for a black person. Objective reality, moreover—that is, the reality of white power—appeared to prove the white person right.

To find a basis for mutual understanding in such a context amounts to demanding the impossible; asking whites to relinquish their dream of safety, their grasp or their hope of power, is the same thing as demanding that they alter, indeed surrender, their identity.

And were the social context less forbidding, this might not be impossible. In terms of the human conflict, this alteration, surrender, and re-creation of oneself keeps life and love and ourselves alive. This is how we re-create each other.

But the virulence of the social conflict has very nearly obliterated the possibilities of the human one, for we cannot reach each other. So long as whites cannot transcend the point of view bequeathed them by their history, blacks can approach them only, in essence, as beggars. Even this was possible, and relatively (and rigorously) fruitful, for a time. But that time is behind us. The white people of this country (to speak *only* of this country) consider that they have now given all that they can give. There is in this a dreadful and despairing accuracy: one has only to consider how little black people have been given, if indeed, upon examining the record, one can conclude that black people have been "given" anything at all.

But who truly can blame the maverick, the outcast, the convict, the immigrant, who became the white American, for moving on up the ladder? That is what a ladder is for. Who can be certain, given such options, that he or she would, or could, have acted differently? The suffering which drove these people to these shores was a real suffering; let us not pretend otherwise. And their suffering here was real; let us not pretend otherwise. For nothing is easier than falling into the human trap—and here, the specifically American one—of forgetting one's own suffering; with this lapse of memory the suffering of others has simply no reality. And the principal American motion is flight: the flight from misery, anonymity, pain, death. The survivor may feel a distant pain for the wretched, but rejoices that he or she is not among them. The poor are always with us, and one may feel obliged to lend the poor a helping hand—what a revealing phrase!—but on the whole it is easier, and finally becomes mandatory, to ignore them.

Perhaps the basis of mutual understanding and racial harmony awaits the day when the wretched become "we"—which means there will be no more wretched. History has not recorded such a day, but the human being records such a vision with tenacity. No person has ever lived to see his or her work finished, but that does not mean that the work was not done.

The very phrase "mutual understanding and racial harmony" is produced by the history and the people responsible for this present devastation. This is not a sneer, but it is not an unfair observation, either. Mutual understanding and racial harmony were not among the British concerns, so long as their empire was intact and visible and their power unchallenged. They were merciless in India and in Palestine, for example, without giving a thought to mutual understanding; and racial harmony was not among their concerns when they sent gunboats down the Chinese river. Neither are the United States Marines famous for their powers of seduction or persuasion, and neither they nor the domestic American police force feel any very vivid need for mutual understanding and racial harmony. The Black Panthers Fred Hampton and Mark Clark (to name but two), who may really have had an interest in understanding and harmony, were simply murdered by the police in cold blood, as they lay in bed, and the police were protected by the American state in the name of the American people. One could multiply examples infinitely; presently, pleas for understanding and harmony will be coming out of South Africa. In short, to put it brutally, mutual understanding and racial harmony are summoned when white people feel in need of them, and not before.

This means that their plea cannot be heard.

It is important, I think, to state the case harshly: a mutual, self-serving courtesy has had its day. It is true that I do not hate white people—now. This is due to mysteries of temperament, luck, and my private history, and my sense that hatred is always, in the depths, self-hatred; I decided, somehow, not to destroy myself that way. But I certainly must have hated white people once, and if I did, no person alive can deny that I would have had profound and unanswerable reasons for that hatred. And this is what we must face, if we are ever to get beyond it: the history of white people includes their sustained attempt to murder me, and mine. By many millions this is all that is known about white people, and indeed, in order to learn anything more than this, one must get beyond the terrifying gate created by white misuse of power.

Black people are human too, but are not intrinsically more noble than other human beings. If the crimes committed against black people were merely historical, located safely in the past, all might be forgotten. But history does not work that way; history *is* the present. It cannot be otherwise, since the human being is the vehicle of history. And in the present, therefore, the panic-stricken, blind intransigence on the part of white people will make yet bloodier the social conflict, and all but submerge the human one.

We cannot hope to establish a basis for mutual understanding and racial harmony as long as so many of the wretched of the earth are doomed to this condition by their color, or as long as so much of the world's riches is exploited by so few. Inexorably, then, we are living through the end of an era, and our children's children's lives will depend on the courage which we must summon now to face this mighty crisis of identity.

Response

Toni Morrison

In *The Historical Statistics of the United States from Colonial Times to 1957*, right after *rice*, and just before *tar* and *turpentine* are the humans. The rice is measured by pounds; the pitch, tar and turpentine by the barrelweight. In the *Historical Statistics of the United States from Colonial Times to 1957* where this information is found, there was no way to measure—by pound, tonnage, or barrelweight—the humans. Head-count served the purpose of measuring. This same reference book of "Statistics" is full of fascinating information, not the least of which is Series Z 281–303 which documents, in chronological order and by point of destination, the import and export of humans in the United States from 1619 to 1769. Every effort seems to have been made to assure the accuracy of the tables. Below the neat columns of figures, footnotes seem to apologize for the occasional lapses from complete information. "We are sorry," the Bureau of Census seems to be saying, "that better records were not kept or available to us. The country was just getting itself together, you understand, and things were less than efficient."

One senses reasonableness and gentlemanly assertion everywhere in these pages. But it is reasonableness without the least hope of success, for the language itself cracks under the weight of its own implications. Footnote 3, for example, under *Slaves* clarifies the ambiguity of its reference with the following words: "Source shows seventy-two Indian slaves imported; 231 slaves died and 103 drawn back for exportation. "Died" . . . "drawn back" —strange, violent words that could never be used to describe rice, or tar, or turpentine. Footnote 5, by far the coolest in its civilized accuracy, is as follows: "Number of Negroes shipped, not those actually arrived." There was a difference, apparently, between the number shipped and the number that arrived. The mind gallops to the first unanswered question: How many? How many were shipped? How many did not arrive? Then the mind slides toward the next question—the vital one that withers all others: Who? Who was absent at the final head-count? Was there a seventeen-year-old girl there with a tree-shaped scar on her knee? And what was her name?

I do not know why it is so difficult to imagine and therefore to realize a genuinely humane society—whether the solutions lie in natural sciences, the social sciences, theology or philosophy or even belles lettres. But the fact is that the Historical Statistics of the United States is pretty much like what the contours of this society are now and have always been: the equating of human beings with commodity, lumping them together in alphabetical order—when even the language used to describe these acts bends and breaks under that heavy and alien responsibility. The gentle souls, these dedicated civil servants of the census bureau, do not create facts, they simply record them. But their work, I believe, reflects the flaw which obstructs the imagination and the realization of a humane society. Such a society would be one in which the thrust of the acculturation process (otherwise known as education) is toward the creation of members of a society who can make humane decisions—and who *do.* It is a society which refuses to continue to produce generation after generation of citizens who are *trained* to make distinctions between the deserving poor and the undeserving poor, but *not* between rice and human beings; to make distinctions between an expedient life and an indispensable one, but *not* between slaves and turpentine; trained to determine who shall flourish and who shall wither, but *not* between the weight of a barrel and the sanctity of a human head.

That is what indexes are like, of course; not the fan-shaped spread of rice bursting from a gunnysack; not the thunder of barrels of turpentine cascading down a plank; and not a seventeen-year-old girl with a tree-shaped scar on her knee—and a name. History is percentiles, the thoughts of great men, and the description of eras. Does the girl know that the reason she died in the sea or in a twenty-foot deep slop-pit on a ship named *Jesus* is because that was her era; or that some great men thought up her destiny for her as part of a percentage of national growth, or expansion, or Manifest Destiny, or colonialization of a new world? It is awkward to differ from a great man, but Tolstoi was wrong. Kings are not the slaves of history. History is the slave of kings.

The matrix out of which these powerful decisions are born is sometimes called *racism,* sometimes *classicism,* sometimes *sexism.* Each is an accurate term surely, but each is also misleading. The source is a deplorable inability to project, to become the "other" to *imagine* him. It is an intellectual flaw, a shortening of the imagination, and reveals an ignorance of gothic proportions as well as a truly laughable lack of curiosity. Of course historians cannot deal with rice, grain by grain; they have to deal with it in bulk. But dependence on that discipline should not be so heavy that it leads us to do likewise in human relationships. One of the major signs of intelligence, after all, is the ability to make distinctions, small distinctions. We judge an intellect by the ease with which it can tell the difference between one molecule and another, one cell and another, between a Bordeaux of 1957 and one of 1968, between mauve and orchid, between the words *wrest* and *pry*, between clabber and buttermilk, between CHANEL No. 5 and CHANEL No. 16. It would seem then, that to continue to see a race of people as one single personality is an ignorance so vast, a perception so blunted, imagination so bleak that no nuance, no subtlety, no difference among them can penetrate—except the large differences: who shall flourish and who shall wither, who deserves state assistance and who does not, which may explain why we are left with pretty much the same mental equipment in 1976 that we had in 1776. This intelligence is so crippled that it could, as a white professor did in 1905, ask W. E. B. DuBois "whether colored people shed tears"; is also crippled enough to study the "genetic" influences on intelligence of a race so mixed that any experimental data similarly performed on mice would fall apart at the outset.

If education is about anything other than being able to earn more money, that other thing is intelligent problem-solving and humans relating to each other in mutually constructive ways. But the education (the acculturation process) in this country has always considered the cooperation among human beings, and mutually constructive goals fourth- and fifth-rate concerns where they were concerns at all. The history of the country is all the proof one needs that it is so. The rejection of the concept of what Mr. Baldwin has called "mutual understanding and racial harmony" has pervaded this country from the beginning.

Now no one can fault the conqueror for writing history the way he sees it, and certainly not for digesting human events and discovering their patterns according to his point of view. But we *can* fault him for not owning up to what his point of view is. It might prove a useful exercise, in this regard, to look at some of the things our conquerors (our forefathers), our men of vision and power in America have actually said.

Andrew Jackson, December 3, 1833:

> Indians have neither the intelligence, the industry, the moral habits, nor the desire of improvement which are essential to any favorable change in their condition. Established in the midst of another and a superior race, and without appreciating the causes of their inferiority or seeking to control them, they must necessarily yield to the force of circumstances and ere long disappear.

The Nature of a Humane Society

Theodore Roosevelt (to Owen Wister) 1901:

I entirely agree with you that as a race, and in the mass, the [blacks] are altogether inferior to the whites.

I suppose I should be ashamed to say that I take the Western view of the Indian. I don't go so far as to think that the only good Indians are the dead Indians, but I believe nine out of every ten are, and I shouldn't inquire too closely into the case of the tenth. The most vicious cowboy has more moral principle than the average Indian.

General Ulysses S. Grant (to General Webster):

La Grange, Tenn., November 10, 1862

Give orders to all the conductors on the road that no Jews are to be permitted to travel on the railroad southward from any point. They may go north and be encouraged in it, but they are such an intolerable nuisance that the department must be purged of them.

General Order:

Holly Springs, Miss., December 8, 1862

On account of the scarcity of provisions all cotton speculators, Jews, and other vagrants having no honest means of support, except trading upon the misery of the country . . ."

Sam Houston, U.S. Senate, 1848:

The Anglo-Saxon (must) pervade the whole southern extremity of this vast continent. . . . (The) Mexicans are no better than the Indians and I see no reason why we should not take their land.

Freeman's Journal, March 4, 1848:

Our object is to show, once more, that Protestantism is effete, powerless, dying out though disturbed only by the proper gangrenes, and conscious that its last moment is come when it is fairly set, face to face, with Catholic truth.

Richard Pike, Boston, 1854:

Catholicism is, and it ever has been, a bigoted, a persecuting, and a superstitious religion. There is no crime in the calendar of infamy of which it has not been guilty. There is no sin against humanity that it has not committed. There is no blasphemy against God which it has not sanctioned. It is a power which has never scrupled to break its faith solemnly plighted, wherever its interests seem to require it; which has no conscience; which spurns the control of public opinion; and which obtrudes its head among the nations of Christendom, dripping with the cruelties of millions of murders, and haggard with the debaucheries of a thousand years, always ambitious, always sanguinary, and always false.

New York Tribune, 1854:

The Chinese are uncivilized, unclean and filthy beyond all conception without any of the higher domestic or social relations; lusty and sensual in their disposition; every female is a prostitute of the basest order.

General William Sherman:

We must act with vindictive earnestness against the Sioux, even to their extermination—men, women and children. Nothing else will reach the root of this case. The more we can kill this year, the less will have to be killed the next war, for the more I see of these Indians the more convinced I am that all have to be killed or maintained as a species of pauper.

Benjamin Franklin:

Why increase the sons of Africa, by planting them in America, where we have so fair an opportunity (by excluding all blacks and tawnies), of increasing the lovely white and red?

William Byrd, Virginia, 1710–12:[1]

2/8/09: Jenny and Eugene were whipped.
4/17/09: Anaka was whipped.
5/13/09: Mrs. Byrd whips the nurse.
5/23/09: Moll was whipped.
6/10/09: Eugene (a child) was whipped for running away and had the bit put on him.
9/3/09: I beat Jenny . . .
9/16/09: Jenny was whipped.
9/19/09: I beat Anama . . .
11/30/09: Eugene and Jenny were whipped.
12/16/09: Eugene was whipped for doing nothing yesterday.

(In April I was occupied in my official capacity in assisting the investigation of slaves "arraigned for high treason"—two were hanged.)

7/1/10: The Negro woman ran away again with the bit on her mouth.
7/8/10: The Negro woman was found and tied but ran away again in the night.
7/15/10: My wife against my will caused little Jenny to be burned with a hot iron . . .
8/22/10: I had a severe quarrel with little Jenny and beat her too much for which I was sorry.
8/31/10: Eugene and Jenny beaten.
10/8/10: I whip three slave women.
11/6/10: The Negro woman ran away again.

1. His diary. Its editors describe him as Virginia's most polished and ornamental gentleman . . . a kindly master who inveighed in some of his letters against brutes who mistreat their slaves.

Such is the language, the vision, the memory bequeathed us in this society. They said other things, and they did other things—some of which were good. But they also said, and more importantly felt, *that.* When Mr. Baldwin speaks of the failure of social conflict that arises out of the failure of human conflict I believe that I know precisely what he means.

Our past is bleak, our future dim. But I am not reasonable. A reasonable man adjusts to his environment, an unreasonable man does not. All progress, therefore, depends on the unreasonable man. I prefer not to adjust to my environment. I refuse the prison of "I" of which Mr. Baldwin spoke, and choose the open spaces of "we."

With such a past we cannot be optimistic about the possibility of a humane society ever becoming imagined and therefore realized. We cannot be optimistic, but we can be clear. We can identify the enemy; know the difference between fever and the disease, between racism and greed. We can be clear and we can be careful, careful to avoid the imprisonment of the mind, the spirit and the will of ourselves and those among whom we live. We can be careful of tolerating second-rate goals and second-hand ideas.

We are humans, humans who must have discovered by now what every three-year-old can see: "that the whole business of reproducing and dying by the billions is unsatisfactory and clumsy." We are humans, not rice, and therefore "we have not yet encountered any god who is as merciful as a man who flicks a beetle over on its feet. There is not a people in the world who behaves as badly as praying mantises. We are the moral inhabitants of the globe. To deny this, regardless of our feeble attempts to live up to it, is to lie in prison. Of course there is cruelty. Cruelty is a mystery. But if we see the world as one long brutal game, then we bump into another mystery, the mystery of beauty, the light of the canary that sings on the skull. . . . Unless all ages and all races of man have been deluded . . . there seems to be such a thing as grace, such a thing as beauty, such a thing as harmony . . . all wholly free and available to us."

Meaning, Purpose, and Belonging in Life

Norman Cousins

The assignment given me is concerned with human purpose. Clearly this involves philosophy. Yet philosophy is never a finished garment. One grows into it. Year by year individuals are shaped by the sights, the sounds, the ideas around them. Consciously or not, we are forever adding to or subtracting from the sum total of our beliefs or attitudes or responses, or whatever it is we mean when we say that a person has a certain outlook on life. This is not to say that clearly defined philosophies are inevitably subordinated to the total impact of individual experience. My purpose rather is to suggest that it is one of the prime glories of the human mind that the same idea or experience is never absorbed in precisely the same way by any two individuals who may be exposed to it.

In this sense, each human being is a process—a filtering process of retention or rejection, absorption or loss. The process gives a person individuality. It determines whether one justifies the gift of human life or whether one lives and dies without having been affected by the beauty of wonder and the wonder of beauty, without having had any real awareness of kinship or human fulfillment.

There is a question, however, of whether any individual is capable of recognizing and defining the essence of his own individuality. Can a camera photograph itself? In a mirror, perhaps; but even the mirror sees only the outside of the box. A mind that attempts to perceive itself uses the tools of language and logic. But the material with which it deals is beyond mere words or reason. The marrow of human thought or personality eludes its own product, human analysis—even with the most scientific instrumentation.

My own philosophical garment was the product of two world wars. When I was old enough to think creatively about politics and philosophy, the aftermath of war and depression laid strong hands on my ideas, and the old and accepted systems of thought and politics seemed feeble and irrelevant, fit for museums or textbooks but not for the throbbing issues of the day. I was being propelled into a world which was as reluctant and unprepared to receive my generation—or so we thought—as we were to become a part of it. When the New Deal came along, the more conservative among us took hope and root in it, for which we were damned as timid experimentalists by our more politically adventurous contemporaries, and as irresponsible revolutionaries by our elders.

The books we read and the plays we saw and the things we talked about added up to a sort of philosophy of orphanism; to paraphrase Mr. Housman and Mr. Farrell, we were in a world we never made, and there was nothing to indicate that it would ever be any different. When we surveyed the future, it was like looking out over a frozen tundra; if the thaw ever came, we were certain it would be in some far-off age. To be sure, there was excitement over the Oxford pledge and over Marxism and over the economic interpretation of history and over the debunking of the hero. But all these were flurries and not the real thing. For the fact was that we lacked any real adhering surface to which ideas might stick.

Archibald MacLeish some years later summed it up in the word *irresponsibles*. It was the irresponsibility of default rather than of design. How did you go about being responsible when you weren't sure what responsibility meant?

The paradox, of course, was that we were being intellectually static in a politically dynamic world. This is not to say that we were unaware of, or uninterested in, the bulging and threatening shape of things to come. But these were things without impact; we could see them and take note of them, but they were outside us. It was like blinking at the size and speed of an oncoming locomotive while standing on the track.

Such was the curious sense of unreality and wasted motion, the sense of separation from our times. It didn't last—it couldn't. But the circumstances of the awakening weren't the same in every case. Some of us emerged gradually, moved along by the momentum of events; others had to be blasted out of it by the war, and still others by the continuing crisis following the war. And some of us, apparently, haven't come out of it yet.

In my own case, at least, the winds that blew from the East helped to ventilate my thinking and to clear off the foggy negativism that was the fashion of the time. I remember reading in 1937 about Gandhi for the first time in a form more substantial than scattered newspaper accounts. It was a book by Romain Rolland. It combined a short, highlight biography of Gandhi with an account of the ideas of Gandhi and those of Tagore, dramatizing the importance of this dualism in awakening India. In some respects it was like the Hamilton-Jefferson controversy, with important elements of the philosophy of each coming together to create a vital blend. Gandhi approached mankind through India; Tagore approached India through mankind.

What impressed me most about Gandhi was not only his philosophy, impressive though it was under the special conditions in India, or the effectiveness of nonviolence, for the technique was frequently at odds with the philosophy behind it. What impressed me most was the dramatic proof that individuals need not be helpless against massed power—that they need not be overwhelmed by any supposed inexorabilism or fatalism, that there was scope for free will and conviction in the shaping of society, that history could be fluid, not fixed, if people were willing to transcend their egos in order to merge themselves with the larger body of mankind.

It is difficult to describe adequately my sense of wonder at all this, for an idea that until then seemed beyond debate or even speculation was that of the utter domination of the individual person by his or her times. Since you had never questioned it, you never had to think about it. History was the ocean—alternately calm and turbulent—and the individual was the rudderless vessel. As for the great leaders and commanding figures of history, you had been in the habit of seeing them as products rather than as architects of their times. But Gandhi didn't fit into the conventional role of the historical leader. He was in no position of power, nor did he seek power. He exercised leadership without being an official leader. He was a person, "Anyman," demonstrating the practical value of ethics as applied to political problems. The response of the Indian people to him is one of the most stirring chapters in history.

In reading Rolland, it was clear that Gandhi's teaching and his noncooperation movement were enriched and invigorated as the result of Tagore's ceaseless prodding in behalf of universalism. Tagore recognized the danger to the world of yet another purely nationalist movement. He could see that the Gandhi movement might get beyond Gandhi, that the heat generated by noncooperation could become the fever of a national authoritarianism. India's problem, as Tagore saw it, was inseparable from the world problem. "No nation can find its own salvation by breaking away from the others. The awakening of India is bound up in the awakening of the world." I can recall now the thrill I felt in reading Tagore's poetic definition of universalism:

> Where the mind is without fear and the head is held high;
> Where knowledge is free;
> Where the world has not been broken up into fragments by
> narrow domestic walls;
> Where words come out from the depth of truth;
> Where tireless striving stretches its arms toward perfection;
> Where the clear stream of reason has not lost its way into
> the dreary desert sand of dead habit;
> Where the mind is led forward by thee into ever-widening
> thought and action—
> Into that heaven of freedom, my Father, let my country awake.

What was happening in India made me feel foolish for having been mired so long in the futility that was the fashion of my generation. Compared to India's, our problems were as wisps of smoke alongside a thunderhead. And yet, India was moving toward freedom precisely because a philosophy compounded of affirmation, action, compassion, and universalism was giving inspiration and direction to countless millions who were learning to think about the idea of freedom for the first time.

It was natural that the momentum generated by Gandhi and Tagore should carry me back to a reappraisal of American history and the American philosophers, and it was even more natural, perhaps, that I should begin with Emerson, with whom the Indian thinkers seemed to have such a rich affinity. What formerly had seemed to me in Emerson to be a collection of bland philosophical truisms somewhat in the lavender tradition now came alive with force and distinction. As in Gandhi and Tagore, there was the rigorous assertion of individual integrity and purpose as a foundation for service to the general welfare. There was the Gandhian disdain in Emerson for conformity and convention: "Every true man is a cause, a country, and an age; requires infinite spaces and numbers and time fully to accomplish his design; and posterity seems to follow his steps as a train of clients." Then, in a one-line distillation of the Gandhi philosophy, Emerson wrote, "Nothing can bring you peace but the triumph of principles." Dozens of others had said it before Emerson; he brought it into rich focus.

Emerson defined both the power and responsibility of the individual in a complex society. He saw a wide and fertile field for individual action in advancing the general welfare. He didn't believe that mankind collectively or people individually need feel they were incarcerated by history. The individual did belong. No state, no custom, no convention, could alter or destroy that fact. Then, almost as though he were anticipating one of the great debates of the twentieth century—the debate over inevitability and the "wave of the future"—Emerson wrote that we were not at the "mercy of any waves of chance. . . . In dealing with the state, we ought to remember that its institutions are not aboriginal, that they are not superior to the citizen, that one of them was once the act of a single man, that every law and usage was a man's expedient to meet a particular case, that they are all limitable, all alterable."

Emerson led to Holmes, and Holmes to William James, and James to John Dewey. The combination led me to question the direction in which my education had taken me. My conventional education had prepared me for life in Western civilization and, beyond that, for a bird's-eye view of the world. Terms such as *Western civilization* or *Christendom* became stock phrases or slogans—without any real comprehension of the fact that what is finest in the Western tradition is universal and not geographic. We read books or articles about the uniqueness of our Western values with little acknowledgement of the cross-fertilization of ideas and cultures between East and West. We blandly assumed that everyone knew precisely what it was we were talking about when we used the term *Western values.*

These values, of course, were connected to human individuality and to philosophical affirmation. Even here, qualifiers were necessary, for the natural rights of man have never been more finely defined than under Confucianism. We can also reflect that the political and philosophical corruption of Platonism led in a direct line to authoritarianism in the modern world. Nor ought we ever to forget that Christianity originated in the East, or the fact that there is an organic connection between the Koran and the Old and New Testaments.

The result of this exaggeration of the nature of the separation between East and West was a new illiteracy, the illiteracy of those who can read or write but who are unable to comprehend the totality and interrelationship of history. It is the illiteracy of those who exist in the second half of the twentieth century but who do not participate in it. It is the illiteracy of those who are unprepared for the building of a world community. They may have been educated to make them aware of the differences that keep people apart, but they are tragically ignorant of the basic similarities that can bring people together. No community neighborhood has ever been smaller than the world neighborhood is today, in the sense that every person's welfare and destiny is interlocked with everyone else's, yet the preparation for living in that community is severely deficient.

Whatever the uncertainties about the future may be, of one

fact we can be sure. The present generation of Americans and the next generation and the generations after that will have to operate in a world arena. They will have to be at home in many lands and among many peoples. They will have to talk many languages and comprehend many philosophies, psychologies, and approaches that are still uncharted in much of present-day education. They will need special knowledge, certainly; but they will need something far more important—an intense awareness of the conditions under which those values can be created and maintained.

The basic reality in our time is geographic compression. Far-flung areas that had been secure in their remoteness have been jammed together in a single arena. "Higher education" had indeed become a misnomer in light of the new needs. What seemed adequate at the turn of the century for the purposes of top-level education fulfills only an intermediate function at best. The danger described so well by Whitehead—that events might outrun mankind and leave it a panting and helpless anachronism—has become more than a figure of speech.

How to educate for a decompartmentalized world? How to gain acceptance for the idea that life is the highest value? How to prepare for citizenship in the human community? The place to begin, it seemed to me, was with the fact that the universe itself does not hold life cheaply. Life is a rare occurrence among the billions of galaxies and solar systems that occupy space. And in this particular solar system life occurs on only one planet. And on that planet life takes millions of forms. Of all those countless forms of life, only one, the human species, possesses certain faculties in combination that give it supreme advantages over all the others. Among those faculties or gifts is a creative intelligence that enables mankind to reflect, anticipate, and speculate, to encompass past experience and also to visualize future needs. There are endless other wondrous faculties, the mechanisms of which are not yet within the understanding of their beneficiaries—the faculties of hope, conscience, appreciation of beauty, kinship, love, faith.

Viewed in this planetary perspective, what counts is not that the thoughts of people lead them in different directions but that all people possess the capacity to think; not that they pursue different faiths but that they are capable of spiritual belief; not that they write and read different books but that they are capable of creating print and communicating in it across time and space; not that they enjoy different art and music but that something in them enables them to respond deeply to forms and colors and ordered vibrations of sounds.

These basic lessons, then, would seek to provide a proper respect for humanity in the universe. However friendly the universe may be to mankind, it has left the conditions of human existence precariously balanced. All people need oxygen, water, land, warmth, food. Remove any one of these and the unity of human needs is attacked, and man with it.

The next lesson would concern the human situation itself—how to use self-understanding in the cause of human welfare; how to control the engines created by mankind that threaten to alter the complex conditions on which life depends; how to create a peaceful society of the whole.

With such an education, it is possible that some nation or people may come forward not only with vital understanding but with the vital inspiration that people need no less than they need food. Leadership on this higher level does not require mountains of gold or thundering propaganda. It is concerned with human destiny. Human destiny is the issue; people will respond.

In terms of a working philosophy, out of this expedition in ideas and morals came the confirmation and enlargement of the doctrine not only of natural liberty but of natural scope in creating liberty. I had come a long way from the cynicism and disillusion which had soured much of my earlier thinking. And little by little, I could see the evidence growing all around me that many others of my generation were reexamining their beliefs against the background of an accelerating history. Nazism and nihilism were joined and mobilized, and people were being killed; it dawned on many of us that notions of futility were an intellectual luxury, that the threat was alive and real, and that decisions might have to be made that we had thought need never be made again.

It was at this point that the second step or challenge in the general design of my reeducation asserted itself. Admitting that there was no retreat for the individual and that he or she could find no refuge in fatalism or determinism, what kind of world were people trying to build—assuming that the world could be saved for the rebuilding? T. S. Eliot said it about Munich:

> The feeling which was new and unexpected was a feeling of humiliation, which seemed to demand an act of personal contrition, of humility, repentance and amendment; what had happened was something in which one was deeply implicated and responsible. . . . Was our society, which had always been so assured of its superiority and rectitude, so confident of its unexamined premises, assembled round anything more permanent than a congeries of banks, insurance companies and industries, and had it any beliefs more essential than a belief in compound interest and the maintenance of dividends?

Just as earlier I had to reexamine my own place in society, and the potentiality of the individual for ethical action, so now I reexamined my ideas on the nature of society itself, on the potentialities within the group for ethical ideas and action, and, in general, on government as an organism with a metabolic rate of its own, a conscience of its own, and a life cycle of its own. Unlike the previous search, which began with Gandhi and went weaving in and out with no fixed pattern, stretching over the entire history of ideas, this search came to rest in two areas; classical Greece and late eighteenth-century America.

Greece offered the example of a civilization that, on the basis of the evidence, seemed to have passed into decay, not because it had become moribund, but primarily because of sheer human error. America was a nation designed on a drawing board. The architects understood error in government as did no other group assembled before or since. Greece's golden age was abruptly terminated precisely because the city-states themselves, in their dealings with one another, lacked a mechanism for destroying or correcting the errors of the whole. With the American Constitution-makers, the concept of the inevitability of error, and the specific means required to deal with it, represented one of the chief building blocks of the new government.

I use the word *error* not just in the familiar sense of blunder or mistake, but in the broader sense of avoidable failure. For history can be viewed as an accumulation of error: the nature of the error and the thought proceeding out of error often determine the rate of progress and the type of progress. Indeed, the story of people and nations is largely the story of their attitudes toward error. The less democratic a society, the smaller the margin for error of its subjects and the greater the margin for error of its rulers. The more arbitrary the definition of error, the less important the machinery of justice. The more protection error receives in high places, the less scope for public opinion and an ungoverned press.

Apart from the errors committed by the highly privileged citizens of Greece under the double standard of virtue and morality that existed between themselves and their slaves, there was the endless series of errors in the dealings among the Greek city-states themselves. The great similiarities among the peoples were no bar to war; indeed, it almost seemed as though their mutualities lubricated their antagonisms. What was missing was the means of bringing order into their collective life—the life of the city-states in their relations with one another. They made the mistake of attempting to seek national security through military coalitions or balanced power. They failed to face up to the need for federation among themselves and the need for a rule of law which federation alone might have provided. Their leaders were unwilling to effect a larger junction except on their own terms, which is to say, domination of all others. Besides, as James Madison later observed, the last place in the world to look for the basic motive power for federation is officialdom, for it is unreasonable to expect rulers voluntarily to turn in their seals of office and accept a lesser role; the psychology of power and leadership has little margin for subordination. The motive power for larger law would have to be supplied by the people themselves. But this, too, was lacking.

These failures and mistakes made a profound impression on the American federalists. The function of the Constitution-makers, as Hamilton and Madison saw it, was to build "monuments" to experience. They recognized two broad categories of error. The first grew out of the neglect or violation of principles. The second was on the operational or functional level, and proceeded out of the fallibility of humanity. As they saw it, then, theirs was a dual responsibility. They had to establish a framework of principle within which states could live side by side on a fairly rational basis. Next, they had to provide the people with the means of coping with error—inevitable error—by their elected and appointed officials.

On the level of principles, this meant that states within a geographic unit must have binding obligations among themselves for the greater safety of all. But these obligations were to be limited to those matters affecting the common security and welfare. In all matters pertaining to the relationships of the states to one another, particularly when and where there were disputes, the central government was to have jurisdiction.

On thc operational level, error was taken for granted. No person was deemed wise enough to be free of error. The important thing was to limit the effect of those errors by depriving their makers of the natural secrecy in which errors breed and multiply. If one branch of the government made the error of attempting to arrogate too much power to itself, another branch of the government should be able to correct it, or at least to call public attention to it. The highest office in the land, for example, must not be immune to or isolated from free and open criticism. The general term to describe the process was *checks and balances*; more accurately, perhaps, it was the "error theory of government." In short, there must not only be an accounting *of* error, but an accounting *for* error.

The history of early Greece and the constitutional period of American history deepened and reinforced my conviction against historical determinism. Greek civilization died, not because of any natural laws or life cycles affecting nations, but because the Greek peoples were unable to avert the final error of war. It was only a matter of time before they would fight the one war from which they could not recover. Nor did historical determinism operate in the founding of the United States. Here was a magnificent example of the scope and power of free will and decision in the affairs of humanity. It was a bold validation of the long-challenged theory of human progress. And here, finally, was the specific application of historical experience and principle to the deliberate creation of a structure of government possessing the form of law and the substance of justice.

When the United States became part of a larger geographic unit—the world entity—it was as though it had been thrown all the way back to the unworkability of the nation-state system of ancient Greece. Nothing threw a brighter light on the ultimate failure of that system than what happened at Hiroshima on August 6, 1945. Overnight, the human species had come face to face with the problems of human destiny. Mankind had conquered nature only to discover that the forces inside itself were more powerful and terrifying. Humanity had beaten back every natural challenge thrown its way: heat, cold, water, ice, sun, sand, and wind; but it had yet to comprehend that far more menacing was the environment it had created for itself. All at once, the planet became too small for mankind's competitive urge and its quarrelsomeness. A sword was fixed with the point over its heart, and it was stumbling around in a darkened arena full of pits and obstacles.

All my life I had been a gradualist; in my thoughts on universalism and world government I had been concerned primarily with the requirements of a world community organized under law and justice, and it had seemed self-evident that it might take several generations at least before such a community could be brought into being. But with Hiroshima it became clear that a long-range ideal had become an immediate necessity and that no amount of talk about the difficulties in the way of this universalism could dispose of the danger of trying to survive without it. The question was not whether we needed it, but only how we would have to go about getting it within the required time.

That night—the night after the day that mankind revealed the great design of its own destruction—I tried to sort my fears and hopes in an editorial. The gist of that editorial was that "modern" mankind had become obsolete, a self-made anachronism becoming more incongruous by the minute. We had exalted change in everything but ourselves. We had leaped centuries ahead in inventing a new world to live in, but we knew little about our own part in that world. Given time, we might be expected to bridge those gaps normally; but by our own hand we had destroyed even time. Communication, transportation, and war no longer waited on time. Whatever bridges had to be built and crossed would have to be built and crossed immediately.

The purpose of that editorial, I am afraid, was somewhat misunderstood. It was said that I had written a farewell to mankind, that I had defined a predicament from which there was neither retreat nor escape. Such was not my intention, and I have only myself to blame for not having made my purpose clear. I believed there were rational grounds for hope—tremendous hope—and I said so, but I made the mistake of bearing down so heavily on the danger that by the time I tried to discuss the possibilities of meeting that danger the dominant mood of the editorial had been established in the minds of many readers.

I am no pessimist. I doubt that any person knows enough to be a pessimist. Neither am I a reckless optimist. I do not think that things necessarily come out all right in the end if left to themselves. I do not believe that any nation or any people enjoys a natural immunity against catastrophe or a special dispensation against disaster. Survival depends on ideas and action; and before we decide what the ideas are or what the action is to be, it is essential that we become supremely aware of the danger and resolve to meet it. It was in that spirit that I wrote the editorial, which seemed to me a logical expression of everything I had learned during the process of my "reeducation." Far from subtracting from an affirmative, activist philosophy built around the plastic nature of history, atomic fission added something: the powerful ingredient of urgency. I never wavered in my confidence in the *capacity* of humanity to eliminate war and build a just peace, or to make the changes in itself in order to meet the problems and opportunities; what I tried to do was to emphasize that capacity rested on decision, and decision on recognition of the challenge.

On the political level, one of the most compelling reasons for urgency was that time was working against us. With each passing day after the end of the war, the classic and natural causes for tension and conflict between two giant nations outside a power vacuum would assert themselves unless some way could be found of eliminating the competition for power and security. When the United States and Russia looked at each other across this vacuum, the struggle to fill it would be on in earnest unless a world organization were invested both with preponderant force and with a judicial structure which would be able to command the confidence of the world's peoples.

Two months before Hiroshima, it seemed regrettable but not unnatural that the delegates at San Francisco should fail to invest the United Nations with the power of world law. Nor did it seem strange that the United States should propose the veto, and indicate its unwillingness to submit itself to a higher sovereignty. Russia, as the other great power, was no less anxious to avoid binding commitments, and served notice at San Francisco that its foreign-policy objectives were not to be made subordinate to the Charter.

But Hiroshima made San Francisco ancient history. It was as though a man-made ice age were descending, reducing all man's political bickerings and quarrels to a preposterous thimbleful alongside the universality of the threat. For the issue was not the nation but mankind itself; and the peoples of the world were waiting for leadership which would enable them to break out of the old level on which they argued and fought, and onto a new level of awareness and responsibility equal to the danger and the opportunity.

But while peoples everywhere had been drawn together within a single potential battlefield, and while they shared a common destiny, they were without common representation, and had yet to define the basis of a common hope. The nation was no longer able to protect persons, their property, or their welfare, and the nation had ceased to be the ultimate outer protective ring. The nation had been the natural product of a geographic community. But what about the human community now that the geographic community was one? Something beyond the nation had to be created—adequate to meet the challenge and the opportunity, adequate to create the conditions of peace, adequate to make peace meaningful, adequate to speak for mankind.

All these problems call for thought—and we are encouraged by Hegel to believe that every problem is penetrable by thought. This is encouraging enough, but Hegel lived at a time when the problem of scrutinizing living history was not yet battered and confounded by acceleration. The trouble with trying to penetrate the vitals of the past few decades is that 1900 was more than a thousand years ago. Into a few decades have been compressed more change, more thrust, more tossing about of men's souls and gizzards, than had been spaced out over most of the human chronicle previously. The entire metabolism of history has gone berserk.

What is most significant, therefore, about the past fifty or sixty years is not the extent of change but the pace of change. In little more than a generation, our legs have become forty times longer than they ever were, in terms of speed and mobility. During this time we have developed more new sources of energy and new resources than in any previous period. And the rate of acceleration continues to increase, a specific reflection of the fact that the number of scientists now alive is larger than all the scientists in all the ages of mankind put together before 1920.

The acceleration has done more than impair the faculty of human observation and comprehension. It has created a tendency toward disorientation. It has unhinged the sense of vital balance that enables a person to locate himself or herself in time and place. In the centrifuge of the twentieth century, mankind is whirling away from the center of its own being. The farther out one spins, the more blurred one's view of oneself, of what one might be, and of one's relationship to the nameless faces in the crowd. The separation is not just between body and place, it is between mind and reason.

Ultimately, the acceleration produces irreverence. Men in increasing motion cover ground but have none to stand on. Values take on a free-floating quality. The disconnection makes for distortion and an unfamiliarity that breeds contempt. It is not just a matter of rejecting values; it is a matter of being disconnected from the things that give rise to values. Obviously, not all irreverence is bad. The irreverence that challenges, that peels back the layers of sham, that releases bitterness or anger against attempts to indignify life—this in itself is an assertion of values. But the main vein of irreverence in our time is quite different. It is nihilistic, brutal, antihuman. Basically, it is directed against life itself.

The symptoms are fundamental. They are not just a street mob goading someone on a ledge to take the plunge. Nor a crowd in a subway passively observing one person carving up another. Nor people paying for the privilege of seeing people get hurt. Nor rapacious comedians mistaking verbal brutality for wit. These grisly manifestations seem to come with the human situation. But irreverence in the twentieth century has a more pervasive accent. It involves the basic mood of large numbers of people and the kind of culture they are prepared to support. It is visible in the abrasiveness of human relations that many people either prefer or seem to take for granted.

These things haven't occurred because of some historical quirk. They are the product of specific gravity and direct cause. They reflect and are part of a dominant theme. The theme is the volcanic eruption of the scientific intelligence, throwing hot lava over the whole of humanity's estate, most especially over the national structures. A nation meant many things to an individual, but most of all it meant protection—protection against other tribes, protection against disorder from within. This protection, from without or within, required force. Then, suddenly, out of the acceleration came a new kind of force that changed everything about the state except its awareness that a fundamental change had come about. Mankind became deprived of its protection. The power was total, obliterative, suicidal.

The ultimate effect of the acceleration, therefore, was to make life tentative. From there it was the shortest of steps to make it cheap. Does it mean nothing to live in an age when the defensive level of human beings has been reduced to that of insects against a blowtorch? The most enshrined phrase in the lexicon of philosophers is *the dignity of man*, yet dignity does not depend only on political charters or declarations. Dignity also means solidity; it means a moral contract accepting life as infinitely precious. How much reverence for life is possible when everyone knows that the flick of a finger can incinerate a billion human beings and that a nod can release tons of disease germs? A painful world mankind can train itself to endure, but a world that on the whim of a madman can become a crematorium or a disease chamber—this is the giant thief that steals a person's dignity.

All over the world today, regardless of ideological systems, people in ever-larger numbers are turning to crime and brutality. Violence has become a universal pastime. This is not a sudden fad or aberration. People and their society are in a constant condition of interaction. At a time when nations can vaporize civilization, the individual takes on the temper of the total organism of which he or she is a part. One doesn't have to react on the level of conscious decision; one can reflect an environment that no longer fully comprehends the fragility and uniqueness of human life.

Any attack on the problem must begin not so much with a definition of acceleration as with a definition of mankind. If mankind and its limitations are regarded as a constant, then it may be only a matter of time before it becomes ground up in the wheels it has sent spinning so furiously. But if human uniqueness is defined as the capacity to conceive that which has never been conceived before, then acceleration can be relieved of its terrors. Mankind's difficulty has never been in doing things; it has been in knowing what to do. The ultimate test is not of its skills but of its purposes and desires. It has already transformed nature; are we to say it is unable to transform itself? Is it reasonable to believe that a species that has demonstrated a capacity to lift itself off its planet is unable to raise its sights in devising a rational future? If awareness of the consequences of the present drift leads to a desire to avert them, the Age of Acceleration can lead to an Age of Balance.

Thomas Jefferson looked forward to a time when all barbarism would disappear from the earth. If he were alive today he would take note of the persistence and extension of barbarism but, as a believer in human perfectibility, he would warn against the conclusion that men are essentially barbarous. With Franklin, Emerson, William James, and Holmes, he would resist theories of historical inevitability. He would not be intimidated by the momentum of events into believing that a great reversal could not be brought about. He would also probably try to remind us that no idea figured more largely in the making of American society than that history was what men wanted it to be, and that civilization is what happens when people have intelligent desires.

There is hope, then, in a plastic definition of man. This goes beyond the recognition of a divine itch or the sudden notion that there is an extra minute before midnight. Hope today—and it may be the only hope—resides in the worldwide emergence of the articulate and communicating citizen. What people want and what they do means more and more to the governments of which they are a part. The American experiment has succeeded in the way that Madison and Hamilton never dared dream it would. Its essential claim—that nothing is more important than man—has been echoed in every continent. The individual person has come into his own. Thinking, feeling, musing, complaining, fending, creating, building, evading, desiring, indivuals have become more important to the operators of their governments than ever before. The question, therefore, is not whether mankind is capable of prolonging and ennobling its stay on earth. The question is whether it recognizes its prime power—and also its duty—for accomplishing that purpose.

What will cause Everyman, who lives everywhere, who is preoccupied about different things and who lives under different systems, suddenly to find both unison and resonance in calling for safety and sense on earth? Next, what is it he or she is expected to say? Finally, who will do the effective listening?

On the first question: Despite national boundaries and belligerently different ideological systems, the main confrontation in today's world cuts across national boundaries and ideological lines. The ultimate divisions take place within the societies, not between them. On one side are those who comprehend or sense the meaning of the acceleration, who perceive that new connections among men have to be created regardless of their diversity, and who move almost instinctively toward building those universal institutions that can serve the city of mankind. On the other side are those who think in terms of separatism, the perpetuation of group egos, the manning of tribal battle-stations, and the benefits of compartmentalization. It is out of this transcendent confrontation that Everyman will make his or her voice and weight felt. People need to be encouraged to believe that what they feel and want to say can be part of a universal thrust. And it is here that writers, especially novelists, poets, and playwrights, have their finest opportunity. If nothing else, we have learned that the ideas of the poets and artists penetrate where everything else had failed. The question, therefore, is not so much whether Everyman is capable of response, whatever his or her station, as whether he or she has something and someone to respond to.

On the second question: It would be exhilarating, to say the least, if a shout were to go up all over the world for a human society under law. This is not likely to happen. It is not essential that it happen. All that is necessary to happen is the direct expression of raw concern. There is primitive, colossal energy in the simply stated but insistent call by enough people for a situation of reasonable safety on earth, for an end to anarchy in the dealings among states, and for easier access by members of the human family to one another.

On the third question: Even the most insulted and arbitrary

government or system has to be concerned today about the turnings of the popular mind. Some systems may be less attuned than others but at some point all must pay attention.

The same acceleration that has produced disarray and irreverence can give mankind confidence in achieving big goals within the short time it is necessary to achieve them. It can give it confidence, too, in the reach of its intelligence for finding answers of almost infinite complexity. Progress lies not in a rejection of acceleration but in a proper respect for the possibilities of mind.

Hesiod's *Works and Days* cried out for a return to the good old days, when life was less complicated and more trusting and when, presumably, one's illusions were intact. The remote but remembered past always tends to impart a quality of innocence to bygone times.

The scrutiny of the past encounters far fewer barriers to the understanding of causes and effects than does the scrutiny of the present. You assemble your reference materials about the past; there they rest, accessible and obedient, waiting to be sorted out and judged. But the facts of the present won't sit still for a portrait; they are constantly vibrating, full of clutter and confusion.

Today's elusive and complicated facts are apt to be viewed as simplicities a generation hence. The current sophistications will probably seem like a species of innocence. What happens, of course, is that people never lose their innocence; they just take on new perspectives. This is where nostalgia begins. It is also what makes the reading of history so engaging and the writing of it so precarious.

The individual who believes it important to consult the past would do well to respect two caveats. One is to avoid becoming a captive of chronology, neither being charmed by the submissiveness of materials dealing with the past nor intimidated by the complexities and loose ends of the present.

The second is to resist cynicism. Complexities are the natural habitat of cynicism, if only because they set the stage for concealment and manipulation. Especially is this true of complexities that embrace manifest injustice or malevolence or special privilege or corruption or callousness. And the disillusion that is joined to cynicism breeds distrust. This is how societies begin to fall apart. John Middleton Murry, the English critic, had this to say fifty years ago of the generation of his countrymen which emerged from the First World War:

> If they had the luck not to die, their brothers had no such luck. From the very beginning, they had to face ultimate questions. The whole civilization which had been taken for granted by their elders was to them an object of suspicion and a cause of despair. . . . They did not become revolutionaries, for revolution seemed to them as futile as war itself. They became nihilists; they touched the bottom of an abyss of despair. . . . It is not easy to create out of despair. . . . They are struggling to create for themselves a philosophy of life by which they may live; they are trying to discover for themselves a justification of their own activity. . . .
>
> The perennial academic question: What is the function of art? has suddenly taken on an almost agonized actuality. . . . So long as this effort at criticism remains purely intellectual, a cynical pessimism is its inevitable conclusion, and the function of the writer is fixed as one of mere amusement. . . . Certain things have to be accepted as beyond the scrutiny of the intellect; chief among them is life itself. The system or the society of which the individual is a member is profoundly mistrusted. The individual cannot trust the system; he must trust himself. So that the critical problem with which modern English literature is trying to grapple is twofold. Is there in the universe at large a general process man may trust? Has he a self he can trust?

What Murry was doing, a quarter of a century before Sartre, Camus, and Tillich, was posing the supreme existentialist questions. His description of the philosophical position of the young English writers following World War I was also prophetically true of the new generation of writers in France and Germany following World War II and, in a sense, of the American writers much later in their reaction to the Vietnam War. This significant difference between the Europeans and the Americans, of course, was that the Europeans manifested their opposition through bitterness and withdrawal, whereas the Americans turned to scorn and activism. Common to both, however, was the deep and corrosive distrust of established institutions and even, in a subliminal sense, of life itself.

Middleton Murry didn't feel that a purely intellectual response was adequate to the challenge of life. He never explicitly defined intellectuality, but it must be assumed he was thinking of it in terms of sophisticated indifference or disdain. The intellectuality he criticizes has to be juxtaposed against the positivist attitudes—a belief in the perfectibility of the individual; the notion of an accountable society; confidence in the use of the rational intelligence; faith in the regenerative capacity. The ability to think creates the obligation to define purpose: that is, the need to probe for, and constantly refine, the values by which humans add meaning to existence.

Creativity is an aspect of human uniqueness that needs special tending. Creativity can be stifled or throttled not just by political juggernauts but also by brutality or wickedness or squalor. It is folly, therefore, to assume that the editor or the writer or the artist has no obligation to the conditions that make creativity possible.

Arguments over the ivory tower versus the arena are usually a waste of time. They tend to set art against involvement. They assume that creativity never needs its champions, that there is no connection between the shape of the society and the condition of the arts, and that the world of ideas is somehow separate from the world in which great books are written or great music composed or canvases painted or great drama staged. What is the good society if not the creative society? The conditions of life are inseparable from the conditions of art. The truly creative writer or artist never has to choose between the ivory tower and the arena. He or she moves freely from one to the other according to his needs and concerns.

Nothing is more vital for the creative artist than access to the arena. Repressive and insecure societies keep artists under control not by forbidding them to write or paint but by separating them from their audience. What Solzhenitsyn protested was not that he was forbidden to write but that his writing was not available to his countrymen. And great audiences, as Walt Whitman reminded us, are necessary if we want to have great poets. For it is the audience that ultimately has to uphold the values of the ivory tower.

One of the prime characteristics of a monolithic society is not just that it tries to expunge the free and creative spirit but that it cuts off a free and creative response. When Nikita Krushchev tried to release the Russian people from the paralyzing effects of Stalinism, one of the first things he did was to permit artists to exhibit works of their own choosing, as apart from those approved by political controllers. Paintings by the thousands came out of cellars. The dominant character of those paintings was not exactly what one might find in a showing of uninhibted abstractionism, but it was remarkably devoid of exhortation or "poster naturalism." What was most significant about that exhibition perhaps was that the audience seemed tentative in attitude, as though the people weren't quite sure it was really safe to see what the artist himself wanted them to see. The habit of selective encounters with art had become so strong that the great audience, in Whitman's phrase, was not ready.

C. P. Snow has been concerned about the gap between the artist and scientist. Even more serious is the gap between artist and audience. Both have their needs; both have their rights. Neither exists in splendid isolation. Yet it has not been an easy time—the fifties and sixties especially—for creating a rapport between the two. In the fine arts, we have been passing through a period of estrangement between practitioner and public. Artists properly insist on their right to express themselves and to experiment as fully as they wish. They do not believe they should be asked to explain what they mean or to justify their belief that what they have produced deserves to be exhibited. But the art-loving public, even more than the critic, holds the ultimate power. The empty galleries that greeted many of the showings of experimental art during the sixties flashed the danger signal that people, almost as a Tolstoian prophecy come true, insist on their own definition of art and cannot be pushed beyond certain limits. Today, the swing is back to realism and romanticism, but the heavily imitative and repetitious nature of much of the work may dim public enthusiasm.

If the audience seems detached from the arts today, then it is not a solitary phenomenon. There is evidence on every hand that the American people are in a general mood of withdrawal. The clamorous activism of the sixties has given way to the distrust and disillusion of the seventies. There is little disposition to rally around banners, whether new or old. It is a lean time for leaders.

The problem is not that persons of stature are vanishing. The problem is that the American people right now are not in a heroic mood. Their history has been disfigured by government itself. The deepest and most nourishing part of their tradition is the principle that government cannot make secret commitments which the people are then compelled to redeem. Yet through at least two presidencies, such commitments were made. The fact that the government would deliberately and consistently lie to the American people has cracked open the wall of confidence that they instinctively believed would never be breached. The endless horrors of Watergate have compounded that distrust and added to the disillusion.

We are back again, then, at the question Middleton Murry asked with reference to England fifty years ago: Is there anything or anyone people can trust? Can the individual trust him- or herself?

Useful answers to those questions are not likely to come out of cynicism. The society cries out for regeneration and reintegration. Beyond that, the world has to be kept from sliding into a grotesque downward spiral. The nation has always been the ultimate form of human organization. Yet that institution is the principal factor in the downward spiral. It is no longer able to perform its historic function. It cannot protect the lives or property of its people; it cannot uphold their cultures or their values. The sudden compression of all the nations into a single geographic unit has produced no corresponding response in terms of an organization of the whole. Instead, there is virtual anarchy in the world arena.

The problems inside the arena demand a world view, a world philosophy, a world sensitivity to the dangers that now extend to the whole of the human race. Chief among these dangers is the bulging stockpile of nuclear weapons that could produce a global holocaust. The stockpile has long since passed the point at which it has any relationship to any theoretical military need. Yet the nuclear explosives pile higher each year, as though the nations are dctermined that, if war should come, no leaf or grain of sand would escape the furnance nor any evidence remain of a world exquisitely suited to life in all its forms.

A world dimension applies to the other major problems as well—contamination of the total environment, squandered resources, limping societies, too little food and too many people, persistence of social injustice, shrinkage in the conditions of creative growth.

These problems call for the highest energies and keenest perceptions of which the human race is capable. Cynicism blocks off access to those energies and dulls those perceptions, if only because the cynic positions himself for defeat. Progress begins with the idea that progress is possible. Cynicism begins with an unnatural respect for the supposedly impossible.

Nothing is more false historically or more dangerous than the notion of helplessness. The past half-century, perhaps more than any previous period in history, has demonstrated that history is not immutable and that existing forces are not inexorable. In our lifetime, we have witnessed a vast enlargement in the definition of human uniqueness. The human species is unique because it alone can do things for the first time. The big problem, however, is to convince people that human beings are equal to their needs, that a problem can be resolved if it can be perceived, that progress is what is left over after the seemingly impossible has been retired, and that the crisis today in human affairs is represented not by the absence of human capacity but the failure to recognize that the capacity exists.

In our time, notions of helplessness are derived from at least four main causes. One cause is represented by the collective sense of an imminent self-inflicted defeat. The particulars, as mentioned a moment ago, are familiar: Population is swelling but the food supply is shrinking. Energy needs are growing faster than new sources of energy can be generated or developed. Oxygen is being depleted by disappearing vegetation and contamination of the seas. Water tables are being increasingly infected. The sky has become an open sewer. The conditions of life on this planet are running down.

The second and related cause of despair grows out of imperfect human organization. The ease with which human aggregations can organize for destructive purposes is exceeded only by their difficult in meeting common survival problems. The human race is primed for apocalyptic war but not for enduring peace. The effect on the individual is to make life tentative, dispiriting.

The third cause of helplessness or hopelessness is onrushing depersonalization. The new technology has produced the theoretical basis for the greatest liberation from drudgery in human history, but the pervasive effect so far is not new options but the quantification of life. Human beings are becoming spindled artifacts; they are losing their faces. They are also losing their secrets. Their mistakes and indiscretions are metabolized by a data base, never to be forgotten. Nothing is more univeral than human fallibility; nothing is more essential than forgiveness or absolution. Yet statistical maintenance is as remorseless as it is void of redeeming judgments nourished by intangibles or the passing of time. Hope must be associated with names, not numbers. Helplessness, therefore, increases in direct proportion to numbering mechanisms unmodified by acts of faith or grand leaps of intuitive splendor.

The fourth cause of helplessness or hopelessness is related to a timeless condition—the dread of ultimate loneliness. It is here that existentialism finds its greatest appeal. The eternal quest of the individual human being is to shatter his loneliness. It is this condition that enables philosophers and theologians to make common cause with poets and artists. Loneliness is multidimensional: There is the loneliness of mortality. There is the loneliness of time that passes too slowly, or too swiftly. There is the loneliness of inevitable separation. There is the loneliness of aspiration. There is the loneliness of squandered dreams. There is the collective loneliness of the species, unable to proclaim oneness in a world chained to its tribalisms.

And now, finally, there is the loneliness of life in the universe, always a philosophical preoccupation but now a presiding reality reinforced by man's forays into space. The change is greater than was represented by the Copernican revolution. Copernicus's contribution was primarily to knowledge, only secondarily to philosophy. After Copernicus, there was the challenge to the human mind that came for knowing that the earth was not the center of all things—but this challenge did not substantially change the fact that mankind continued to see itself as the hub of the universe. People were astounded that previous generations should ever have believed that the earth did not revolve around the sun; but they still lived in an anthropocentric world in an abstract universe.

In our time, however, the liberation of human beings from earth gravity has enabled the species to become less theoretical about, and detached from, the universe. What was most significant about the lunar voyage was not that men set foot on the moon but that they set eye on the earth. They perceived larger relationships. They had an increased sense of human uniqueness. The effect was philosophical. To be able to rise from the earth; to be able, from a station in outer space, to see the relationship of the planet earth to other planets; to be able to contemplate the billions of factors in precise and beautiful combinaton that make human existence possible; to be able to meditate on journeying through an infinity of galaxies; to be able to dwell on an encounter of the human brain and spirit with the universe —all this enlarges the human horizon. It also offers proof that technology is subordinate to human imagination. An objective had first to be conceived. The conception fathered the technology. The technology became successful only through the application of both brain power and will power.

Humans are not helpless. They have never been helpless. They have only been deflected or deceived or despirited. This is not to say their history has not been pockmarked by failure. But failure is not the ultimate fact of life; it is an aspect of life in which transient or poor judgments play larger roles than they should. So long as people do not persuade themselves that they are creatures of failures; so long as they have a vision of life as it ought to be; so long as they can comprehend the full meaning and power of the unfettered mind—so long as they can do all these things, they can look at the world and, beyond that, the universe with the sense that they can be unafraid of their fellow humans and can face choices not with dread but with great expectations.

In this sense, the main challenge confronting us is not ideological or economic but philosophical. Yet we live at a time of philosophical poverty. The vast increase of new knowledge and therefore of problems has not produced new philosophies that speak uniquely to the new condition in human affairs.

One of the primary obligations of philosophy, of course, is to avoid becoming trapped in a contemporary setting. Philosophy seeks to make connections in the human mind between the memories of the race and ways of thinking about life. It constructs principles for asking meaningful questions and for disciplining the speculations those questions produce. But the test of philosophy is in its ability to contribute to its own time while remaining independent of it.

Yet the problems of the twentieth century have not generated specific and systematic philosophies for thinking about major problems. The most active philosophical ideas in our time, of course, are those associated with existentialism. It is important to note, however, that existentialism is primarily the creation of a nineteenth-century thinker, Søren Kierkegaard of Denmark. It was not until the early part of the twentieth century that Kierkegaard's ideas made a substantial impact—not in Denmark but in Germany, a natural consequence considering the economic and political chaos that followed Germany's defeat in World War I.

The end of that war produced a pronounced pendulum swing in Germany from a widely held sense of national omnipotence to a sense of national failure and emptiness. Various German intellectuals took up the existentialist idea that an individual's first obligation is to maintain a circle of sanity, responsibility, and awareness around his or her own existence. Life was surrounded by dread, yet the individual could protect himself against intellectual, spiritual, and physical paralysis. He could be guarded in his commitments. Even if his choices were limited, even if he could have no confidence that his choices might be correct, he had the obligation to live out his life and to extract from it what he could. His connections with, and obligations to, his fellow human beings were important facts of his existence, but not necessarily the overriding facts. What was predominant was his need to survive in an unpredictable, harsh, and not very controllable world.

Just as it is understandable that existentialist thought should have taken hold in Germany after World War I, so it is equally understandable that existentialism should figure prominantly in the intellectual climate of France after World War II. The course of the war provided little support for philosophical idealism or for positive ideas celebrating human purposes. Yet French literary figures such as Sartre and Camus, even though both were reluctant to describe themselves as existentialists, responded to the general intellectual mood of disillusion and despair in much the same way that Heidegger and Jaspers had responded in Germany. The mood of their plays and books was bleak, but the human spirit was sustained nonetheless. The individual was not justified in turning away from the reality of his own existence, even though his efforts to protect it were probably doomed.

This, then, was the curious mixture of existentialism at the end of two worlds wars—a compound of limited aspiration, despair, dread, and a sense of the individual's obligation to put himself ahead of the collective mechanism called society.

Whatever its appeal to a European, however, existentialism—even as modified affirmatively by later writers, notably Teilhard de Chardin—did not completely satisfy those whose history had not taken them to a dead end. For any American whose national society had been created mainly by young philosophers who knew how to transform ideals into institutions; for an American who had grown up in a tradition that regarded the search for progress as an enduring and positive obligation; for an American whose intellectual underpinnings came from the transcendentalist thinkers and from William James, Charles Sanders Peirce, and John Dewey; for an American who believed that historical logic supported the idea of a positive frame for human events—for such an American, existentialism lacked dynamic thrust. It didn't present itself as a philosophy of resignation, but this seemed to be its message. By accommodating itself to helplessness and hopelessness, existentialism fostered the very mood of negation it originally sought to dispel.

Yet existentialism did great honor to the concept of human individuality and to the things that belong to the individual and not to society. If it appeared to sanction cynicism, it also fortified and enlivened the philosophical process, one reflection of which is the diversification of existentialism itself. It also had a world impact—far greater, perhaps, than the pragmatic philosophy of William James or the related logical positivism of John Dewey.

In the main, however, existentialism has not been an effective or appropriate response for the present human condition and the predicament it has been unable to resolve; the human species has the means to expunge itself but not the unifying ideas for creating a shelter against disaster. Nor is existentialism an antidote to the growing feeling of helplessness or hopelessness among individual human beings all over the world. Quite the contrary, what ties most existentialists together is precisely this feeling of helplessness—helplessness to shape the collective destiny, helplessness to preside over erratic and painful events, helplessness in recognizing and facing up to anguishing choices.

Yet the greatest of all historical truths, as we said a moment ago, is represented by the ability of the human species to do that which has never been done before. The notion of individual helplessness is therefore unhistoric and unnatural. It is a notion that has gained currency at certain times, of which the present is an example. What generally happens is that supposedly inexorable forces gather strength in combination with personified malevolence. At such times, enough evil is inflicted on enough people to produce a lowering ceiling over human hopes. The result is that the individual becomes spiritually devitalized and despairing.

Against this mood is the excitement created by new lines of connection with an expanding universe. A great adventure opens out before us. We have new worlds to contemplate. We have new connections to make. A rendezvous with infinity becomes us.

Some have reacted to the widened consciousness of the surrounding universe, and to the evidence that life exists elsewhere, with morose feelings about the discovery that the universe was not constructed for our particular benefit. Yet what is most important is that, whatever its place in infinity, life is infinitely precious. It is precious because of what it is, not because of any universal prevalence it may have.

It is precious because the human mind can contemplate questions such as these. We do not have to experience infinity in order to encompass it. It is precious because we have access to the phenomenon of cause and effect, thus being able to create our own causes and to shape our own effects. We can dwell on the experiences of past lives and thus enhance our own time. Life is precious not because it is perfectible but because human beings can comprehend the idea of perfectibility. It is precious because there are no limits to the fineness of human sensitivities. We are capable of responding to the good, the true, and the beautiful. We have the capacity to love and to respond to love. Life is precious because humans can continue to create in ways they have never created before. We can do the impossible.

Finally, nothing about human life is more precious than that we can define our own purpose and shape our own destiny.

We do this in many ways: by being aware both of its preciousness and its fragility, by developing to the fullest the potentialities and sensitivities that come with life, by putting the whole of our intelligence to work in sustaining and enhancing the conditions that make life possible, by cherishing the human habitat and shielding it from devastation and depletion, by using our free will to the utmost in advancing the cause of life. The individual can make choices. So long as the ability to choose can be matched with options of consequence, there are strong grounds for hope. There is hope that enough individuals will use their free will to make the life-giving and life-sustaining choices.

Each individual is capable of both great altruism and great venality. He has it within his means to extend the former and exorcise the latter.

The individual is capable of both great compassion and great indifference. He has it within his means to nourish the former and outgrow the latter.

The individual is capable of maintaining great societies and staging great holocausts. He has it within his means to fortify the former and avert the latter.

The individual is capable of ennobling life and disfiguring it. He has it within his means to assert the former and anathematize the latter.

If he recognizes that his basic purpose is to justify his humanity, he will have no difficulty in addressing himself to these choices.

It may be argued that determinism works against such choices and that we have a place in the universal design that we will never be in a position to alter, however strong our free will and however majestic our acceptance of the need to justify our humanity.

The next great development in humanity may be represented by our liberation from the idea that we have no command over our destiny. Even if it could be demonstrated that we are moving steadily toward a negative destiny, we might be able to change direction. The ability to create choices and to choose correctly may be the ultimate divine gift. Being able to make the fulfilling choice may be the highest exercise of our intelligence and spirituality. To paraphrase Descartes, we are human; therefore, we justify life.

The kind of response to human purpose which I have been describing is juxtaposed against negative existentialism and might be called *consequentialism.* By consequentialism I am thinking of the whole sequence of ideas by which human beings —the living, the dead, and the unborn—are related to one another and also to the universal order. Consequentialism is concerned with the need for complete integration—integration of intellect, conscience, knowledge, and experience—also, essential integration with the outside world. Progressive integration is a basic law of life. The development of the complex mechanism of a human being from a single cell is only one example. Similarly, each individual human being is only one part of a larger being or body that we call the human species. The challenge to the individual is to comprehend this oneness and then live it out.

The significance of reality is of lesser importance than the fact of life itself. For life is rich in its consequences. Consequences give reality to man's capacity to struggle between good and evil, nobility and venality, altruism and selfishness. A human being fashions his consequences as surely as he fashions his goods or his dwellings. Nothing one says, thinks, or does is without its consequences. Just as there is no loss of basic energy in the universe, so no thought or action is without its effects, present or ultimate, seen or unseen, felt or unfelt. Reality *is* consequences. At every step in life we are coping with the consequences of ideas and actions, most of them long since forgotten. These consequences or effects are the unseen factors in individual life and the affairs of mankind; they are imponderables only in the sense that they are not directly identified. But they are no less vital than that which is explicit and accessible in human experience. In short, life is of consequence—literally so. Wisdom consists of the anticipation of consequences, and consequences can be both good and bad.

For all of humanity's lofty philosophical excursions, we are still earthbound. We are overly fond, perhaps, of applying our concepts about size, direction, time, space, energy, to situations in which those concepts may be completely extraneous. Man is measurement-minded. In fact, we have to be, because our plane of existence necessarily utilizes such concepts. Yet there is a larger plane on which those approaches may have no validity.

We have tried to throw our arms around infinity and have been left not with the universe in our arms but with a closed and empty circle. Hence the more we know about the discernible and the theoretical universe, the more confused we become. Boundlessness or endlessness at first fascinates us, then appalls us.

We have a tendency to superimpose God on a design—in fact, to equate our speculations about infinity with God. This tendency may be neither wrong nor bad. It may be merely irrelevant—at least in the sense that we may be looking in the wrong direction. Even if it could be proved that the universe was a nothingness, it would make no difference so long as what happens inside that "nothingness" takes place within reach of our own experience, or our own function and essence, or, to call it by its philosophical name, reality—reality being the manifestation of cause, effect, interaction, and finally, consequences.

The main point, therefore, is that there has to be a *something* in "nothingness." The universal vacuum cannot complete itself. It cannot because there is a rejection of absolute nothingness. It is not the enormousness or the scope or the grandeur of what results from the rejection of nothingness that is primarily significant here. What is most significant is that true nothingness is impossible. Infinity would swallow us up but it cannot. Nothingness surrounds us but it cannot claim us. Not even science can conceive of pure nothingness; pure nothingness nowhere exists. The universe may be only a particle, but it asserts itself, and the nothingness is kept from becoming absolute. Thus the universe is a vital particle. And there are vital particles inside it, the most vital of which is mankind.

The true contemplation of the Deity, therefore, should proceed not out of manifest phenomena but out of a void. This is the final test of spiritual substance. If our spirituality proceeds out of awe, it loses substance as soon as awe is dissolved. God emerges in fullest glory not when made to sit astride infinity or when regarded as an architect of cosmic spectacles, but when contemplated as the ultimate force that prevents the cosmic void from becoming absolute.

Whether the great design of creation exists within a microcosm or macrocosm is unimportant; the vital particles inside it have order and purpose and they exist. And there is a place inside that order for mankind, for consciousness, for conscience, for love. This is what is important. We are not children of relativity. We are brothers and sisters. And we enjoy or suffer the consequences of our ideas, our acts, our hopes, and our fears.

Against this background, let me recite some articles of faith:

I am a single cell in a body of three billion cells. The body is mankind.

I glory in the individuality of self, but my individuality does not separate me from my universal self—the oneness of mankind.

The portion of that substance that is mine was not devised; it was renewed. So long as the human bloodstream lives I have life. Of this does my immortality consist.

I do not believe that humankind is an excrescence or a machine, or that the myriads of solar systems and galaxies in the universe lack order or sanction.

I may not embrace or command this universal order, but I can be at one with it, for I am of it.

I see no separation between the universal order and the moral order.

I believe that the expansion of knowledge makes for an expansion of faith, and the widening of the horizons of mind for a widening of belief. My reason nourishes my faith and my faith my reason.

I am diminished not by the growth of knowledge but by the denial of it.

I am not oppressed by, nor do I shrink before, the apparent boundaries in life or the lack of boundaries in the cosmos.

I cannot affirm God if I fail to affirm humanity. If I deny the oneness of humanity, I deny the oneness of God. Therefore I affirm both. Without a belief in human unity I am hungry and incomplete.

Human unity is the fulfillment of diversity. It is the harmony of opposites. It is a many-stranded texture, with color and depth.

The sense of human unity makes possible a reverence for life.

Reverence for life is more than solicitude or sensitivity for life. It is a sense of the whole, a capacity for inspired response, a respect for the intricate universe of individual life. It is the supreme awareness of awareness itself.

I am a single cell. My needs are individual but they are not unique.

I am interlocked with other human beings in the consequences of our thoughts, feelings, actions.

Together we share the quest for a society of the whole equal to our needs, a society in which we neither have to kill nor be killed, a society congenial to the full exercise of the creative intelligence, a society in which we need not live under our moral capacity, and in which justice has a life of its own.

Single and together, we can live without dread and without helplessness.

We are single cells in a body of three billion cells. The body is humankind.

Response

Martin E. Marty

Norman Cousins, more than any other speaker in the symposium, has addressed himself to the overall topic. He has tried to spell out "The Nature of a Humane Society." His attempt was part of his assignment. While others were to speak out of and within the limits of a discipline—law, history, science—or to address the issues that focus in specialized human sectors or problems—race, womanhood, and the like—he was to accept the universe as a whole. People reluctant to make the effort have no right to accept the task of speaking on "meaning, purpose, and belonging in life." Cousins is not reluctant. His whole career and outlook prepare him for this kind of task.

If his ideas and hopes are to be put to work in any way by others, it is important for us to understand his *mode* and style of discourse. He is not here a "mere" journalist, historian, analyst, or reporter, though many of us might hope that journalists and historians would more frequently lay bare their own assumptions and presuppositions as he does, since none of them is a "mere" anything, either. He wants to be reckoned as doing more than straight reporting. Whatever persons think they are getting cool, detached chronicling will be hopelessly confused by what is going on in this address.

Mr. Cousins is decisively and rather consistently speaking creedally, using the language of faith, in a time when many are reluctant to be caught doing so. His last remarks he even calls "some articles of faith." *That they are.* In some circles it is an insult to be charged with using articles of faith or speaking creedally. In the context of the sponsorship of this symposium I would suppose and hope that the charge will not embarrass the speaker or the listeners. "That's just rhetoric" is a phrase that has to be fought by professors of rhetoric or editors of journals devoted to rhetoric. "That's just a creed, that's just faith," might be intended to sound condescending, but professors of faith ought to ask, "Is there anything that is 'just faith,' and what is wrong with creed, with faith?" Yet so unaccustomed is the public to hearing the language of creed or the admission that it is being used outside the sanctuary that we are likely to be utterly confused if we do not discern it in this address.

Whenever serious humans address the large themes of the human venture, they will be using the language of faith. Most cover up the traces to it and fit it with disguises. Jacques Monod was typical of the new physicists who wanted to purge all philosophical and religious traces from his analysis. Yet his reviewers found him even in his most rigorous moments unwittingly and apparently necessarily talking about "purpose" and "design." I have no doubt that psychological behaviorists and ethologists believe that they are often talking the language of laboratory or field, because they have worked with white mice or various species of baboons. Theirs is paraded as discourse unblighted by any faith. Yet I have no doubt—this is an article of faith born of historical inquiries—that in the 1990s a new generation will look back on the work of B. F. Skinner or Konrad Lorenz and observe that they were in no small measure giving voice to a myth of the 1970s.

Creeds have not only form but also *content*, and it is proper to ask, What is the center or core of Mr. Cousins's faith? The details are not important here. It is possible to reduce the complex creed of Maoism to a few essentials. The enormously elaborate Christian system of dogma can be expounded at book and even library length. Yet its core is condensed in a short Apostles' Creed and, according to some scholars, can be reduced to a New Testament baptismal formula: "Jesus is Lord." The Cousins creed centers in the possibility of progress and the reality of human capability. Humans will find meaning, purpose, and belonging in life only if there is a chance that their efforts will add up to a contribution to progress, and they will be motivated to make efforts only if they overcome the constrictions of fate and the paralysis of futility. Norman Cousins says:

> Humans are not helpless. They have never been helpless. They have only been deflected or deceived or dispirited. This is not to say their history has not been pockmarked by failure. But failure is not the ultimate fact of life; it is an aspect of life in which transient or poor judgements play larger roles than they should. So long as people do not persuade themselves that they are creatures of failures; . . . so long as they can comprehend the full meaning and power of the unfettered mind—so long as they can do all these things, they can look at the world and, beyond that, the universe with the sense that they can be unafraid of their fellow humans and can face choices not with dread but with great expectations.

Cousins speaks of "the gift of life," which implies a giver; "there was scope for free will" is an observation of faith; "life is the highest value" is a commitment; that there are "rational grounds for hope" is an assertion that lies as much in the zone of hope as it does of reason. The reader who underlines all the times Cousins speaks of "capability" or says that humans are "capable" will soon learn his accent. His choice of heroes also suggests his tilt; he speaks, partly inaccurately, I think, of Thomas Jefferson as "a believer in human perfectibility."

What is wrong with speaking of progress, capability, and perfectibility? I am not here attacking the validity of this profession or confession but simply and strenuously pointing out that it *is* a creed, not an object of sight or easy empirical verification if it is verifiable at all. In intellectual circles the creed is today rarely asserted. Philosophers are cautious about using language that points to the future, since its references cannot be checked out. If historian J. H. Plumb is correct, "among professional historians the idea of progress is out." Among historicists and relativists, who dominate today, "the idea of progress is hopelessly naive."

According to Plumb, the idea of progress supplanted earlier creeds of providence in the eighteenth century Enlightenment, only to fall into decline in the twentieth. Plumb would agree with Cousins: "To ignore the implication of the concept of progress seems to me to lead to disintegration, nihilism, and to the proliferation of meaningless investigations." One can combat nihilism only "if the idea of historical progress is made once again the core of our historical philosophy, and is taught to all who wish to understand man and his nature."[1]

That humans have made some kinds of progress in many areas of life is demonstrable. That these kinds add up to balance against failures, and that they can help assure a better future is quite debatable. If we could compute the faiths of the whole human race, it is likely that more millions still believe in "providence" than ever took up "progress." Most people in the world's Biafras and Bangladeshes are not in range of the luxury of believing in perfectibility or capability. Many humanists believe that one can act positively in history while rejecting the Cousins creed; thus Paul Tillich told how he was a religious socialist in order to act in history, while retaining his Lutheran "consciousness of the 'corruption' of existence, a repudiation of every kind of social

1. J. H. Plumb, ed., *Crisis in the Humanities* (Baltimore: Penguin, 1964), esp. pp. 43–44.

Utopia (including the metaphysics of progressivism, an awareness of the irrational and demonic nature of existence. . . ."[2] Cousins recognizes such possibilities also among existentialists. Tillich's kind of Christian and Camus' type of existentialist found reasons for hoping against hope, acting against futility, even without sharing faith in progress or perfectibility and without being sure about all the dimensions of capability.

Cousins quite rightly stresses that he is neither an optimist nor a pessimist. At times he sounds like Herman Kahn: "Nevertheless, on the whole I remain cautiously pessimistic." Yet, given all that he knows late twentieth century humans have a right to fear, he tilts toward a positive reading of the signs of the times. By page 272 I had written on my margin, "he knows all the problems but he stresses the other side." This in answer to the query my reading led me to address myself: "Doesn't he know what the odds against a humane society in the future are?" He knows. His faith leads him to appropriate this knowledge and accent something else. One can learn much about a philosophy of history by listening to an author's use of the word *still.* Cousins says, "for all of humanity's lofty philosophical excursions, we are still earthbound." Many a Christian reverses this and says, "Humans still retain some part or reflection of the image of God," or "despite the 'fall,' humans can still do good things."

Once it is established that we are hearing a creed and that we know something of its contents, it is important to ask the question of a humane society: "What is the humanistic and social *function* of such a creed?" In the churches creeds are "symbols" to rally the faithful. Or they might help define the boundaries of a church, to provide believers with a sense of identity and group bonding, to help them glorify God or taunt others or equip heresy-hunters with definitions. Cousins has few of these uses or intentions in mind, but his purposes seem clear. A comparison might illumine the case.

What was the function of presidential language from Jefferson through Lincoln and, in pale shadowings beyond them, when it was asserted that America was "the last, best hope of earth?" Is

2. Paul Tillich, *On The Boundary* (New York: Scribners, 1966), p. 75.

that proposition empirically verifiable? Of course not. It might be established that from 1776–1826 or from 1861–65 America was the best extant hope among the nations. But to say "last, best" requires a vantage no one is allowed. He who speaks it would have to be aware that the day of his speaking was the last in human history. Otherwise there would always be the possibility that a later, better hope could emerge. Jefferson and Lincoln must have known this. Yet there was no reason to care. Their language had a different function. They posited the idea, a psychologically sophisticated one, that humans in large groups would not act positively unless they saw some worth in themselves and their fellow citizens and unless they found enough validity in their ventures to take risks for them, to make sacrifices —even unto death—for them.

In the Christian community, to use a second example, there is sometimes realism and anxiety in the remembered words of Jesus in the Gospels. At times one hears disciples recalling Jesus in great discouragement as he looks down on his beloved Jerusalem. He asks whether "when the Son of Man comes" he "will find faith in the earth." At times the Apostle Paul seems overwhelmed by circumstance. Yet Jesus is also described as asserting that the disciples' faith is "the victory that overcomes the world." Paul looked at "principalities and powers" that trapped Christians in a cosmos and still asserted that nothing of these should separate them from the empowering love of God in Christ. He claimed in the face of what looked like a triumphant "old creation" that if "anyone is in Christ there is a new world." And while the old order prospered on all hands, he went on to say that for such who were in Christ, "the old order has already passed; the new order is already here" (2 Cor. 5:17). Jesus and Paul are trying to provide new spectacles and to ask for new commitment.

Using contemporary ideas of human capability and faith in the worthwhileness of the universal human family, Cousins is rallying the troops or groups to put forth efforts against the almost all-encompassing apathy, anomie, acedia of our time, the inabilities to "get up" for anything, to find norms and purpose, to rejoice or affirm in the presence of the good. Since his universal-sounding language is probably congenial to only a minority of the human race at a time when the language of progress and purpose are relatively "out," it is appropriate to ask what in his vision will give trouble to others, and what those who do not share the center of his creed can appropriate in his intentions?

First, those who have a qualified belief in capability and progress will have almost no difficulties. No one asserts his or her creed more consistently than Cousins. Second, those who have unqualified beliefs in perfectibility will be troubled by all his gloomy cautions. And third, those who have a tragic sense of life will not read his responses to human particulars as he does. We have already noted that both Christians and existentialists of many sorts are "capable" of acting without believing in the details of his views of capability and free will and free choice. I believe that any of these, if they are serious and caring about the human future in its natural planetary environment, will profit from the Cousins example as implied in all three words of his main title.

Meaning

Norman Cousins knows that humans are, as Sartre calls them, "stalkers of meaning." People can endure any "how" of living if they have a "why" (Dostoievsky). "Because we are present to a world, we are condemned to meaning" (Merleau-Ponty). He does not settle for us the modern question that philosophers, historians, and lay people regularly raise: whether meaning is manifest in history or whether history acquires meaning only from the meanings humans bring to it, but he successfully demonstrates or at least effectively reports on the dangers to a world in which the number of people who consciously care to articulate "meanings" diminishes below a certain level. If too many are apathetic or despairing, all will be at the mercy of the worst.

Purpose

The Cousins address illustrates how ideas have consequences. He does not say "sit on the curbstone and weep," or "throw in the towel," or "give in to existential despair." He believes and thinks that belief can focus in purpose. Other beliefs lead to other purposes. In *The Spectator* (7 April 1967, p. 398), the English physicist John Rowan Wilson, after favorably reviewing Robert Ardrey's *Territorial Imperative,* a book that suggests biological reasons for seeing humans as essentially predators or defenders of territory, concludes: "Perhaps we should stop aiming at the impossible task of trying to love and understand our neighbours. It might well be better if we kept ourselves to ourselves, barking across our fences now and then, and baring our fangs in ritualized aggression, but never going so far as to engage in open conflict." One revises purposes in the light of different beliefs about capabilities or possible outcomes.

Belonging

Norman Cousins's lifework, or at least the image he has acquired in his mature years, is preeminently that of one who calls capable individuals to choose participation in the immense journey of planetary man, in the whole venture of the whole human family. National sovereignty may have some benefits but is essentially a necessary evil. He wants others to share what he here calls "the planetary perspective." His instincts have led him to seek world federations, unions, councils, laws, and philosophies, without, of course, doing injustice to the value of local tradition.

As one sees the misfortunes that have befallen the United Nations, the World Council of Churches, the planetary and global organizations and designs, one is tempted to conclude that Cousins's universal creed must look very sectarian and private, a faith for the few. He must almost have to turn theological and, in "the true contemplation of the Deity" cry out, "Though he slay me, yet will I trust in him." For most trends are against "planetary perspective" at the moment when such a vision may be most needed. New nationalisms, often absurdly complex and demanding, are far stronger trends, portending what must look to Cousins like a future characterized by jungle, not civility. Every new state asserts itself with the full regalia of old empire, as if the world had room for a couple of hundred autonomous empires.

Norman Cousins knows he must even go a step further than nationalism. He properly perceives the growth of new tribalisms everywhere. Over against his side, "on the other side are those who think in terms of separatism, the perpetuation of group egos, the manning of tribal battle stations, and the benefits of compartmentalization. . . . People need to be encouraged to believe that what they feel and want to say can be part of a universal thrust." At that point writers, novelists, poets, playwrights are called into action.

New tribalisms do appear on all hands today, as people seek identity in the sprawling, bewildering world in which Cousins moves with more ease than most. Separatism, group ego, tribalism, and compartmentalization, for good reasons and bad, have been the order of the day for a decade now. In the bicentennial year the motto that seems to have been invoked on all days but the Fourth of July was not e pluribus unum, ("out of many, one"), but rather ex uno plures, ("out of one, many," or even, "against many, many"). The lines follow divisions of gender, race, ethnic group, religious denomination, and the like.

Harold R. Isaacs describes the situation:

> We are experiencing on a massively universal scale a convulsing ingathering of people in their numberless grouping of kinds—tribal, racial, linguistic, religious, national. It is a great clustering into separatenesses that will, it is thought, improve, assure, or extend each group's power or place, or keep it safe or safer from the power, threat, or hostility of others. This is obviously no new condition, only the latest and by far the most inclusive chapter of the old story in which after failing again to find how they can co-exist in sight of each other without tearing each other limb from limb, Isaac and Ishmael clash and part in panic and retreat once more into their caves.[3]

Lebanon, Northern Ireland, the Middle East, the India-Bangladesh border, Rhodesia and South Africa, Ethiopia, and almost wherever else one turns provides illustration of the principle, often in context of inevitable assertivenesses. But even in the United States such a tribalism is apparent. In *America*

3. Harold R. Isaacs, *Idols of the Tribe* (New York: Harper & Row, 1975), p. 1.

magazine (9 January 1971, pp. 10–11), Thomas H. Clancy typically drew the conclusions from the *Zeitgeist:*

> For a long time now we have been exhorted to love all men. We have finally realized that for sinful man this is an unrealistic goal. The saints and heroes among us will still face the challenge in a spirit of unyielding despair. The rest of us will try first to love our own kind. This is the year when 'brother' and 'sister' began to have *a less universal and hence truer meaning.* [Emphasis mine].

Unless I misread Cousins's life and this address, he would consider such an approach to be the enemy. For him it is necessary to point to the largest possible common areas of philosophical and ethical agreement or potential agreement. He would no doubt find congenial the summary of R. E. Money-Kyrle:

> The basis of morality is therefore neither *a priori* and universal as the metaphysicians claimed, nor empirical and relative as critical philosophers and anthropologists maintain, but empirical and universal in the sense that it is a quality, like binocular vision or an articulated thumb, which is found to be common to all mankind.[4]

To this one anthropological base Cousins would add some dazzling universal philosophy born of his own "sense of wonder" and his reading of Gandhi, William James, Ralph Waldo Emerson, and other congenial spirits. His approach has much that is attractive, but it will be more congenial to those whom Clancy typed as our "saints and heroes," or at least to those who have the luxury of gaining universalizing visions without losing their own identity, as Cousins manifestly has done. Some attention should be paid to thoughtful people with fewer talents and opportunities, and Cousins may neglect this zone.

Thomas Mann has said: "The world has many centers." It is not likely that a single planetary philosophy or even perspective will or should prevail—unless accompanied by coercions that Cousins would find repulsive. Most people will have to make their way through their "many centers," without falling into the tribalisms he fears and condemns. This means that there might be more stress on the intermediate zone of institutions, forms, and

4. Quoted in Richard Kluckhohn, ed., *Culture and Behavior: Collected Essays of Clyde Kluckhohn* (Glencoe: The Fress Press, 1962), p. 269.

philosophies with which we live: nation, church, association, and family. There "private meanings" can of course become ends to themselves; group "purposes" alone can be served; "belonging" can end with the huddled gathering of the like-minded. But some of these can also point toward the universal.

If we line up the gallery of the "saints and heroes" of our own time—the planetary people who would "love all men"—one common feature stands out. For various tastes there might be different portraits in the gallery, but without doubt many of the following would be remembered: Pope John, Gandhi, Martin Buber, Albert Schweitzer, Martin Luther King, Dietrich Bonhoeffer, Dorothy Day, and the like. Each of them was deeply steeped in the treasure trove, the lores and the loves of a particular tradition—Catholic, Hindu, Jewish, liberal Protestant, black Baptist, confessing Protestant, moderate Catholic. They went so deep that they penetrated to the universal embrace and intention of each tradition not stopping with the exclusivisms that are associated with each at certain stages and for certain purposes. With Cousins, they shared concern for the res publica, the "commonweal," in a time of privatism, narcissism, as in what Tom Wolfe now calls the "me decade."

Something—was it the voice of God, the achievement of philosophy, the signal of the "Yes" in the events of history, the anthropological condition, the love of their own deepest tradition, their care for what was familiar and close?—led them to freedom for risk, exposure, and hope. They responded and were responsible. Eugen Rosenstock-Huessy's motto speaks for them: *Respondeo Etsi Mutabor*, "I respond, even though I have to be changed." And, changed, they effect change. This is the purpose of the creeds shared with us by people like Norman Cousins—professions of faith more important to many of us for the example we can share, than for the content that divides us still.